Dispute Resolution

EXAMPLES & EXPLANATIONS

EXAMPLES & EXPLANATIONS

ASPEN PUBLISHERS

Dispute Resolution

Michael L. Moffitt
Associate Dean for Academic Affairs
James O. and Alfred T. Goodwin
    Senior Faculty Fellow
Associate Professor of Law and
    Associate Director, ADR Center
The University of Oregon School of Law

Andrea Kupfer Schneider
Professor of Law
Marquette University School of Law

Wolters Kluwer
Law & Business

AUSTIN   BOSTON   CHICAGO   NEW YORK   THE NETHERLANDS

Aspen Publishers
Attn: Permissions Department
76 Ninth Avenue, 7th Floor
New York, NY 10011-5201

To contact Customer Care, e-mail customer.care@aspenpublishers.com,
call 1-800-234-1660, fax 1-800-901-9075, or mail correspondence to:

Aspen Publishers
Attn: Order Department
PO Box 990
Frederick, MD 21705

Printed in the United States of America.

1 2 3 4 5 6 7 8 9 0

ISBN 978-0-7355-7088-7

Library of Congress Cataloging-in-Publication Data

Moffitt, Michael L., 1968-
    Dispute resolution : examples and explanations / Michael L. Moffitt,
Andrea Kupfer Schneider.
        p. cm.
    Includes bibliographical references and index.
    ISBN 978-0-7355-7088-7
    1. Dispute resolution (Law) — United States. 2. Arbitration and award — United States.
I. Schneider, Andrea Kupfer. II. Title.

    KF9084.M655 2008
    347.73'9 — dc22

                                                            2008033523

About Wolters Kluwer Law & Business

Wolters Kluwer Law & Business is a leading provider of research information and workflow solutions in key specialty areas. The strengths of the individual brands of Aspen Publishers, CCH, Kluwer Law International and Loislaw are aligned within Wolters Kluwer Law & Business to provide comprehensive, in-depth solutions and expert-authored content for the legal, professional and education markets.

CCH was founded in 1913 and has served more than four generations of business professionals and their clients. The CCH products in the Wolters Kluwer Law & Business group are highly regarded electronic and print resources for legal, securities, antitrust and trade regulation, government contracting, banking, pension, payroll, employment and labor, and healthcare reimbursement and compliance professionals.

Aspen Publishers is a leading information provider for attorneys, business professionals and law students. Written by preeminent authorities, Aspen products offer analytical and practical information in a range of specialty practice areas from securities law and intellectual property to mergers and acquisitions and pension/benefits. Aspen's trusted legal education resources provide professors and students with high-quality, up-to-date and effective resources for successful instruction and study in all areas of the law.

Kluwer Law International supplies the global business community with comprehensive English-language international legal information. Legal practitioners, corporate counsel and business executives around the world rely on the Kluwer Law International journals, loose-leafs, books and electronic products for authoritative information in many areas of international legal practice.

Loislaw is a premier provider of digitized legal content to small law firm practitioners of various specializations. Loislaw provides attorneys with the ability to quickly and efficiently find the necessary legal information they need, when and where they need it, by facilitating access to primary law as well as state-specific law, records, forms and treatises.

Wolters Kluwer Law & Business, a unit of Wolters Kluwer, is headquartered in New York and Riverwoods, Illinois. Wolters Kluwer is a leading multinational publisher and information services company.

Dedications

To Roger Fisher, who gave us our passion for this field.
To Bruce Patton, who taught us to teach.
To Bob Mnookin, who made teaching possible for us.
To Frank Sander, who taught us to take responsibility for the
future of the field.

Michael & Andrea

Summary of Contents

Contents

Chapter 7   Must This Dispute Go to Arbitration? The Question of Arbitrability   165

Chapter 8   Federal Preemption and the Law(s) of Arbitration   183

Chapter 11   Analyzing Settlement Decisions   247

Preface

No matter what kind of law you choose to practice, we are confident that the topics covered in this book will play a central role. Transactional lawyers negotiate the terms of deals. Litigators, in modern times, resolve far more cases voluntarily than through trial. Family lawyers and their clients routinely attempt to mediate agreements before turning to a court to impose the terms of a parenting plan or a division of marital assets. Defense attorneys and prosecutors spend considerable energy negotiating plea agreements. Estate planners and probate attorneys anticipate (and sometimes clean up after) disputes that arise following the death of a family member or business partner. Regulatory agencies often engage in negotiated rulemaking. Court administrators routinely direct cases away from traditional litigation paths, in favor of voluntary dispute resolution mechanisms. Arbitration clauses are commonplace in commercial contracts, employee handbooks, and consumer agreements. And so on. Dispute resolution, in short, is everywhere in the practice of law.

Despite its importance, the law of dispute resolution often finds itself scattered throughout a range of courses. Your Contracts class will teach you about the law of fraud. Your Ethics class will teach you about your duty to advise your client about settlement opportunities. Your Trial Practice class will teach you about the integration of settlement talks into the cadence of modern litigation. And entire law school courses (like Negotiation or Mediation or Arbitration) focus on specific dispute resolution processes. Each of these is important. But none of these courses fully paints the legal landscape within which dispute resolution occurs.

This book aims to provide a comprehensive view of that legal landscape, and we are delighted to offer it in the EXAMPLES & EXPLANATIONS format. Much of dispute resolution is about practices — the actual application of principles and ideas to concrete circumstances. What opportunities for creative settlement exist? What are the boundaries of legally acceptable behavior by negotiators? What constraints and opportunities does mediation present? To what extent can disputants be diverted from traditional litigation processes? What powers does a court have to enforce or avoid dispute resolution mechanisms and their outcomes? Understanding the practice of dispute resolution requires an understanding of the legal contexts in which these processes take place. This book, therefore, offers:

Clear, readable, and up-to-date **overviews of important and complex legal doctrines and analytic frameworks**, including:

- The Federal Arbitration Act, federal preemption, contractual challenges to arbitration, and the evolving federal policy favoring arbitration
- The Uniform Mediation Act and state confidentiality laws
- Legal Ethics relating to dispute resolution, including those rules governing the role of lawyers in dispute resolution
- Court-mandated dispute resolution, its requirements, forms, and limits
- The economics of deal structures and the decision analytic approach to dispute resolution
- The three primary ADR processes and their relationships to each other and to the courts

Practice applying legal concepts and analytic frameworks to specific dispute resolution circumstances

A **logical organization** that traces the coverage in most survey courses on Dispute Resolution

Liberal use of **visual aids**, diagrams, charts, and conceptual illustrations

Hundreds of law students have read and commented on drafts of the EXAMPLES & EXPLANATIONS book you are about to read. In a range of courses, including ADR, Negotiation, Mediation, Arbitration, and even Civil Procedure, we have offered these materials as a mechanism to enhance our students' understanding of the law. Our students have taught us how to explain the law of dispute resolution, how it works, and why it sometimes doesn't. It is no exaggeration to say that our students helped to write this book. For that reason, we are confident it is tailored to students' interests and needs. Dispute resolution is a permanent and increasingly important component of legal education and law practice. We hope that you find this book helpful as you study its contours.

Michael Moffitt
Andrea Schneider
August 2008

Acknowledgments

We would like to express our appreciation to our generous colleagues in the field of Dispute Resolution, many of whom provided formal and informal assistance in the creation of this book. We specifically want to thank our co-authors in *other* writing endeavors, including Bob Bordone, Liz Borgwardt, Roger Fisher, Brian Ganson, Chris Honeyman, Lela Love, Carrie Menkel-Meadow, Jamie Henikoff Moffitt, Scott Peppet, and Jean Sternlight. Collaborating with them shaped and enriched our understanding of dispute resolution. We also drew inspiration from the scholarly works of Sarah Cole, Chris Drahozal, Bob Mnookin, Len Riskin, Nancy Rogers, Frank Sander, and Nancy Welsh. And we benefited enormously from the anonymous external reviewers whose suggestions consistently made this book stronger.

We are grateful for the support we have received from our law schools, our faculty colleagues, and from our Deans. They have provided not only financial and research support, but also the academic leadership and encouragement that sustained our enthusiasm for this project.

This book would never have come together without the tremendous contributions of our talented, careful, professional, energetic, and beautiful assistants, Carrie Kratochvil and Jill Forcier.

More than three dozen student Research Assistants helped to conceive, craft, and edit this book. Through a genuine collaboration and mutual learning experience, we came better to understand this book's potential. For their contributions, we thank Adam Anderson, Tiffany Baack, Neal Bartlett, Noah Chamberlain, Matthew Clabots, Jilian Clearman, Michael Emer, Matthew Faust, Jonathan Fritz, Emilia Gardner, Matthew Garner, Kathleen Goodrich, Katherine Grant, Jeremy Guth, Starla Hargita, Tiffany Keb, Jessica Kumke, Courtney Lords, Travis Miller, Jonah Morningstar, Kathleen Murray, Hal Neth, Erika Norman, Jessika Palmer, Laura Panchot, Ron Phillips, Tiffany Ray, Andrew Sadjak, Jonathan Scharrer, Adam Schurle, Sara Scoles, Christine Slawson, Rachel Sowray, Paul Tassin, Nick Toman, James Tschudy, Michael Tuchalski, and Michael Watson.

Finally, we thank the hundreds of students on whom we have imposed various versions of these materials over the last three years. We look forward to continuing to learn from our students in the years to come.

Dispute Resolution

An Introduction to Negotiation

§1.1 INTRODUCTION

Most disputants, in most disputes, turn first to some form of negotiation. Understanding negotiation is, therefore, foundational to understanding dispute resolution. When one attorney calls opposing counsel and tries to secure a commitment on a revised lease term, both attorneys are negotiating. When an insurance adjuster offers a financial settlement in exchange for a release, the adjuster and the policyholder are negotiating. When disputing parties appear before a mediator, they are negotiating (with the assistance of a third party). Disputants routinely communicate with each other, in one form or another, in an effort to persuade the other to a particular course of action. In other words, they negotiate.

Not all disputes are resolved through negotiation, of course. Most of the court opinions you have read in law school casebooks are the product of disputes that were resolved through litigation. And as you will study in the arbitration sections of this book, an increasing number of disputes are resolved by the pronouncement of a privately hired arbitrator. Still, even in these circumstances, the disputants had an opportunity to resolve some or all of the issues through negotiation. Negotiation is so prevalent today that few disputants arrive at court (or at an arbitration) without having attempted to negotiate a settlement previously.

Though most recognize the prevalence and importance of negotiation in the practice of law, the negotiation process itself is the subject of ongoing examination. Scholars and practitioners alike continue to search for the best ways to describe the dynamics between two or more disputants who seek to persuade each other to some course of action. Compared with some aspects of legal practice, negotiation is relatively unstructured. There are few "rules" — at least not in the same way that there are rules of pleadings, of evidence, or even of professional responsibility. At the same time, some consensus is emerging about the structures underlying legal negotiation.

In this chapter, we outline some of the basic vocabulary, frameworks, and concepts central to negotiation.

§1.2 INTERESTS

Every negotiator enters a negotiation with a set of "interests" — the concerns, fears, desires, and dreams that motivate them at the negotiation table. A party will be happy with a negotiated outcome based, in large measure, on how well it satisfies that party's interests. Interests are the primary currency of negotiation — the things that guide negotiators' decisions — but they are often unspoken or masked. One key to understanding negotiators' actions, therefore, lies in understanding the interests underlying their negotiation decisions.

Negotiators are sometimes unaware of the relevant interests in a negotiation because they focus too heavily on one or both sides' negotiation *positions* (what they say they want), rather than on their *interests* (why they want that). A plaintiff might demand "a million dollars" to settle her claim against her former employer. Her position is perfectly clear: $1 million from her former employer will settle her claim. Without knowing more about the plaintiff, however, we cannot know for certain what her underlying interests might be. Having financial security for retirement? Having a face-saving story to tell her family? Removing roadblocks to her future career development? Restoring her reputation among her former colleagues? Covering short-term expenses? Punishing the company for what she perceived to be despicable treatment?

If this plaintiff's attorney fails to ask enough questions to understand her client's true motivations — her true interests — the attorney will be constrained to seek only one type of settlement: one that produces a million dollars. As a result, the attorney will be negotiating without some very important information. (Is it possible to satisfy the client with a settlement that includes different terms? Is the client indifferent to the payment form? Does the client care about the scope of the release? Is the client operating within important time constraints?) For similar reasons, even counsel for the defendant would do well to inquire about the plaintiff's underlying interests, despite the fact that the plaintiff's demand suggests that only one outcome would satisfy her.

This distinction between positions and interests is not the only articulation of this dynamic. Some authors describe differences between needs, wants, or objective values, for example. However one thinks about these terms, the idea is that negotiation involves an effort by each side to satisfy its interests as well as it can.

§1.3 BATNA

BATNA, an acronym originally developed in the book *Getting to Yes*,[1] stands for Best Alternative To a Negotiated Agreement. The idea behind BATNA is that every negotiator has some alternative to reaching an agreement with the other side. It may be attractive, or it may be awful. (Don't let the "Best" part fool you.) A negotiator's BATNA is the thing he or she would do if the present negotiations broke down and produced no agreement. What steps would the negotiator take to try to satisfy his or her interests? The answer is that he or she would pursue his or her BATNA.

One benefit of understanding your BATNA in a negotiation is that it serves as a reality check on what the other side has offered. In short, a negotiator should never settle for something that is worse than his or her BATNA. If you knew you could buy your favorite car elsewhere for $20,000, it would be against your interests to buy your second-favorite car for $21,000, unless there is something important at stake beyond the quality of the car and its price tag. Using the same logic, it would not be sensible to enter an agreement if it satisfies your interests *less well* than some other course of action you could take.

Alternatives, in the language of modern negotiation theory, refer to actions that one negotiator can take without the consent of the other(s). If a party walks away from the negotiation table (either literally or figuratively), he or she walks to whichever alternative he or she believes is most attractive.

The initial step in determining a BATNA, therefore, is to assess the full range of possible alternatives to an agreement. In many disputes, one conspicuous alternative is pursuing legal actions of one form or another. You do not need the consent of the other side in order to file a lawsuit. But negotiators typically have multiple alternatives. Could you pursue another potential business partner? Could you go above the head of the negotiator on the other side? Could you go public with the dispute? Could you just let it drop? Without knowing the full range of alternatives, a negotiator cannot accurately assess his or her BATNA.

After assessing the range of possible alternatives, the second step in calculating a BATNA is to compare the relative merits, risks, and

---

1. Roger Fisher, William Ury & Bruce Patton, *Getting to Yes*, 2d ed. (1991).

opportunities of each course of action. The alternative that presents the most attractive package, on balance, is your BATNA. If one alternative is litigation, then obviously you will need to conduct considerable research to assess how attractive it would be to go to court. What substantive law(s) likely control this set of circumstances? What is the likelihood of success at trial? How much will discovery, trial, and possible appeals cost? How long will it take? What will be the effects of the publicity associated with the trial? And so on.

§1.4 BOTTOM LINES (AND RESERVATION VALUES)

According to some visions of negotiation, each negotiator has a bottom line — a limit beyond which he or she will not or cannot go. Economists typically refer to these limits as each party's "reservation value."

A party's reservation value is a function of his or her BATNA, but the two are not the same thing. A negotiator's BATNA is often an action — go to court, buy another house, accept the other employment offer, etc. But one action is not easily compared with another action without translating these actions into the same currency, whether this is money or something else. As a result, a negotiator might reasonably seek to translate the value of his or her BATNA into strictly economic terms, so that it might be compared with a similarly translated offer during the negotiation.

In other words, a negotiator's reservation value is what the other side would have to offer in order to make the negotiator indifferent between accepting the offer and walking to his or her BATNA. If you are the plaintiff in a lawsuit and the defendant offers you $50,000 to settle the claim, should you accept? The answer depends, of course, on your interests and on your expectations of what would happen if you went to court.

Imagine that you are holding an offer to work for Company A for $75,000 per year. You are about to enter discussions with Company B about the prospect of working for Company B. What is your reservation value in those negotiations? If you found the two companies completely identical, your reservation value would probably be very near to $75,000. If you preferred the line of work, the job responsibilities, and the people at Company B, your reservation value in those negotiations would probably be less than $75,000, because you'd be willing to sacrifice some money in order to secure the benefits Company B would provide. How much less would you be willing to take? That depends on the strength of your interests, your financial situation, etc. For purposes of illustration, assume that you decided that you would be willing to give up $5,000 in salary in order to take the job with Company B. Your reservation value, therefore, would be around $70,000 as you entered negotiations with Company B. In short, if they offer more than $70,000, you'll take it.

To continue with this example, Company B also enters the negotiations with both a BATNA and a reservation value. Assume that Company B has also interviewed a more experienced job applicant — a person they consider slightly better qualified for the job. (Sorry!) The more experienced applicant is Company B's BATNA in its negotiations with you. Assume that the more experienced person has also made it clear that she will not accept the job for less than $110,000. In determining its reservation value, Company B would have to determine how much *more* valuable the experienced applicant would be as compared with you. How much more would they be willing to pay to get her instead of you? For purposes of illustration, assume that the company thinks she is worth $20,000 per year more. Their reservation value entering negotiations with you would be around $90,000. If they can get you for less than $90,000, Company B would prefer to hire you. Otherwise, they'll hire the more experienced applicant.

Negotiators sometimes face far more complex decisions, and the process of identifying a reservation value is correspondingly more complex. Consider, for example, an unhappy consumer who is trying to decide whether she should file a lawsuit against the manufacturer of a piece of allegedly defective computer equipment. Perhaps the company has offered a modest coupon to settle the consumer's complaint. How would she go about assessing whether to accept the offered coupon? Even if she viewed the decision in only monetary terms, she would have to consider the costs of drafting a complaint, filing fees, the prospects of winning at various stages in the litigation, the costs of litigating, the likelihood of recovering various amounts at trial, and the prospect of appeals. She would also have to take into account the question of *when* each of these expenses and possible awards would take place. That list of variables is long enough to cause many decision makers (particularly those who are making decisions about large sums of money) to seek some mechanisms for organizing and making meaning of the various factors, rather than merely "eyeballing" the case or going with their instincts. In Chapter 11, we describe a more detailed set of mathematical processes for making assessments like these. For purposes of this chapter, the important concept is that the consumer, like any negotiator, would have *some* reservation value. There is something the manufacturer could offer the consumer that would make the consumer indifferent between suing and settling.

§1.5 ZOPA

ZOPA, or Zone of Possible Agreement, refers to the space between the two negotiators' reservation values — the points at which mutually satisfactory agreement is theoretically possible. Some scholars refer to this as a "bargaining zone."

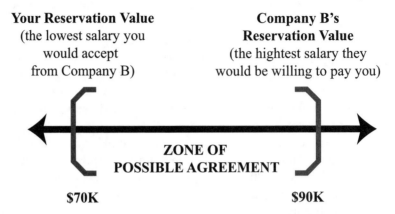

In the employment situation described above, your reservation value was $70,000 and Company B's was $90,000. This produces a ZOPA spanning $20,000. Economists would look at this situation and say that you and Company B should reach a deal, because by doing so, you can each do better for yourselves than you could by walking to your respective BATNAs.

Of course, the world does not always pay perfect attention to the analysis suggested by economists. There are many reasons why negotiators might not arrive at a deal, even when one is possible. Maybe they don't have adequate time to find a possible deal. Maybe one or both of them is lacking appropriate decision-making authority. Maybe one or both of them engages in gamesmanship or other strategic behaviors that result in a failed negotiation. As a matter of theory, though, a ZOPA signals that a deal should be possible.

§1.6 OPTIONS AND THE OPPORTUNITY FOR VALUE CREATION

The benefit of the framework involving reservation values and ZOPAs is that these concepts provide for ready comparisons. They are simple. Unfortunately, their simplicity also presents an important limitation. In the real world of negotiations, parties will rarely be comparing one strictly monetary offer with another strictly monetary offer.

In fact, the predominant negotiation theories of the day suggest that negotiators should *avoid* negotiating based on positional haggling. That is, negotiators should not behave as though money were the only thing in issue. Instead, according to the prevailing advice (advice with which we agree), negotiators should "focus on interests, not on positions," and in doing so, should develop multiple options for satisfying those interests.

In the language of negotiation scholarship, "options" are the label given to various elements of a possible deal between the parties. A lump-sum cash payment is an option. An annuity is an option. A confidentiality clause is an option. And so are a joint press statement, a contingent payment, a late fee, a dispute resolution clause, and a choice of law provision. (Notice the distinction between words that hold apparently similar definitions: "Alternatives" are those actions one side can take on its own, and "options" are possible pieces of a deal both sides might consider putting into an agreement.)

If they are well structured, options are vehicles for "expanding the pie" — for presenting deal packages that are more attractive to both sides than any mere exchange of dollars could make them. Economists describe a limited set of circumstances in which negotiators can "create value." Wise negotiators recognize these circumstances and capitalize on them in order to satisfy their interests as well as possible in an agreement. Below, we survey seven categories of circumstances in which negotiators have an opportunity to craft value-creating options that go beyond a simple, zero-sum exchange of dollars.

§1.6.1 Shared Interests

In some circumstances, both negotiators will hold at least some interests in common. If negotiators are able to identify these shared interests (sometimes called "noncompetitive similarities" by economists), they can structure deal terms that make both sides better off. In a negotiation between a star soccer player and her team, for example, one risks falling into the trap of assuming that all of the relevant interests are opposed. (The player wants to be paid more, and the team wants to pay her less.) Even if those interests exist, they are not the only possible interests. For example, both the player and the team want the team to play well. Both the player and the team also want full stadiums, good press coverage, and a successful season. In this case, they might build incentives into the contract, establish agreements on media appearances, or structure payments in ways that permit the team flexibility in hiring other star players.

Even parties to a dispute sometimes hold shared interests. For example, divorcing parents differ in plenty of ways. Both, however, likely have a noncompetitively similar interest in seeing that their children's health and education will be provided for. They may disagree about the details of how best to accomplish this, but each can be made better off in the event these interests are addressed. Labor and management often have conspicuously divergent interests in negotiating the terms of a future contract, but both of them share an interest in the long-term health of the company. A newspaper and a person accusing the paper of having published an inaccurate statement will likely disagree about whether the statement constituted libel, but they may have a shared interest in having the inaccurate statement corrected. Business partners in a dispute over a delivery of widgets may share an interest in resolving the dispute quickly and amicably enough to continue to do what has been an otherwise mutually profitable business with each other.

§1.6.2 Economies of Scale

Negotiators also sometimes create value in an agreement by capitalizing on "economies of scale." In virtually all circumstances, the more of something you need to buy, the cheaper each unit will be (hence the bargains at stores that sell goods in bulk). And the more of something you produce, the more cheaply you can produce each unit (one of the reasons it can cost you more to make your own dinner than to eat out at a high-volume restaurant).

Disputants sometimes have expenditures that are redundant with each other. An easy example is that there is no reason for each party to pay separately to have a deposition recorded and transcribed. The parties could easily split those costs, and each would wind up with the same product for less than it would have had to pay independently. In some cases, disputants might even agree mutually to hire a single expert to perform an analysis relevant to the dispute. In theory, the two disputants could split the cost of a single land surveyor, for example, to resolve a property boundary dispute. Sometimes, of course, each party may have strategic reasons to think that the extra costs of having "its" expert outweigh the potential for savings from economies of scale. Still, the basic concept underneath economies of scale is that negotiators can create value (or at least prevent the loss of value) by sharing redundant expenses.

§1.6.3 Differences (in Risk Preference, Predictions, Time Frame, Resources and Capabilities, and Priorities)

It is no surprise that negotiators often differ. Indeed, the reason they enter negotiations is typically precisely because they have some differences. What may be less intuitive is that these differences between negotiators can be an important source of value-creating trades.

Differences in Risk Preference Not everyone holds the same attitude toward risk. Some people can't stand to roll the dice, and some can't stay away from the gambling table. In a negotiation between parties with different risk tolerances, the party who is more risk averse should be willing to pay a premium for the more risk-tolerant party to assume the risk in a deal. For example, in a deal between business venture partners, the more risk-tolerant party should be willing to offer the other party more of a guaranteed revenue stream in exchange for receiving a greater percentage of any "up side" in the business.

Differences in Prediction   Mark Twain once wrote, "It is difference of opinion that makes the horses race." Similarly, if two negotiators disagree about the future, they can reach a deal that amounts to a "bet" on what will happen in the future — and in so doing, can make each happier with the agreement than they would have been with a straight exchange of dollars. A landowner believes that the environmental damage caused by the defendant has only begun to be unearthed, and the defendant insists that everything is now discovered and remediated. If the defendant believes that no further environmental damage will be discovered on the landowner's property, it can promise to pay the landowner an enormous sum of money in the event of future hazard, in exchange for a smaller payment today. If each is confident of its prediction, each prefers this outcome to a split-the-difference cash payment.

Differences in Time Frame   A dollar today is worth something different than a dollar tomorrow. In virtually all circumstances, one would prefer a dollar today over a dollar tomorrow. But negotiators may differ in the extent to which they prefer a dollar today. (In economic terms, the parties may have different discount rates.) If negotiators recognize differences in time frames, they can craft deals in ways that capitalize on these differences. These differences explain why settlements are sometimes paid over time, and why settlements are sometimes announced immediately after the end of a company's fiscal year.

Differences in Resources and Capabilities   Negotiating parties may also come to the table with different skills, different endowments, and different assets. Rather than creating dissension, these differences can also help facilitate a deal. Many joint ventures or partnership deals are predicated on the fact that one party has more time (or greater skills) to carry out the deal while the other party is willing to finance but cannot spend (or has no interest in spending) the time to oversee the investment. Two friends, for example, who jointly invest in a rental property may divide their responsibilities by who has more abilities in home repair, who has more time to visit and oversee the property, who has more knowledge of the real estate market, or who has more cash on hand to buy the property when it comes on the market. The allocation of these responsibilities will be most efficient if they recognize the relevant differences between themselves.

Differences in Priorities   Virtually no negotiation of any importance is really about only one issue. Instead, negotiations usually involve multiple issues. Any time multiple issues are on the table, it is likely that the parties will attach different relative valuation to those issues. In other words, each negotiator may attach a different significance to each issue. Recognizing these differences in priorities, negotiators can trade off one issue for another (often called "logrolling" in negotiation literature). If the prospective employee cares more about salary and job training, and the employer cares relatively more about benefits and vacation, they should structure a deal in which the employee gets more of what he wants on the issues of greater importance to him, in exchange for the employer getting a more favorable deal on the other terms.

§1.7 MODELS OF NEGOTIATION

None of the frameworks, vocabulary, or concepts we describe above actually tells a negotiator what to say or do in a particular setting. Should I make the first offer? How should I respond to what they just suggested? Should I make this proposal or that one? Should I include other people in the conversation? Should we talk here or there? Now or later? Negotiation is filled with strategic or **tactical decisions**. And it is far beyond the scope of this book to suggest specific answers to these complex questions. (They may look like simple questions, but if you take an entire course on Negotiation, you will start to see that they have layers and layers underneath.)

Virtually everyone agrees that negotiations in the real world involve more than just cold, economically rational calculations. Negotiators are real people, with all of the beautiful features and problematic baggage that go with being a real person. Negotiators have partial information and their decision-making processes sometimes suffer from cognitive biases and failures. Negotiators also have wisdom, intuitions, and creativity. No accurate picture of negotiation would discount the importance of **psychological dynamics** involved in negotiation. In fact, some textbooks spend considerable time surveying a range of different cognitive and psychological dynamics underlying negotiators' decisions. But these, too, are beyond the scope of this introductory survey of negotiation practices.

Some have suggested that there are two basic models of negotiation advice. On the one hand, there is a set of advice for helping negotiators figure out how to explore interests, how to make sure that communication is clear and efficient, how to maintain relationships, how to persuade based on objective criteria, and how to solve problems creatively. Advice along these lines has taken on many different labels, though the most common are "principled negotiation," "integrative negotiation," "mutual gains negotiation" and "win-win negotiation." On the other hand, a different set of advice focuses on how to secure advantage over the other side, how to get a bigger slice of the pie, how to claim value that has been created, and how to manipulate the other negotiator's decision. Advice along these lines has been called "competitive bargaining," "distributive negotiation," or "hard bargaining."

We are not convinced that the lines between these two models of negotiation are as clear as the labels suggest. "Principled" negotiators who create an enormously efficient and creative agreement must still eventually figure out how to allocate costs or benefits — an activity that involves dividing the figurative pie. And even the most steadfastly "competitive" bargainer would not be so foolish as to forgo a potentially beneficial trade merely because it somehow also benefits the other side. Negotiators may come into negotiations with a particular default or instinct about how best to try to persuade the other party. But negotiation is a dynamic, evolving process, and the most skilled negotiators would never limit themselves to merely one approach.

Examples

The Apartment of Ralph's Dreams

Ralph is hoping to find a new apartment to rent. He knows of four apartments currently available, any of which would at least minimally satisfy his interests. The first is on Main Street, and it is a bit smaller than Ralph was hoping to find. He has already negotiated with the landlord at Main Street, and the best rate he could get was $1,700 per month. The second apartment is on Broad Street. It is beautiful, but at $2,500 per month, Ralph has decided that he cannot afford it. The third apartment is in a neighborhood on High Street, far from where Ralph hoped to live, and it would cost him $1,600 per month. Of these three, the Main Street property presents the most attractive combination of price, size, and location, though it is not ideal. The fourth apartment, on University Street, is large, convenient, and located in an attractive neighborhood. The University Street apartment is owned by Laura, who listed its rental price at $2,000 per month. Ralph thinks the combination of the extra space and the better neighborhood makes the University Street apartment worth at least a couple hundred dollars per month more to him than the apartments on Main Street or High Street.

1. **Ralph's BATNA.** As Ralph considers beginning a negotiation with Laura over the University Street apartment, what is his BATNA?
2. **Ralph's Reservation Value.** What is Ralph's Reservation Value in a negotiation with Laura?

Laura owns a number of apartments, including the one on University Street. The current tenants of the University Street apartment have been paying $1,600 per month, and they are leaving at the end of this coming month. Laura plans to move into the apartment herself in 12 months, but she is hoping to rent the apartment to a new tenant from now until she is ready to move in. Laura has advertised the apartment as being for rent, and she is asking for $2,000 per month. So far, only a man named Terrance has shown interest in the apartment, and he was unwilling to pay more than $1,600 per month, so Laura turned him down. As far as Laura knows, Terrance has not yet found an apartment, so it might be possible for her to go back and strike a deal with him for $1,600 per month. Laura's expenses, including rent, utilities, taxes, upkeep, etc., take virtually all of the $1,600 per month, leaving her with no profit and no cushion in the event of unforeseen expenses. She thinks there is about a 50-50 chance she would be able to find a renter immediately if she dropped the rent to $1,800 per month, and she is absolutely confident that if she didn't get someone this month, she could find someone by next month at that price. She would like to get more than that, but she also doesn't want to let the apartment stand unoccupied (and therefore receive no rent) in the coming months. She knew there was only a small chance that anyone would agree to pay $2,000 per month for the apartment, but she saw no harm in at least asking.

3. **Laura's BATNA.** Assuming Laura is preparing to negotiate with Ralph about the possibility of Ralph renting her apartment, what is Laura's BATNA?

4. **Laura's Reservation Value.** What is Laura's Reservation Value in a negotiation with Ralph?

5. **A ZOPA for Ralph and Laura.** Based on your responses above, in a negotiation between Laura and Ralph about renting this apartment, do you think a Zone of Possible Agreement exists? If yes, what would you estimate that zone to be?

Musical Shares

MusiCo is a small but growing company that has several dozen recording artists under contract. According to the contract with these artists, MusiCo owns the intellectual property rights to the songs in all formats — including CDs and downloadable electronic formats. MusiCo has a small production facility for producing CDs, and it has a powerful and popular internet site through which it does most of its sales. The MusiCo board of directors has been making plans to make a public stock offering in the near future, but the company's sales over the past several months have lagged without any obvious explanation — until a MusiCo employee noticed a MusiCo artist's work for sale in a Distribyouth retail store at the local shopping mall. Distribyouth is one of the largest music labels in the nation, though industry insiders are somewhat concerned that the company has not been signing as many new artists as it may need to sustain its growth. Distribyouth has enormous production facilities, a robust distribution network, and a growing chain of retail operations. MusiCo has filed a lawsuit against

Distribyouth, alleging that Distribyouth has been unlawfully producing, distributing, and selling works by artists under contract with MusiCo.

6. **Options to Explore.** Beyond the question of a possible exchange of dollars, what potential value-creating options should Distribyouth and MusiCo at least explore in settlement conversations, based on the facts above?

Teachers in Turmoil

The School Board and the Teachers Union have been unable to reach an agreement regarding the terms of the teachers' contract for the coming years. Each has threatened to take action if a settlement is not reached soon.

The union has publicly announced that its priorities are (1) receiving an adequate compensation package, and (2) caring for members who are approaching retirement. Consistent with the teachers' second priority, the union has demanded that the district insert a clause in the contract that prevents the school district from transferring any teachers involuntarily once they have 15 years of service. The union considers this transfer limitation even more important than its normal opposition to any contract provisions that would allow the district to treat some teachers differently than others.

The school board has stated publicly that its priorities are (1) not agreeing to a compensation package that would threaten the financial well-being of the district or cause cutbacks in levels of service, and (2) attracting talented, entry-level teachers to the district. Related to the second of these, the board has proposed that the district be given discretion to award certain new teachers the equivalent of a "signing bonus." It opposes the idea of a transfer limitation, but it considers the signing bonus an even more important issue.

Regarding compensation, the board and the union disagree fundamentally about the district's economic outlook. The board believes that the state legislature will cut funding for local schools again this year, making even less available to pay for teacher contracts. The union insists that the state legislature will *increase* funding in the coming year, thus providing the backdrop for the board to approve significant increases in teacher compensation.

Beyond salaries, the two parties disagree about how the district ought to handle insurance premiums for teachers' health insurance. In years past, the district has guaranteed that it will contribute a certain percentage of teachers' insurance costs. This year, over the union's objections, the district is proposing that it provide a flat sum insurance contribution for each member. The board has explained that it "needs" to implement such a system because it is fearful that health insurance costs will skyrocket, moving the district's percentage-based insurance contribution commitments beyond its ability to pay.

7. **Options to Explore.** Beyond the question of how many dollars the district will pay the teachers, what value-creating opportunities should the board and the union at least explore in their negotiations?

Explanations

The Apartment of Ralph's Dreams

1. **Ralph's BATNA.** Ralph's Best Alternative To a Negotiated Agreement is whatever he considers the best course of action in the event he can reach no satisfactory arrangement with Laura over the University Street apartment. The facts suggest that Ralph has at least three alternatives to doing a deal with Laura (the apartments on Main Street, Broad Street, and High Street). He may have even more — for example, it may be that he could stay in his current apartment, that he could share space with someone else, or that he could buy a home rather than rent. With the facts we are given, however, it appears that the course of action Ralph thinks is most attractive (putting aside the prospect of the University Street apartment) would be to rent the Main Street property for $1,700 per month. The Main Street property at that rate, therefore, is Ralph's BATNA.

2. **Ralph's Reservation Value.** At what price point would Ralph be indifferent between renting the University Street apartment and the Main Street apartment? We know that Ralph can get the Main Street apartment for $1,700, and we know that he would prefer to rent the University Street apartment. The question is *how much more* does Ralph value the University Street apartment over the Main Street apartment? The facts suggest that Ralph thinks the University Street place is worth "a couple hundred dollars" extra, because of its size and location. We could, therefore, reasonably estimate his reservation value at $1,900 ($1,700 for Main Street + $200 for the added attractiveness of the University Street features).

3. **Laura's BATNA.** Laura's Best Alternative To a Negotiated Agreement is whatever she judges to be the best course of action in the event she can reach no satisfactory arrangement with Ralph.

In this case, Laura has at least two obvious alternatives: (1) try to rent to Terrance for $1,600 per month over the coming year, or (2) wait and hope to find another renter. If we assume that Laura's estimates are correct, there is a 50 percent chance she would get a renter at $1,800 this month, and a 50 percent chance she would have to have the apartment stand empty for one month before getting a renter at that price.

To determine Laura's BATNA, therefore, requires us to decide whether Laura would prefer the certainty of Terrance at $1,600 or the expected value of the wait-and-see approach. The math involved is not complex. Laura could simply lay out the revenue streams each alternative would provide her and compare them. For example:

Month #	Expected income from Terrance	Expected income from wait-and-see
1	$ 1,600	$ 900
2	$ 1,600	$ 1,800
3	$ 1,600	$ 1,800
4	$ 1,600	$ 1,800
5	$ 1,600	$ 1,800
6	$ 1,600	$ 1,800
7	$ 1,600	$ 1,800
8	$ 1,600	$ 1,800
9	$ 1,600	$ 1,800
10	$ 1,600	$ 1,800
11	$ 1,600	$ 1,800
12	$ 1,600	$ 1,800
TOTAL	**$19,200**	**$20,700**

The calculations for the alternative of going with Terrance are straightforward. Laura is assuming that she would receive $1,600 from him each month, so Laura's expected revenue with Terrance over the coming year would be $19,200. (That's 12 months × $1,600/month.)

Calculating the expected value of the wait-and-see approach is only a little more complicated. The facts tell us to assume that if Laura drops the asking price to $1,800/month, there is a 50 percent chance of an immediate renter, and a 50 percent chance of someone coming along one month later. Laura's expected rental return for the first month under this strategy, therefore, is $900. Of course, Laura will not be receiving $900 in rent this coming month. She'll either be receiving her $1,800 asking price, or she'll be receiving $0 because the apartment will be standing empty. But there is a 50-50 chance of each of those, so $1,800 × $\frac{1}{2}$ = $900 expected for the coming month. Laura then assumes that she would be able to rent the place for the remaining 11 months at $1,800/month. Laura's expected revenue with the wait-and-see approach, therefore, would be $20,700. (That's 1 month at $900 + 11 months at $1,800/month.)

If Laura makes her decision entirely based on her expected rental revenue, it looks like her BATNA is to drop the asking price and wait for another renter. But of course, Laura may base her decision on something other than the cold calculations described above. Perhaps she is extraordinarily risk averse. Or perhaps she has an immediate need for cash. Or perhaps she likes Terrance enough to be willing to forgo the extra expected dollars. Assessing the course of action that represents someone's BATNA requires an understanding of all of that person's interests — not merely his or her financial interests. Nevertheless, in this case, because we have no additional information about Laura, we would judge that her BATNA is to wait for another renter because doing so maximizes her expected return on her investment.

4. **Laura's Reservation Value** is the price point at which she is indifferent between renting to Ralph and walking away to her BATNA. In the answer above, we determined that her BATNA is to drop the asking price and wait to see if she can find another renter — a course of action that yields an expected rental return in the coming year of $20,700. If Laura is otherwise indifferent between renting to Ralph and renting to a currently unknown renter, Laura's reservation value would be the rate at which the two would yield identical total expected rental payments over the coming year. The basic math involved is this:

$$(\text{rate}) \times 12 \text{ months} = \$20,700$$
$$(\text{rate}) = \$20,700/12 \text{ months} = \$1,725/\text{month}$$

So, according to this calculation, Laura's reservation value in her negotiations with Ralph would be $1,725. She would prefer to walk to her BATNA rather than accept less than $1,725 from Ralph, and she would prefer to rent to Ralph if he is willing to pay anything above $1,725.

Of course, these calculations, like the BATNA calculations above, make a fair number of assumptions about probabilities, about Laura's preferences, about her risk profile, and so on. (See Chapter 11 for more on the mechanics and limitations of a decision-analytic approach to understanding negotiation.) As a simple means of estimating, however, the $1,725 figure captures well the idea that there is some price point at which Laura would say "no" to Ralph, in favor of seeking someone else.

5. **A ZOPA for Ralph and Laura.** If we juxtapose Ralph's Reservation Value and Laura's Reservation Value, we see that the two have a Zone of Possible Agreement.

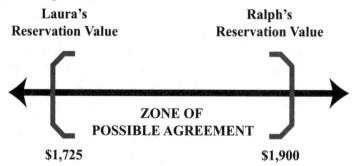

Laura would prefer to rent for anything above $1,725, and Ralph would prefer to pay anything under $1,900. The ZOPA, therefore, is between $1,725 and $1,900.

Of course, this simple analysis ignores the possibility that Laura and Ralph might discover value-creating trades during the negotiation process. Perhaps they will discover that Ralph has little furniture and Laura needs a place to keep some of her furniture for the coming months. Perhaps they will find that Ralph has flexibility at the end of the coming year and would be willing to let Laura move in earlier if her plans change. Maybe they will find that Laura has no short-term need for cash and Ralph would be willing to pay a higher rate in later months in exchange for a lower rate sooner. (For more on value-creating, non-zero-sum settlement options, see the examples below.)

6. **Musical Shares.** Assuming the two parties are able to get past the differences that led to their immediate dispute at least well enough to have a conversation, there are at least four different categories of options MusiCo and Distribyouth should explore, based on these facts.

First, they should consider whether there are ways the two companies could capitalize on their **differences in resources and capabilities**. Distribyouth has production facilities, distribution networks, and retail outlets. MusiCo has artists under contract and an internet presence. The two could consider a joint venture to better capitalize on the resources each company brings to the table.

Second, they should explore whether they can capture value by achieving **economies of scale**. MusiCo's facility for producing CDs is much smaller than Distribyouth's, and it is likely that MusiCo has to spend more per CD than it would cost Distribyouth to produce identical CDs. Even if the two did not enter a formal joint venture, perhaps MusiCo would be willing to pay Distribyouth to produce MusiCo CDs — at a price both companies would consider favorable. If they can arrange their business appropriately, it may not make sense for *both* companies to have their capital tied up in separate, expensive production facilities.

Third, the companies may have **different time frames** that are important to them. If MusiCo is considering a public stock offering, it is reasonable to assume that they would not want to have expensive and uncertain litigation on the books. In fact, they probably need to show some real prospects for immediate growth. Distribyouth may have a longer time horizon for its business planning. Perhaps the two could explore an arrangement that provides MusiCo the greater share of initial opportunities or profits, in exchange for terms that are more favorable to Distribyouth's longer-term plans. Alternatively, if MusiCo's interest in doing the public offering is to try to raise some capital in the short term, maybe Distribyouth would be willing to front dollars for MusiCo's endeavors, in exchange for either a fixed return or a share of the profits.

Fourth, Distribyouth is in need of new artists, and MusiCo has apparently had success in signing artists. A joint venture might, therefore, be in order. But it may also be that each side places a different **relative valuation** on the artists, on various of the rights currently being bundled together, or on the stock of the to-be-public MusiCo. If the parties can identify which of these they value differently, they may be able to craft a trade.

7. **Teachers in Turmoil.** At least three categories of options suggest themselves, beyond the simple, distributive question of how many dollars the teachers will receive.

First, the parties have a difference in **relative valuations** or **priorities**. The union cares more about the transfer limitation than about the signing bonus. The district cares more about the signing bonus than about the transfer limitation. The two might be satisfied with a straight trade (the union gets the transfer limitation, and the district gets discretion to award signing bonuses). Or it may be that one side cares deeply about both issues, while the other side cares relatively less. (For example, if the union cares relatively less about these two issues, it might trade both of them for a more favorable salary.)

Second, the parties' **differing predictions** about the future funding levels may present an opportunity for the two sides to strike a contingent agreement that both sides will view as favorable (at least in the short term). If the union is convinced that the funding will go up, and the district is convinced that funding will drop, both should be willing at least to explore the following deal: If the funding drops, teachers' compensation will be set very low — at a level very favorable to the district; if the funding increases, teachers will receive a very large salary increase — one far larger than the district would normally provide. If the union truly believes its prediction, they should be willing to live with the low-pay provision, because they expect that funding will increase, triggering the favorable raise. And the district, because it expects the opposite state funding decision, should view the contingent arrangement as favorable. An alternative way of structuring the deal would be simply to tie the salary increase to a percentage in the state budget. Note that proposing either of these kinds of arrangements has the additional benefit of helping to uncover "false" predictions from one or both sides. Only if they are truly confident of the thing they are predicting will they be willing to go along with a contingent arrangement with harsh consequences.

Third, the question of health insurance premiums may present a situation in which the parties have **differing risk preferences**. It may be that the district is so fearful of the prospect of out-of-control insurance costs that it would be willing to pay the union the equivalent of a premium to have the union bear the risks involved. The union might be able to get more dollars from the district in a "flat contribution" arrangement than it could get trying to negotiate a particular percentage of premium coverage. In this way, assuming the union is more tolerant of risk, both sides may benefit from capitalizing on that difference.

CHAPTER 2

When Bargainers Go Bad: Lying and Other Misbehavior

§2.1 INTRODUCTION

This chapter focuses on the line between negotiation behavior that is formally punishable and negotiation behavior that is not formally punishable. We are not talking about the line between what is effective and what is not. (That is a question of strategy.) We are not talking about the line between what is acceptable and what is not. (That is a question of reputation and community norms.) We are not talking about the line between what is ethical and what is not. (That is a question of personal norms and philosophy.) We are simply asking the question, "If I engage in this kind of behavior, can I get into trouble under the law?"

Please do not understand us to be suggesting that the question of "what is legal" is the only (or even the most important) question relevant to a negotiator who is selecting a set of behaviors. In fact, our experience suggests the opposite. Reputations matter, both in the short term and in the long term. Further, deception and other forms of "misbehavior" in negotiation often prove to be both costly and ineffective. This book is not written as a best practices guide. But you should understand that the ABA's Model Rules of Professional Conduct and the cases discussed in this chapter represent an ethical floor — something below which you should never fall. In fact, most lawyers operate well above that level.

The legal boundaries around negotiation behavior, however, are most likely to be the focus of your law school courses. So, in this chapter, we focus most of our attention there. Legal boundaries, for the most part, are drawn from two sources. First, the Model Rules of Professional Conduct outline a variety of ethical duties for lawyers, including duties related to negotiations. Second, the common law of both contracts and torts creates boundaries on legally tolerable bargaining behavior.

Many people have drawn analogies between negotiations and poker. The analogies are imperfect at best. The imagery of poker likely ignores those aspects of negotiation that involve value creation, relationship building, and problem solving. (See Chapter 1 on Negotiation for more on these.) Nevertheless, in at least one limited way, the analogy to poker may be on point because in both negotiations and in poker, people sometimes perceive a competitive advantage if they are able to deceive the other side effectively. In some sense, it almost does not matter how often this advantage actually exists in negotiation. The perception that deception (and other misbehavior) creates an advantage is so strong that understanding the boundaries of deception is an important part of understanding negotiation.

We begin this chapter by exploring the (limited) utility of a "good faith" requirement that would somehow purport to preclude all misbehavior. We then focus specifically on the question of lying in the context of negotiation. After briefly surveying some of the other forms of negotiator misbehavior, we conclude by examining the kinds of sanctions a negotiator may face if he or she is found to have stepped across one or more of the lines of permissible negotiation behavior.

§2.2 WHY "GOOD FAITH" IS NOT (NECESSARILY) THE ANSWER

This chapter is devoted to examining the boundaries between what bargaining behavior is formally punishable and what is not. If all negotiators operated under a system akin to the familiar Golden Rule ("Do unto others as you would have them do unto you"), we might expect to see few instances of misbehavior. But the reality is that no such duty commonly attaches to negotiators. Even for attorney-negotiators, the boundaries of what is tolerable are nuanced and ambiguous.

At the outset, we want to address the question of "good faith" in the context of negotiations. There are two reasons why the concept of good faith in bargaining does not serve as a guarantee against misbehavior. First, it is not clear what boundaries result from the determination that the negotiators must act in good faith. Second, it is not clear that a duty to act in good faith applies in a wide range of negotiation contexts.

First, even if an obligation to negotiate in good faith applies, it is not always clear what this obligation requires. Even statutes requiring good-faith negotiation in the relatively narrow context of court-annexed ADR programs almost never define good faith. Given this lack of clarity, one commentator suggests that "perhaps [good faith] is like obscenity: you know it when you see it."[1]

In the broader context of voluntary negotiation, good faith obligations present a constraint only against the most horrible negotiation behavior, leaving a vast gray area unpunished. Nevertheless, some examples of actions punished under this admittedly loose good-faith standard exist. Courts have found parties in violation of a good-faith obligation for delaying negotiation, for failing to seek approval for agreements, for breaching an agreement of exclusivity by making a deal with a competitor during negotiations, and for improperly delaying investments.

The definition of good faith may also depend on the type of dispute the parties are trying to resolve. In the context of labor-management negotiations, for example, each side is under an obligation to refrain from engaging in a wide set of behaviors that would otherwise be permissible. For example, in a negotiation outside of the labor context, either side is free to walk away from the table, or even to refuse to enter negotiations. But in the context of collective bargaining, such behavior risks being treated as an unlawful violation of the statutory duty to bargain in good faith. Similarly, even though negotiators in a broad range of contexts commonly present take-it-or-leave-it offers, such behavior in the context of a labor negotiation could be considered an unfair labor practice because it violates the duty to bargain in good faith (as explained in the well-known case *NLRB v. General Electric Co.*, 418 F.2d 736 (2d Cir. 1969), outlawing "Boulwarism"—a particular form of take-it-or-leave-it negotiating named after the GE vice-president Lemuel Boulware).

Second, even if we could define good faith, it is not always clear that there is a duty to negotiate in good faith. Although the Uniform Commercial Code and the Restatement (Second) of Contracts both refer to a duty of good faith in performance and enforcement of contracts, neither specifically mentions a duty to negotiate in good faith. Consistent with this approach, courts generally reject a general good-faith requirement that would apply to every party in every negotiation. The most well-known pair of cases demonstrating the complexity of good faith as a standard for negotiators is *Hoffman v. Red Owl Stores*, 26 Wis. 2d 683 (1965), and *Gray v. Eskimo Pie Corp.*, 244 F. Supp. 785 (D. Del. 1965), both of which were decided in the same year and turn on the question of detrimental reliance (discussed later in the chapter).

In *Red Owl*, Joseph Hoffman operated a bakery but wanted instead to own a Red Owl franchise for a grocery store. Red Owl Stores expressed interest in the project, and when Hoffman indicated that he had only $18,000 available

---

1. Kimberlee K. Kovach, *Good Faith in Mediation—Requested, Recommended, or Required? A New Ethic*, 38 S. Tex. L. Rev. 575, 600 (1997).

to invest in the project, the Red Owl representative assured him that he would not need more than that. Hoffman sold his bakery, bought and sold an interim grocery store, moved his family, and purchased fixtures in anticipation of opening a Red Owl store. Red Owl then told him that he would need more capital after all. The Wisconsin Supreme Court upheld a jury verdict in favor of Hoffman against Red Owl, citing the injury resulting from Hoffman's reliance on Red Owl's promises.

Compare this to *Eskimo Pie*, in which negotiations between two prospective business partners went awry, but the court rejected a claim based on reliance damages. In *Eskimo Pie*, the Grays approached Eskimo Pie Corporation about a new idea for marketing a donut-shaped ice cream pie. (The Grays called it a "Snonut.") Eskimo Pie expressed initial interest, but then dragged out negotiations for more than two years, citing excuses ranging from its president being out of town, to a corporate reorganization, to an insistence that negotiations take place face to face (but never being available for such meetings). During the course of these negotiations, the Grays did not approach any other companies about marketing their idea. Eskimo Pie eventually declined the Grays' offer to do business on the ice cream pie idea. Shortly after that, the Grays discovered that Eskimo Pie had been testing the idea internally the whole time and had begun production of a Snonut-like product. The court in *Eskimo Pie* dismissed the Grays' complaint, acknowledging the possibility that Eskimo Pie may have acted in bad faith, but finding that the Grays had not adequately demonstrated any reasonable, detrimental reliance on any assertions from Eskimo Pie.

As we discussed, modern courts typically recognize a good faith obligation only in specific, relatively limited contexts. For example, many courts recognize a limited obligation to bargain in good faith when the parties in question have already established a preliminary agreement. If the parties sign a letter of intent to lease space in a shopping center, a court will likely find that the parties are obligated to negotiate the details of the lease in good faith. (Knowing this, many parties now explicitly write into their letters of intent that there is *no* duty of good faith attached.) Similarly, if one party makes a preliminary agreement to lend the other money, a court will probably find that the parties are obligated to negotiate the amount of money and repayment schedule in good faith. Some negotiations occur under a court order, and that order frequently carries with it an obligation to act in good faith. (For more on court-affiliated ADR, see Chapter 9.) Other contexts may include a statutory duty to bargain in good faith, such as labor-management negotiations, which occur in a wide range of settings. But as a general matter, good faith does not constrain the behavior of many negotiators, in many contexts.

The problem with good-faith requirements, therefore, is twofold: First, even if a duty to act in good faith exists, the scope of the duty is not typically clear enough to prevent all ambiguity. And second, it is not necessarily clear (even in a given jurisdiction) whether a duty to act in good faith attaches to negotiators. We are not suggesting that good faith is irrelevant. Far from it. But your inquiry into the boundaries of punishable behavior cannot end with an inquiry into good faith.

§2.3 WHEN A LIE ISN'T A LIE

Negotiators face a number of tensions as they sit across the table from their counterparts. Among the most significant of these is the perceived tension between wanting to disclose information (in order to promote efficient communication and better outcomes) and wanting to withhold information (in order to prevent being exploited by the other side). Some believe that this tension is so pervasive and so significant that they simply label this as "the negotiator's dilemma." Taken to its extreme, a negotiator might even feel pressure to mislead the other side in order to gain a strategic advantage with respect to the distributional aspects of the negotiation. This leads to the simple-sounding question: Are negotiators permitted to lie?

No legal duty directly revolves around the term "lying." The law speaks, instead, about fraud, misrepresentation, deception, and other legal concepts. So, it is important to understand what kinds of behaviors are permissible and what kinds are not. The boundaries of permissible behavior are clearly not the only things that matter in negotiators' decision making. There are plenty of good reasons why people might not do everything they are technically permitted to do. But, in theory, people will be particularly hesitant to do things they are definitely *not* allowed to do.

Elements of Fraud
1. Knowingly
2. Misrepresents
3. A Material Fact
4. Causing Detrimental Reliance

To begin to describe the boundary between that which is permitted and that which is not, we start with two fundamental concepts: the mental state of the speaker (did she or he have the intention to deceive?), and the falsity of what is being said (was it a misrepresentation?).

§2.3.1 Knowing

Liars know they are liars. Embedded in the concept of lying is the idea that the speaker has an intention to deceive, which only occurs if the speaker knows his or her statement is untrue. Take a simple example: The plaintiff's lawyer tells defense counsel that the plaintiff has suffered severe injury, requiring extensive hospitalization. If the plaintiff's lawyer knows that the plaintiff has not suffered severe injury and was never hospitalized, we would be comfortable saying that the lawyer is lying.

Now, what if the plaintiff's lawyer *believes* that the plaintiff has suffered severe injury, tells the defense counsel that the plaintiff has suffered severe injury, and it turns out that the plaintiff has not suffered severe injury? Would we say that the plaintiff's lawyer is lying? Probably not. Though the statement turned out to be untrue, the plaintiff's lawyer did not know it was untrue at the time she said it. *Knowledge* matters. (As you will see below, there is a difference in the way tort law and contract law treat the question of knowledge. In short, knowledge is required for recovery in tort, but it may not be necessary in order to avoid a contract's terms.)

Of course, the term "knowledge" is not self-defining, and there are a number of different legal twists, clarifications, and complications that can arise. For example, some parties might try to get cute by advancing an argument along the lines of, "Well, really now, who can *know* anything, anyway? In this post-modern world, the concept of knowledge is out-dated. . . ." We cannot speak to the kind of success such an argument would meet in a philosophy class. But negotiators charged with defending themselves against an accusation that they lied should certainly hope to have something more to stand on than this. Courts virtually never treat a knowledge requirement as "100 percent absolutely certain."

Similarly, courts will be more likely to frown on assertions of lack of knowledge if the accused person is responsible for her or his own lack of knowledge. This concept can be labeled "contrived ignorance." For example, imagine a corporate executive who specifically informs his accounting and finance department *not to tell him* any bad news related to a particular business initiative. The executive goes to the media and to investors and tells them all kinds of wonderful things about the initiative. If the executive's comments were not accurate, has the executive lied? The executive may not *know* that what he was saying was untrue, but *he* was the reason he did not know it to be untrue. In most contexts, the law would not look favorably on the behavior of the executive, despite his lack of knowledge.

§2.3.2 Misrepresentation

Falsity is another component of figuring out what constitutes a lie. Short of revealing something like state secrets or trade secrets, the law doesn't generally punish people who say things that turn out to be true. Or more accurately, if we get upset at a truth-teller, it is for some reason other than for being a liar. (For example, they may have said something impolite, something that breached confidentiality, or something that caused injury.) Embedded in the concept of lying is the idea that the statement in question was a misrepresentation of the truth.

---

§2.4 WHEN IT MIGHT BE A LIE, BUT ISN'T PUNISHABLE

Not all knowingly false statements are treated the same. Some are treated as fraud. (See the next section for more on fraud.) But there are a number of different categories of knowingly false statements to which legal and professional institutions are apparently indifferent. Again, we remind you that there may be reasons — reputation, for example — why a person might not choose to lie, even if lying is not punishable. Still, it is important to understand the limits of legal sanctioning. Three concepts — materiality, puffery, and detrimental reliance — will help to clarify the boundaries of what is punishable.

§2.4.1 Materiality

Both the common law of fraud and the ABA's Model Rules of Professional Conduct draw a distinction between misrepresentations about *material* facts and misrepresentations about facts that are not material. It is only the former category of misrepresentations that commonly land a speaker in hot water.

Most courts find that a misrepresentation is material if it would influence a reasonable person's decision or course of action. Some examples may help to illustrate the boundary. A client walks into your office one day, opens his wallet, points proudly to a picture of his new granddaughter, and asks, "Isn't this an adorable little girl?" What do you say if, in fact, you hold an opinion about the cuteness of the granddaughter that would be likely to disappoint your client? This is the concept of the "white lie." Many (though not all) lawyers would immediately respond with a statement affirming the cuteness of the baby, in spite of their actual opinion. They have knowingly misrepresented their assessment, but the misrepresentation is not material because it is not a misrepresentation concerning the particular business that the lawyer and the client are about to transact. (Of course, telling someone their granddaughter is *not* absolutely adorable may very well affect the relationship.)

Further, an issue does not become material simply because it is somehow related to the negotiations. Imagine that the owner of a car is negotiating with a buyer. The owner tells the buyer that she took the car to a specific garage for the car's most recent maintenance inspections, forgetting that she actually took it to a different, more reputable garage. The buyer makes an offer on the car. This misrepresentation is probably not material, because it would not have changed a reasonable buyer's decision to make an offer.

On the other hand, in some circumstances, a fact will plainly be material to the negotiations at hand. For example, in negotiations over a joint venture, each party might make representations about its production capacity, its client base, or its existing assets. Any of these representations would be considered material to the negotiations, because a prospective business partner would contemplate a joint venture precisely because of these issues. A misrepresentation about any of these material issues, therefore, would create a risk of fraud. The Uniform Commercial Code also provides guidance on the materiality of any description of goods that might be the subject of negotiation. UCC §2-313 provides that a seller can make an express warranty in a number of ways, including:

> (a) Any affirmation of fact or promise made by the seller to the buyer which relates to the goods and becomes part of the basis of the bargain creates an express warranty that the goods shall conform to the affirmation or promise.
> (b) Any description of the goods which is made part of the basis of the bargain creates an express warranty that the goods shall conform to the description.

An express warranty (which can be oral and need not even be explicitly "incorporated" into the agreement) is a term of the contract, and it is part of the "basis of the bargain."

§2.4.2 Puffery

One vision of negotiation largely mirrors the kind of haggling one might expect to find in a flea market: each side makes outrageous initial demands, concedes only reluctantly, vigorously opposes any assertions made by the

---

Model Rule of Professional Conduct 4.1

Truthfulness in Statements to Others

In the course of representing a client a lawyer shall not knowingly:

(a) make a false statement of material fact or law to a third person; or

(b) fail to disclose a material fact to a third person when disclosure is necessary to avoid assisting a criminal or fraudulent act by a client, unless disclosure is prohibited by Rule 1.6.

other side, and perhaps eventually reaches an agreement at a point somewhere between the initial offers. As you know from Chapter 1, we think this vision is far too simplistic to capture the reality of most legal negotiations. Still, the image of haggling remains, and it has had some effect on how legal ethicists conceive of the duties that attach to negotiators.

One of the most vivid examples of this image of negotiation is found in Comment 2 to Rule 4.1 of the Model Rules of Professional Conduct.

Rule 4.1, Comment 2:

This Rule refers to statements of fact. Whether a particular statement should be regarded as one of fact can depend on the circumstances. Under generally accepted conventions in negotiation, certain types of statements ordinarily are not taken as statements of material fact. Estimates of price or value placed on the subject of a transaction and a party's intentions as to an acceptable settlement of a claim are ordinarily in this category, and so is the existence of an undisclosed principal except where nondisclosure of the principal would constitute fraud. . . .

The drafters of the Model Rules do not describe how they came to the conclusion that one convention or another is "generally accepted," and it is also not clear why general acceptance should be considered synonymous with "ethical." Nevertheless, this comment to the Model Rules declares various forms of "puffery" to be tolerable, in part because the rules deem the subjects of puffery not to be material facts.

Under Rule 4.1, an attorney can often misrepresent the value of a deal or purchase because it is understood to be puffery. Statements like, "This land will surely house the best shopping mall ever," or "This company has produced the finest cars in Europe," are commonly taken to be sales talk and not considered material facts.

Similarly, under legal ethical rules, an attorney is permitted to misrepresent his client's settlement intentions. For example, imagine that a defendant instructs his attorney to agree to "any deal that costs me less than $200,000," and the plaintiff subsequently asks defense counsel, "Would your client be willing to settle this for $150,000?" What options does the attorney hold for the defendant? The attorney could say, "Yes" and try to finalize that deal. The attorney could evade the question. Or the attorney could say, "No" and hold out for an even better deal. Of course, the latter strategy has some risks — both tactical and reputational — associated with it. But as a matter of legal ethics, the attorney has not run afoul of Rule 4.1's prohibition against making fraudulent statements because the statement would be considered "mere puffery." And under the common law of fraud, none of these options would be actionable — including a knowingly false statement about the client's willingness to settle for a particular price.

There are, however, some ways in which Rule 4.1 and the common law of fraud do restrict negotiators' assertions about the limits of their willingness to agree to particular terms. Imagine an attorney for a landlord who is negotiating with a current tenant at the end of the tenant's lease. If the landlord's attorney says to the tenant, "The landlord has no intention to renew your lease unless you agree to a $500/month increase in the rent," the landlord's attorney cannot be found to have committed fraud or violated Rule 4.1 — even if the attorney knew the landlord would consider renewing the lease for far less. Now imagine that the landlord's attorney says to the tenant, "You had better renew this lease, along with a $500/month increase, because the landlord already has a prospective tenant who is ready to sign on those terms. We're going to close with them tomorrow if you don't agree today" when, in fact, there is no prospective tenant. Unlike the first (vague) assertion about what the landlord was willing to do, the second (specific) assertion about the landlord's Best Alternative To a Negotiated Agreement (see Chapter 1) does create a risk that the attorney has committed fraud, and courts have rescinded lease contracts in cases like this.

What justifies the distinction between lies about what a client is willing to do and lies about what competing offers a client has? Though they are not specific about their logic, most courts seem to explain this distinction with reference to the expectations of the listener. Perhaps the listener has comparatively less reason to trust a general assertion about settlement intentions and comparatively more reason to trust a specific assertion about a fact relevant to the speaker's settlement intentions. If this is true, then that suggests that the law is at least partially driven by a belief that a negotiator should know when to trust what the other negotiator is saying. This leads us to the concept of detrimental reliance.

§2.4.3 Detrimental Reliance

What if a speaker told a lie, but the listener never relied on the speaker's lie? This is not an idle philosophical question along the lines of "if a tree fell in the woods and nobody was around to hear it. . . ." Instead, this question raises the concept of *detrimental reliance*. Without detrimental reliance, it is quite unlikely that the speaker's lie will be punished.

In general, a party cannot recover damages for fraud unless he or she relies on a false statement to his or her detriment. For example, if a father tells his daughter that he will pay for college if she quits her job, but the daughter remains in her job, the daughter is not relying on his promise and has done nothing to her detriment. Similarly, if the father's promise leads the daughter to quit her job, but her employer (in a moment of generosity) continues paying her salary, the daughter may not have incurred a detriment. Only in a case where the father makes the promise, the daughter quits her job, and then the father refuses to pay for college would there be an argument that the daughter suffered a detriment from reliance on her father's promise. Without reliance that causes harm to the listener, no action in fraud will stand.

In most jurisdictions, a party must show not only that she relied on a statement to her detriment, but also that her reliance was reasonable or justified. Reliance on a statement is usually reasonable or justified if the statement appears reasonable on its face and the party has no reason to doubt its truth. For example, imagine an aggressive salesman in a clothing store who tells a shopper looking for new professional attire, "If you buy this suit, your salary is guaranteed to double in a year!" Even if the shopper buys the suit but fails to secure the promised salary increase, a court would be extremely unlikely to consider the shopper's reliance on the absurd assertion to be justified. In contrast, if a father tells his daughter that he will pay for college if she quits her job, and the daughter has no reason to doubt that he will do so, her reliance on his promise would be reasonable. However, if the daughter knows that her father has neither the capacity nor the intention to pay for college, her reliance on his statement might not be reasonable. If there is no detrimental reliance, or if the reliance is not reasonable, a speaker is unlikely to face any legal consequences for his or her misrepresentation. In the lease example above, the tenant can only recover if he reasonably relied on the threat of another tenant and agreed to the lease increase.

§2.5 WHEN A LIE IS A LIE, AND IS PUNISHABLE: FRAUD

Lies can get any negotiator into trouble. Even statements that fall within one of the categories listed above (and are, therefore, not the subject of official prohibitions) may damage a negotiator's reputation or ability to successfully persuade a counterpart. But some lies run not only those risks, but also the risk of legal or professional sanctions. The biggest category of these lies is given the label "fraud."

All negotiators, including lawyers, operate under the strictures of the common law prohibition against fraud. The common law tort of fraud, generally speaking, involves four elements that we have already discussed. A negotiator engages in fraud if she or he (1) knowingly (2) misrepresents (3) a material fact (4) causing detrimental reliance.

The common law of contracts makes it somewhat easier to avoid a contract than to recover in a tort action because the first element of fraud, knowing, is not required to void a contract. The test for avoidance under contract law hinges principally on the materiality of the misrepresentation. Even if the speaker's misrepresentation was made unknowingly, a materially false assertion that causes reasonable, detrimental reliance will suffice. It also turns out that, according to strict contract law, a party can avoid a contract even in the absence of materiality, provided the party can demonstrate misrepresentation and detrimental reliance. Cases illustrating this principle, however, are not easy to find. You are probably on safe ground to assume that successful cases of fraud are going to involve misrepresentations about something material.

In addition to the common law of fraud, as we outlined in §2.4.2 on puffery, attorneys have professional ethical constraints on their behavior as well. All negotiators, therefore, must understand that the law of fraud forms an important set of boundaries on their behavior.

As you might expect, each of the elements of fraud are subject to argument, clarification, and some degree of debate. In the sections above, we have provided guidance on how courts have interpreted each of these four elements. In the sections below, we discuss when *not* talking can still get you into trouble.

---

§2.6 WHEN SILENCE WON'T SAVE YOU

Negotiators do not necessarily shield themselves from difficulty merely by keeping quiet. In most of the examples up to this point, we have described instances in which a negotiator makes an affirmative statement that the negotiator knows to be untrue. That is certainly one form of behavior that can constitute fraud. However, a negotiator's silence, in certain circumstances, can also constitute fraud.

§2.6.1 Omission

In some circumstances, a negotiator who omits information will be treated as having made a misrepresentation. The common law of fraud recognizes the possibility that a misrepresentation might be made either through an affirmative statement or through an omission. The same is reflected in Rule 4.1(b) of the Model Rules of Professional Conduct, which provides:

> In the course of representing a client[,] a lawyer shall not knowingly (b) fail to disclose a material fact to a third person when disclosure is necessary to avoid assisting a criminal or fraudulent act by a client, unless disclosure is prohibited by Rule 1.6.

Comment 1 to Rule 4.1 reads:

> A lawyer is required to be truthful when dealing with others on a client's behalf, but generally has no affirmative duty to inform an opposing party of relevant facts. A misrepresentation can occur if the lawyer incorporates or

affirms a statement of another person that the lawyer knows is false. Misrepresentations can also occur by partially true but misleading statements or omissions that are the equivalent of affirmative false statements. . . .

Silence, therefore, is not always a shield against committing fraud. We should also note that because Rule 1.6 no longer prohibits a lawyer from revealing confidential information if doing so will prevent a crime or fraud, the duty under Rule 4.1 effectively *requires* a lawyer to disclose this information.

A classic example of an omitted fact deemed a material misrepresentation arose in the case of *Kentucky Bar Ass'n v. Geisler*, 938 S.W.2d 578 (Ky. 1997). Geisler represented a pedestrian who was struck by an automobile. During the course of Geisler's negotiations with defense counsel, Geisler's client died, but Geisler said nothing about her client's death. The attorneys eventually reached a settlement, and only following the settlement did the defendants learn that Geisler's client was dead at the time of the settlement negotiations. When she faced a Bar disciplinary action, Geisler argued that she was under no affirmative duty to disclose the information *and* that the information was immaterial. The Supreme Court of Kentucky was unmoved by these arguments. It found the client's death to be plainly material to the settlement of a tort claim for injuries to the client. Citing the Kentucky equivalent of Model Rule 4.1, it also pointed out that "misrepresentations can occur by failure to act." In issuing its order publicly reprimanding Geisler and ordering her to pay the costs associated with her reprimand, the Kentucky Supreme Court wrote:

> [T]his Court fails to understand why guidelines are needed for an attorney to understand that when their client dies, they are under an obligation to tell opposing counsel such information. This seems to be a matter of common ethics and just plain sense. However, because attorneys such as respondent cannot discern such matters and require written guidelines so as to figure out their ethical convictions, this Court [affirms the ABA Formal Opinion on this matter.]

There are also four specialized circumstances, as outlined by the Restatement (Second) of Contracts, where omission can fall under misrepresentation. The first case involves the negotiator who makes a partial disclosure that is or becomes misleading in light of all of the facts. For example, in a negotiation to buy a widget maker, the widget company sends over financial documents to the potential purchaser. As the negotiation progresses, if the financial statements change (for example, the cost of producing widgets triples), the widget company must disclose the change to the potential purchaser.

The second case put forth in the Restatement arises when the parties have a fiduciary relationship. Typical fiduciary relationships include trustees, corporate executives, spouses, and business partners. In each of these cases, omission of material facts will be the same as a misrepresentation of the material facts.

The third case occurs when one party has superior knowledge that is not accessible to the other side. The classic example of this is found in home purchases, where the seller has a duty to disclose that the house is riddled with termites, floods every time it rains, or has a severe cockroach infestation.

Courts in most jurisdictions do not recognize an implied warranty of fitness in commercial leases. For example, in *Richard Paul, Inc. v. Union Improvement Co.*, 59 F. Supp. 252 (D. Del. 1945), the lease provided that the building could only be used "for the purpose of carrying on its business of manufacturing and dealing in textile products. . . ." The court found that this language was intended to protect the landlord and was not intended as a guarantee that the premises would be suitable for manufacturing or dealing in textiles. Therefore, even though the premises were *not* suitable for these purposes, the tenant had no right of action against the landlord for breach of an implied warranty.

Some jurisdictions, however, have extended implied warranties of fitness to both residential and commercial property. For example, in *Davidow v. Inwood North Prof'l Group*, 747 S.W.2d 373 (Tex. 1988), the tenants rented a commercial space to use as a medical office and soon discovered that it had a leaky roof, a broken air conditioner, a rodent infestation, and unreliable electricity. The court found that the landlord violated an implied warranty of fitness for an intended purpose, which the court said implied "that at the inception of the lease there [were] no latent defects in the facilities that [were] vital to the use of the premises for their intended commercial purpose and that these essential facilities [would] remain in a suitable condition." Although only a minority of states currently adopt this view, you should check the laws of your own jurisdiction.

A final instance where omission is the equivalent of misrepresentation is when there are special codified disclosure duties such as in insurance contracts or public securities offerings. Any omission in these negotiations is the same as misrepresentation. In short, misrepresentation may occur through affirmative statements, through silence, or through omissions, depending on the circumstance.

§2.6.2 Duty to Correct

A lie in the form of an affirmative statement has the goal of misleading the other side into believing something that is not true. A lie in the form of an omission has the same goal. According to Restatement (Second) of Contracts §161(b), nondisclosure is equivalent to an assertion. This happens if a party "knows that disclosure of the fact would correct a mistake of the other party as to a basic assumption on which that party is making the contract and if nondisclosure of the fact amounts to a failure to act in good faith and in accordance with reasonable standards of fair dealing." So, in at least these circumstances, a negotiator will be required not merely to refrain from making statements that cause a misunderstanding, but actually to make affirmative statements to correct his or her counterpart's misunderstanding.

You have a duty to correct a misunderstanding if *you* were the one who caused the misunderstanding. For example, imagine that a house guest sustains a serious injury to her ankle while tripping on an unrepaired portion of the homeowner's deck. The guest calls the homeowner from the doctor's office the next day and says, "Thanks a lot. My ankle is broken." Later that day, the guest learns that the ankle is only sprained, not broken. Several days later, the homeowner approaches the guest and says, "I'm really sorry about your broken ankle. I don't have insurance that would cover this, but I've researched the typical award for a broken ankle, and I'm prepared to offer that amount to you." Must the guest correct the homeowner's mistaken impression that the ankle is broken prior to negotiating a settlement with the homeowner? Yes. The guest's statement was not fraudulent at the time of the phone call because the guest did not know it was a misrepresentation of her injuries. But the only reason the homeowner believed the ankle to be broken was his reasonable reliance on the guest's phone call. The guest's nondisclosure or failure to update would be treated as if the guest were renewing his (now knowingly false) statement at the time the guest and homeowner made the deal.

You also sometimes have a duty to correct if you know your negotiation counterpart has made a factual mistake. For our purposes, mistakes can be divided into two categories: mistakes about the law and mistakes about the facts. Each category of mistake brings a unique set of standards for correction. As you might imagine, if opposing counsel has misread the applicable precedent or has misjudged the value of a claim under negotiation, the other side is under no specific duty to correct that mistake. Each attorney is charged with researching and applying the law on behalf of his or her client. Counsel owes no duty to the other side to inform him or her of potential shortcomings in their legal analysis.

Mistakes with respect to *facts*, however, may create a duty to correct in some circumstances. A simple example of a mistake of fact would be an arithmetic error in calculating the value of a set of assets. The often-cited divorce case *Stare v. Tate*, 21 Cal. App. 3d 432 (1971), provides a clear illustration of the consequences of not correcting the opposing counsel. In *Stare*, the wife's attorney made a calculation error in valuing the marital assets, and the wife's attorney extended a settlement offer to the husband based on those miscalculations. In preparing a response to the wife's offer, the husband's attorney spotted the miscalculation immediately. According to the appellate court, "[t]here can be no reasonable doubt that the counteroffer was prepared in a way designed to minimize the danger that [the wife] or her attorney would discover the mistake." The parties' eventual settlement was based on the wife's miscalculations. After the settlement was signed and the divorce was finalized, the husband sent a note to his ex-wife gloating about the mistake she had made. As the appellate court put it, "[t]he mistake might never have come to light had not [the husband] desired to have that exquisite last word." On appeal, the court ruled in favor of the wife and vacated the previous settlement agreement on the grounds that the husband's attorney had a duty to correct the known mistake.

§2.6.3 When Silence Is Required (A Note on Client Confidentiality)

Given the risk that a negotiator may be required to disclose information, is it safe to assume that an attorney cannot get in trouble as long as the attorney spills all the beans? No. As an initial matter, it is likely that a negotiator who divulges absolutely everything to the other side (including not only facts, but also valuations, reservation points, etc.) would be severely disadvantaged in the distributional aspects of the negotiation. Further, in many contexts, an attorney is *prohibited* from divulging certain information about the attorney's client.

The legal ethical rules governing confidentiality are not specific to negotiation. That is, they do not distinguish between disclosures made during bargaining and disclosures made in other contexts. But they are very clearly relevant — sometimes central — to an attorney's decision making in the context of a negotiation.

Model Rule 1.6 provides the baseline rules governing the confidentiality of client information. We discuss the boundaries of confidentiality separately in Chapter 4. For now, you should simply know that Rule 1.6 requires attorneys to keep confidential any "information relating to the representation of a client unless the client gives informed consent, the disclosure is impliedly authorized in order to carry out the representation or the disclosure is permitted" under a list of narrowly constructed exceptions. Exceptions include things like complying with a court order or taking steps to prevent reasonably certain death, substantial bodily injury, or fraud. And even as to these matters, the rules merely state that a lawyer "may" reveal these pieces of information.

The intersection of Rules 1.6 and 4.1 risk being confusing — particularly if one merely skims them. Of note is that, with respect to criminal or fraudulent activity, Rule 4.1 creates a mandate ("a lawyer shall not . . ."), while Rule 1.6 grants permission ("a lawyer may reveal . . ."). Most ethicists now read 4.1 as requiring lawyers to reveal otherwise confidential information to prevent fraudulent activity, since 1.6 does not prohibit it. (See Chapter 4 on attorney-client privileges for more on this point.)

§2.7 MISBEHAVIOR BEYOND LYING

We have focused primarily on the question of lying in the context of negotiation because it is such a prevalent question. But lying is not the only form of misbehavior to which some negotiators are prone, so the law includes other boundaries as well. An unscrupulous negotiator might try to intimidate or coerce a counterpart into signing an agreement. Or a negotiator might try to sneak terrible provisions into the agreement at the last minute, hoping to catch the unsuspecting counterpart unaware. Or a negotiator might take advantage of his counterpart's desperation to demand onerous terms on a take-it-or-leave-it basis. And so on.

A very substantial portion of the common law of contracts seeks to address these forms of misbehavior. In many respects, doctrines such as coercion, unconscionability, mutual assent, and the question of how to treat contracts of adhesion arose in response to bad bargaining behaviors. The length and focus of this book does not permit a complete reexamination of your course on Contracts, but you should recognize that you are already familiar with many (if not all) of the mechanisms available to curtail the misbehavior of negotiators.

Duress, as you may likely recall, is when one side in a negotiation forces the other side to accept the bargain under coercion or threat. Clear examples of duress include physical coercion, threat of physical harm, or a threat of criminal prosecution. Another example of duress is when the threat would harm the victim (such as publicizing unpleasant matters), but would not actually help the person making the threat; rather it is made solely for vindictive or malicious reasons. The threat of a civil action, however, is not seen as duress because civil action is an appropriate legal action to resolve a conflict.

Duress has been found in cases where there is an illegitimate use of power, such as when an employer threatened to fire the employee unless he or she sold his or her stock in the company or when an employer threatened to fire another family member unless the employee agreed to sign a release for a work-related injury. In narrow circumstances, duress can also occur when one side threatens *not* to carry out an already existing contract. For example, if one party threatens not to deliver promised goods, if the remedy for breach would be seen as insufficient, and the parties are already considered to be bound by a duty of good faith under the contract, this threat would be duress.

It is important to note that general hard bargaining and taking advantage of one's better position in a negotiation is *not* duress. As E. Allan Farnsworth, *Contracts* §4.17 (4th ed. 2004), notes, "A party will ordinarily be held to an agreement even though that party's adversity has been taken advantage of, as long as the contract has been shaped by prevailing market forces." When, however, the contract is the result of an illegitimate use of power, this will be considered duress.

Unconscionability is another type of bargaining misbehavior to which contract law has developed a response. Courts can void a contract they deem to be unconscionable, or they can modify the terms of the contract that are particularly problematic. One of the key issues — presenting both a benefit and detriment to the enforcement of the law of unconscionability — is its lack of a clear definition. Unconscionability typically includes both procedural unfairness (an inquiry into how the negotiation was conducted) and substantive unfairness (an inquiry into the merits of the agreement's terms). Procedural unconscionability would include, for example, the use of "sharp" bargaining practices like fine print and confusing language. Procedural unconscionability may also include a lack of understanding and unequal bargaining power. Substantive unconscionability, as the name suggests, looks at the equities of the bargain. A deal is considered substantively unconscionable if one side has reaped the full benefit of the bargain at the expense of the other.

As the court in *Williams v. Walker-Thomas Furniture Co.*, 350 F.2d 445 (D.C. Cir. 1965), outlined, "Unconscionability has generally been recognized to include an absence of meaningful choice on the part of one of the parties together with contract terms which are unreasonably favorable to the other party." In the case, Walker-Thomas sold Williams a stereo on credit, knowing that Williams received only a $218 monthly government check for herself and seven children and that she already owed the store money for several other purchases. The terms of the contract permitted Walker-Thomas to repossess any of these items if Williams failed to make a payment at any time before the entire debt was paid off (rather than credit her with paying off one item, then the next, then the next, and so on). The doctrine of unconscionability has been most typically used in consumer cases, such as this one, as well as cases dealing with franchisees where the courts perceive that one party has significantly less bargaining power and sophistication. Unconscionability is generally rejected in negotiations between two equally sophisticated bargainers — probably because the parties' relative equality in sophistication makes the negotiations more equal (therefore making procedural unconscionability unlikely) and makes it far less likely to be skewed (therefore preventing substantive unconscionability).

As we will discuss later in the arbitration chapters, parties who seek to avoid the effects of arbitration clauses in contracts often appeal to the law of unconscionability to make their case. Such arguments are only occasionally successful, for reasons that will become clear in later chapters. But you should know that some arbitration clauses have been stricken on the grounds that they were unconscionable. For example, in *Brower v. Gateway 2000 Inc.*, 246 A.2d 246 (N.Y. App. Div. 1998), consumers had various complaints related to computers they had purchased from Gateway. Gateway tried to enforce a contractual provision that compelled the consumers to bring any complaints before an arbitrator in Chicago, and required that they follow the International Chamber of Commerce arbitration procedures. One of those procedures included a $2,000 nonrefundable registration fee, akin to a filing fee. Given that the consumers had suffered less than half that amount in damages, they argued (successfully) that the arbitration clause's nonrecoverable filing fee unconscionably deprived them of any recourse in this case.

§2.8 WHAT HAPPENS TO LIARS?

We have spent most of this chapter describing the boundaries of permissible behavior by negotiators. But we have not yet spent time on the "or else what?" question. What happens if a negotiator steps over one or more of the lines described above? There are basically three categories of official "trouble" a negotiator can get into, one of which is particular to attorney-negotiators. There is also a fourth category of trouble that is informal, but powerful nonetheless. We describe each below.

First, as you may recall from your Contracts class, if a deal is reached through any of the forms of bad behavior mentioned above (misrepresentation, coercion, unconscionability, lack of mutual assent, etc.) it is subject to **rescission**. Contract law provides a vehicle for an aggrieved party to attack the enforceability of a deal. At a minimum, the unscrupulous negotiator risks being stripped of whatever benefit he or she sought to gain from the misbehavior in the deal.

Second, a misbehaving negotiator may be subject to private **liability** for certain kinds of tortious behavior. For example, it is relatively common to see tort actions brought in cases of alleged fraud. A negotiator who commits fraud will not only see the benefits of the contract stripped away, but may very well also be responsible for economic injuries resulting from the fraud. (And in a more limited set of circumstances, a negotiator who commits fraud may even be subject to criminal sanctions.) Other kinds of misbehavior—for example, coercion and duress—do not traditionally give rise to a cause of action in tort law. Instead, they are merely grounds for avoiding the contract.

Third, if the misbehaving negotiator is a lawyer, he or she may be subject to **disciplinary actions** from the Bar. This sanction rests on top of whatever other consequences the negotiator may face. For example, if a negotiator commits fraud, the contract in question is subject to rescission, and the negotiator may face private civil liability for the resulting damages. Further, the attorney may be sanctioned for failure to adhere to Model Rule 4.1. For those of you who have not yet taken a course in Professional Responsibility, you should know that the Bar can issue a wide range of different sanctions on attorneys, ranging from a mild censure to permanent disbarment.

Finally, a very important (although not formal or legal) set of consequences of misbehavior in negotiations relates to a negotiator's **reputation**. In short, reputations matter. Good reputations are hard to establish and are relatively fragile. If you have a reputation as a successful *and* ethical negotiator (the two are entirely consistent), you will be better able to persuade your counterpart in a specific negotiation, because he or she will trust your assertions and suggestions. Further, having a reputation for effectiveness and trustworthiness will be useful in the larger picture of your interactions with your colleagues, your prospective clients, and your counterparts.

Examples

The Bargain Basement is a well-known discount mall. The management of Bargain Basement rents out space to individual vendors who display wares ranging from clothing to electronics to musical instruments. The patrons of Bargain Basement are equally varied. One of the new tenants at Bargain Basement is a company called "Vivid Violin Vendors." As its name suggests, Vivid Violin Vendors specializes in violins and violin-related accessories. The management of Bargain Basement was skeptical that Verne Verdison, the owner of Vivid Violin Vendors, had appropriately assessed the consumer habits of the usual clientele of Bargain Basement, but they agreed to rent a space to Vivid Violin Vendors nonetheless.

1. **Knowing What You Don't Know.** A customer comes into the store looking for a violin by Waldo Woo, a world-famous contemporary violin maker. Verne tells the customer that he doubts he has any, but he agrees to search his inventory. To his surprise, Verne discovers a Waldo Woo violin in the back of the store. "It must have come in while I was on vacation," Verne says. Thereafter, the customer buys the violin. Later that day, as Verne was going through old invoices, he was shocked to discover that the violin he had just sold was a Willy Woo violin, not a Waldo Woo violin. Willy Woo violins are cheap knock-offs that typically sell for about a tenth of the price of a Waldo Woo. If the customer discovers that the violin he purchased is actually a Willy Woo, what are his options against Vivid Violin Vendors?

2. **Truth and Fiction About Violins.** A customer comes into the store and tells Verne, "My granddaughter was just accepted by her first-choice music conservatory. She needs a professional violin, and I'd like to buy her one." Verne goes to his rack of beginner violins (worth less than $2,000), hands one to the customer, and tells him, "This is a professional violin, worth at least $10,000." After Verne and the customer discuss the violin's extraordinary qualities, the customer buys it for $10,000. Verne returns to the rack of beginner violins, thinking about the huge profit he just made by substituting a cheaper violin for the one he had described as "professional." Suddenly, he realizes that he accidentally shelved some of his professional violins in the beginner section, and that the violin he just sold to the customer was actually worth at least $10,000. If the customer's granddaughter doesn't like the violin, and Vivid Violin Vendors has a policy against returns, could the customer rescind the deal based on Verne's misrepresentation?

3. **There Once Was a Violin from Nantucket.** Verne planned to go fishing one afternoon, so he left the store in the able hands of his attorney, Alfred. One customer appeared vaguely interested in an old, beat-up violin in the corner of the shop. Alfred told the customer, "This particular model is worth $15,000. You might be surprised to hear that, but let me explain. This is one of only a few remaining violins produced in the early Colonial Period of the United States. We have traced its origin to eastern Massachusetts, and we're almost certain it dates to the seventeenth century." The customer was amazed and told Alfred that her ancestors had inhabited that area around that time. After a little haggling, the wide-eyed customer bought the violin for $12,000. If the customer later finds out that Alfred fabricated the entire story about the violin's origin, what options does the customer have?

4. **Mouse Dropping (a Hint).** When Verne approached Bargain Basement about the possibility of renting a space, he made it very clear that he intended primarily to store and display antique violins. Vivid Violin Vendors' attorney, Alfred Albertson, asked Bargain Basement's attorney, "Is there anything I should know about the appropriateness of this space, given that this is what we intend to do with it?" Bargain Basement's attorney responded, "I'm sure you'll have even more visitors than you imagine. Visitors of all sorts. All sorts." Alfred thought the response was a bit odd, but went ahead and finalized a rental agreement. About a week after setting up shop, Verne discovered that one of his violins (an odd-looking green one) had been damaged, apparently because rodents of some sort had chewed on it. When Verne complained to a neighboring vendor, Verne's neighbor said, "Oh, yeah. This place is filled with mice. Has been for years. That's why we all lock

up our goods in plastic cases at night." Verne is furious that Bargain Basement did not disclose the infestation before renting the space. Would Verne be successful in an action against Bargain Basement based on the mice-caused damage?

5. **One-of-a-Kind Appetizer.** Bargain Basement's attorney offered, "as a good faith gesture, and not as an admission of any wrongdoing," to compensate Vivid Violin Vendors for the mice-caused damage to Vivid Violin Vendors' odd-looking green violin. Alfred, Verne's attorney for many years, told Bargain Basement's attorney, "That violin was one of a kind, and these mice essentially ruined it. I don't know how we could put a price on it, but it's clearly worth at least $10,000." Bargain Basement's attorney was shocked and indicated that she had no authority to go that high, but stated that she would take this information back to her client. Verne overheard the exchange, and later said to Alfred, "You do know that thing was worth only a couple thousand dollars, at most, right?" Alfred nodded, smiled, and said, "Of course." What, if any, trouble would Verne or his attorney face if this information was discovered?

6. **This Violin Won't Stick Around: The Line Between Puffery and Fraud.** When Verne sees a customer admiring a red violin, Verne offers to sell it for $1,000. The customer balks and says, "Maybe I'll come back someday when you're at a more reasonable price." Verne responds, "Listen, I can guarantee you that this particular violin won't be here beyond tomorrow, because Jimmy the String will snap it up when he comes by." The customer asks, "Jimmy the String? The world famous violin collector?" Verne nods, even though he has absolutely no information about Jimmy the String's whereabouts or intentions. Jimmy the String is known both for his discerning eye and for his deep pockets. The customer gets an almost panicked look in his eyes and immediately hands over $1,000 for the violin. A few days later, the customer has buyer's remorse. Does the customer have any chance of having the deal rescinded on the basis of Verne's erroneous assertions about Jimmy the String?

7. **Back and Forth: Like a Violin Bow.** One day, a customer indicated interest in a rather modern-looking, yellowish violin. She made an offer of $500. Verne laughed out loud, and said, "You will not walk out of here with that model for less than $3,000." The customer protested, indicating that the violin had some minor damage and was clearly used. "My price is $3,000," said Verne. The customer said, "I suppose I could go as high as $1,000, but I really don't see. . . ." Verne interrupted and shouted, "I said $3,000. If you can't understand me, get out of my shop! That's a take-it-or-leave-it offer. I assume you're not taking it, so

leave!" The customer left, and came back later with research about the particular yellowish model, saying, "Look, I found it in this catalog, and I could buy it new for $2,000, so I was thinking...." Verne again interrupted, "I said no haggling. Get out of my store." Does the customer have any basis for a formal complaint against Verne?

8. **Back and Forth: Again, This Time with Gusto.** Vivid Violin Vendors and Bargain Basement are still locked in an argument over the mice-caused damage to Vivid Violin Vendors' green violin. Alfred, Vivid Violin Vendors' attorney, agrees to meet with Bargain Basement's attorney, Bettina, again. The following exchange ensued:

> **Alfred:** This is going to cost you $10,000. Not a penny less.
>
> **Bettina:** You'll take $500, and you'll be happy. I can't go any higher.
>
> **Alfred:** I could maybe take $8,000, but that's it.
>
> **Bettina:** I'm not authorized to go above $2,000.
>
> **Alfred:** My client specifically told me not to come back with less than $6,000.
>
> **Bettina:** I am breaking my client's bottom line here, but I could go to $4,000.
>
> **Alfred:** $5,000?
>
> **Bettina:** Deal.

If it was discovered that, in fact, neither Verne nor Bargain Basement had given either attorney any specific limits prior to the negotiation, would either of the attorneys face a risk of sanction for their statements?

9. **I'd Love to Help You with That Violin, but My Client Won't Let Me.** On one of the days when Verne left his lawyer, Alfred, in charge of the store, Ignatius Indigo entered and expressed interest in purchasing a blue violin. Alfred said the only blue violin in the shop would cost $10,000. Ignatius balked and began to walk out of the store. Alfred said, "Wait, make me an offer." Ignatius offered $2,000. Alfred said, "Well, I'll go back and take a look at the owner's notes to see the minimum he'll accept, but I'm not optimistic." Alfred retreats behind the curtain and emerges a couple minutes later shaking his head, "No, I'm sorry, the owner has been clear that he won't part with that one for less than $8,000. I'd love to help you out, but I can't." Ignatius, dismayed, walks out. An hour later, Ignatius comes back and says, "I just can't do without that violin. How about $7,000?" Alfred hesitates but eventually accepts. Two days later, Ignatius is back at Bargain Basement and sees Verne, the owner of Vivid Violin Vendors. Ignatius asks Verne how he comes up with the

price limits written in the book of instructions for his attorney. Verne looks confused. "What are you talking about? My attorney has no limits from me. I trust him to sell for whatever price he thinks a violin will fetch." Does Ignatius have any possible recourse against either Alfred or Vivid Violin Vendors?

10. **The Stradiwhovius Violin.** Henry Heighseed enters Vivid Violin Vendors and asks about an old-looking violin hanging in the back of the store. Verne says, "Oh, you are a wise one. I can tell you have a discerning eye. This is a one-of-a-kind Stradiwhovius, imported from Europe many years ago." Heighseed expresses skepticism, saying, "If the violin is so great, why haven't I ever heard of it before?" Verne replies, "Well, OK, I exaggerated a little. The Stradiwhovius isn't really one of a kind, but they are incredibly rare. And you can have this one for $10,000." They talk a while longer, and Heighseed eventually buys the violin. Days later, Heighseed brags about his new Stradiwhovius to his violin-collecting friends. They burst into laughter, telling him that the Stradiwhovius is a notoriously terrible violin. It is rare because it is awful. And they explain that violin vendors often use a Stradiwhovius to distinguish knowledgeable customers from easy marks. Heighseed is irate (and embarrassed). What options does Heighseed have against Vivid Violin Vendors?

11. **The Stradiwhovius Strikes Back.** Henry Heighseed believes he has purchased a bum violin from Vivid Violin Vendors. He finds the Stradiwhovius unplayable, and he contemplates various legal actions against Vivid Violin Vendors. Heighseed's daughter, a big fan of online auctions, says, "Listen, Dad, before you go after the vendors about this, why don't you try selling the thing on the internet, just to see how much you're really out of pocket?" Heighseed lists the Stradiwhovius on eBay, along with a lengthy disclosure about the violin's considerable flaws. (As a matter of principle, Heighseed does not want to fool others the way he was fooled.) Almost immediately, bids start rolling in, and soon, the highest bid is higher than the price Heighseed paid for the violin at Vivid Violin Vendors. Apparently, the Stradiwhovius is so terrible, and has been involved in such legendary scams, that it has attained a mythic status among elite collectors. Heighseed is shocked and delighted, of course, but still wants to know if he has any possible recourse against the vendor who deceived him. Does he?

12. **Fire!** Fire breaks out at the Bargain Basement. The facility's sprinkler system kicked in quickly, so most of the items at Bargain Basement were not damaged. Unfortunately, the sprinkler head immediately above the

Vivid Violin Vendors store got stuck in the "on" position, giving it a prolonged dousing. When Verne inspected the violins (some of which were now soggy), he declared that he had suffered between $20,000 and $30,000 in damage. Vivid Violin Vendors brought a lawsuit against Bargain Basement for failing to maintain adequate facilities. In settlement conversations, Vivid Violin Vendors' attorney Alfred details the damage to the violins. Alfred says, "My client will not settle for less than full compensation in this case." Alfred presents a written offer to Bargain Basement in which he mistakenly omitted a zero from the demand. Bargain Basement quickly accepts Alfred's offer. Two days later, Verne and Alfred notice the mistake. Can they get out of the settlement agreement?

13. **To Treble or Not to Treble.** Vivid Violin Vendors also suffered fire-related damage to its violins, and it alleges that the fire was caused by the gross negligence of Bargain Basement. Vivid Violin Vendors alleges that it suffered damage in the range of $20,000 to $30,000. Several years ago, the state legislature passed a Vendor-Fire statute under which commercial tenants could recover treble damages against landlords if they could demonstrate that they suffered fire-related losses due to the landlord's "gross negligence." About a year ago, a state appellate court declared the statute unconstitutional. Just prior to sitting down to negotiate with Vivid Violin Vendors, Bargain Basement's attorney learned that the state's Supreme Court had just reversed the state appellate court, bringing the Vendor-Fire statute back into full force. During settlement talks with Bargain Basement, Vivid Violin Vendors' attorney says, "You guys are lucky that the appellate court overturned the treble damage statute, or else you'd be looking at almost $100,000." Bargain Basement's attorney responds, "That's the way these things go, I guess. You win some and you lose some." They agree fairly easily on a settlement for $25,000. A week after the settlement, Vivid Violin Vendors' attorney reads about the change in the law and realizes that he could have recovered treble damages. What are Vivid Violin Vendors' options for additional recovery?

14. **Desperate for Music.** A customer comes into the shop with a panicked look on his face. "My daughter's concert is tonight, and I've lost her violin. I need a replacement right away!" Verne asks a couple of questions about the customer's daughter, and then suggests a brownish model in the display case. Verne indicates that the violin will cost the customer $4,000. The customer sighs, shakes his head, and says, "Well, I guess I don't have a choice." He pays for the violin, and his daughter's concert goes off without a hitch. Later, however, the customer discovers that the

suggested retail price for the violin Verne sold him is only $2,000. Does the customer have any recourse against Verne?

Explanations

1. **Knowing What You Don't Know.** In this case, Verne's misrepresentation was not intentional. It was not even done knowingly. Verne made an "honest mistake." Therefore, the customer would have no recourse against Verne under the tort of fraud because recovery in tort for fraud requires knowledge or intention to deceive.

   However, as a matter of contract law, the customer would be able to rescind the contract for the purchase of the violin because the contract defense of fraud does not require knowledge on the part of the speaker. Instead, the customer would only need to show that this was a misrepresentation of a material fact (whether or not that misrepresentation was intended or made knowingly). Here, Verne's mistaken attribution of the violin maker is clearly material and it is also clear that the customer relied on this attribution in purchasing the violin. Therefore, the customer could return the violin.

2. **Truth and Fiction About Violins.** No. Verne intended to misrepresent the value of the violin, but his comments did not actually misrepresent the value or qualities of the violin. Both tort and contract law require a misrepresentation of a material fact in order to support an assertion of fraud. Verne's mind may have been impure, but his comments turned out to be accurate representations. Intent to deceive (without actual deception) is not sufficient to find fraud. The customer here has no recourse.

   Now, imagine that the discovery had happened differently. Imagine that the customer had discovered the real identity of the violin. The customer would have no duty to correct Verne's mistake. The law treats mistake as to fact (for example, the customer notices that one of the zeroes smudged off the price tag, making it appear to list for one-tenth the price Verne intended) differently from mistakes as to law or valuation (for example, the customer thinks Verne has grossly underestimated the sound quality, and therefore the overall quality, of the violin in question). Verne's mistake in this case is not a mistake of fact but rather that of the value of the violin, which, like a mistake of law, is left to each party's expertise.

3. **There Once Was a Violin from Nantucket.** The customer can almost certainly choose to bring a tort action for fraud or to avoid the contract on the basis of its having been induced by fraud. Alfred knew his story about the violin's history was untrue. And in this case, it is hard to

imagine that a court would consider the violin's history to be immaterial to the deal. From the exchange between Alfred and the customer, it is clear that the price (and perhaps the entire deal itself) was a product of the customer's mistaken understanding about the origin of this violin. The customer's reliance on Alfred's misrepresentations was reasonable, under the circumstances. And that reliance was clearly detrimental to the customer. Further, it is likely that Alfred's misrepresentations would be treated as a breach of an express warranty under the Uniform Commercial Code §2-313.

Finally, Alfred could be subject to Bar disciplinary action for having violated Model Rule 4.1. Perhaps if Alfred had merely asserted that the violin was worth $15,000, the "puffery" exception in comment 2 of Rule 4.1 would provide safe harbor for him. But his assertions were not mere opinion or valuation. They were specific representations about matters that were material to the deal.

4. **Mouse Dropping (a Hint).** Probably not. If this were a private (rather than commercial) rental arrangement, Verne would probably be in luck. A property owner's information about a piece of property is considered so superior to the information a prospective renter has that the owner is often considered to have an affirmative duty to disclose information about things like infestations. In fact, the Restatement (Second) of Contracts uses this scenario to illustrate the principle that an omission can be treated the same as a misrepresentation. Silence (or careful word phrasing like that seen here) will not satisfy a duty to inform. Further, modern courts have increasingly recognized an implied warranty of habitability for residential leases. So if Bargain Basement had a duty to inform, or if there was an implied warranty of habitability for antique violins, Verne would succeed in his action.

Here, however, because the transaction was commercial, Verne's likelihood of recovery depends heavily on the jurisdiction in which the events took place. Some jurisdictions have begun to recognize an implied warranty of fitness for commercial leases. Courts in most jurisdictions currently do not, however.

5. **One-of-a-Kind Appetizer.** Neither Verne nor Alfred is likely to face any formal sanctions. In this case, the statement about the value of the violin is not the kind of statement a court would typically consider a material fact. A party's assertions about the general merits of an item or an issue under discussion are rarely treated as "material." Without materiality, no tort action in fraud could attach, and it is quite unlikely that the contract would even be subject to rescission. The same lack of materiality will safeguard Alfred from running afoul of the requirements of Model Rule 4.1. In fact, comment 2 to Rule 4.1 specifically permits statements that constitute "mere puffery."

Of course, the fact that no formal sanctions will attach to these comments does not speak to the informal and strategic costs of Verne's comments. Because Alfred stated a value so far in excess of the violin's actual value, Bargain Basement's attorney is virtually certain to smoke out this deception. In terms of a bargaining strategy, then, Alfred is unlikely to have achieved much — other than having caused his counterpart to view the rest of Alfred's statements in this negotiation with increased skepticism.

6. **This Violin Won't Stick Around: The Line Between Puffery and Fraud.** Probably not. Verne here is coming very close to the line between fraud and permitted puffery. It is not fraud for you to assert (falsely) that you have a strong BATNA. (See Chapter 1 for more on alternatives to a negotiated agreement.) But the more precise and detail-filled an assertion about a BATNA is, the greater the risk that a court would count the assertion as fraudulent. The language here is probably still sufficiently vague — Verne is not asserting that Jimmy will definitely be there tomorrow or that Jimmy has specific plans to buy the violin — that a court will view Verne's statements as puffing. Verne's statements are more speculative than definite.

   If, however, Verne made specific statements about Jimmy — that Jimmy had already called Verne, that Jimmy asked Verne to hold the red violin, or that Jimmy told Verne he planned on paying $1,000 for it — Verne would certainly run the risk that a court would rescind the contract. These latter statements are more specific assertions about facts directly relevant to the negotiation versus more general assertions about the likelihood of Verne making a deal with Jimmy.

7. **Back and Forth: Like a Violin Bow.** The customer here has no recourse against Verne other than walking out of the store and refusing to shop there. Verne is puffing about his bottom line, but this is permitted under the Model Rules. Unless the used violin is subject to some obscure regulatory system of which we are not aware, Verne has no obligation to sell his violins for any particular price. And he is certainly under no obligation to sell for less than the price he has listed (however inflated the price may be).

   To be certain, Verne is acting like a jerk. But the question asked about Verne's exposure to formal sanctions. Any sanctions Verne faces for his behavior with this customer will come through informal mechanisms (like a damaged reputation), rather than through the formal mechanisms discussed in this chapter.

8. **Back and Forth: Again, This Time with Gusto.** The attorneys here sound more like amateur hagglers at a garage sale than like professionals, but they face no real risk of formal sanction for their behavior.

A client's willingness to settle a claim — particularly at a specific price point — is on the list of things the common law and the Model Rules treat as something other than a "material fact." Therefore, even knowingly misstating figures about a client's bottom line is normally not actionable. Nevertheless, these attorneys' positional haggling may come with some cost. As we discussed in Chapter 1, focusing purely on the single variable of an immediate payment creates a significant risk that both negotiators will leave value on the table in the sense of passing up a deal that both might prefer to a straight cash payment. This kind of haggling also does a lousy job of building a professional relationship, for obvious reasons. Finally, and perhaps most importantly, both negotiators' conduct makes it far less likely that either will believe the other's future assertions. Proclaiming the existence of a bottom line and then immediately showing that declaration to have been false creates very real credibility problems. None of these issues is in the nature of a formal sanction, but they are real costs nonetheless.

9. **I'd Love to Help You with That Violin, but My Client Won't Let Me.** Ignatius has no attractive formal recourse against Alfred or Vivid Violin Vendors. Ignatius' experience might remind you of the classic car buying scenario in which the salesperson must check with a (fictional) manager about how low he can go on the price of the car. Here, Alfred is pretending to check with a fake listing of prices for the violins. Ignatius could take informal steps against the vendor (for example, by calling his local television station to report these sharp practices), but Ignatius has no legal recourse against the store. Alfred's statements, even if false, fall squarely within the framework of permitted puffery because they describe his authority to settle, as well as the value estimations of the violin.

10. **The Stradiwhovius Violin.** Although Verne has not made an affirmative false statement, his nondisclosure may still constitute a misrepresentation. Verne said the violin was rare, which was true, and he named a price, which a seller is entitled to do. However, Verne's nondisclosure caused Henry Heighseed to form a mistaken belief about the quality of the violin. A mistake induced by fraud or misrepresentation, including nondisclosure, may justify a contract's rescission. For example, imagine that a property owner has a piece of land filled with debris, making it very difficult to sell. If the owner covers the land with a layer of sod, making it now appear that the land is just fine, a buyer (who would not have any reason to suspect otherwise) could have the contract rescinded because of the owner's silent misrepresentation. Similarly, Henry Heighseed can argue that Verne failed to disclose that the violin was notoriously terrible, and that Verne's failure to correct his mistake constitutes misrepresentation.

Even under the common law contract doctrine of mistake, Henry may be able to void the contract. Although a party can use an opponent's mistake to his advantage during bargaining, he loses the right to do so if his act or statement causes the mistake. Here, Henry Heighseed can argue that Verne either had reason to know of the mistake or that his fault caused the mistake because Verne's statements about the violin seemed intended to convey that the violin's rarity increased its value. Because Verne's nondisclosure caused the mistake, Henry Heighseed may be able to rescind the contract.

11. **The Stradiwhovius Strikes Back.** No. Fraud requires some detrimental reliance on the part of the listener. Here, Verne thought the violin was worth $2,000. Heighseed, however, thought the violin was worth $10,000. The violin turned out to be worth even more than $10,000. Therefore, Heighseed has suffered no detrimental harm, based on the facts presented to us.

12. **Fire!** Yes, Verne and Alfred can get out of the settlement agreement with Bargain Basement. This is a clear case of a unilateral mistake on a material fact. Bargain Basement knew that Alfred's settlement offer was a mistake because Bargain Basement knew the amount of damage Verne had suffered (Alfred had detailed it during negotiations) and knew that Verne would not settle for anything less than full compensation. Bargain Basement had a duty to correct the mathematical error. This case is very similar to the *Stare v. Tate* case in which the husband and his attorney were liable for not correcting the wife's mathematical error and for taking advantage of it in order to settle on more favorable terms. Because Bargain Basement knew about the mistake and the mistake affects a material part of the bargain, the contract is voidable.

13. **To Treble or Not to Treble.** Vivid Violin Vendors has very little chance to recover additional money from Bargain Basement. This is not an example of the Bargain Basement attorney making an arithmetic error or identifying the wrong item to be included in the deal as in the previous questions. Instead, Vivid Violin Vendors' attorney made a mistake of law, and presuming the other side did not cause the mistaken impression, they have no obligation to correct such inaccuracies. Therefore, Verne will have no recourse against Bargain Basement and cannot rescind the contract.

Note, however, that Verne may well have a case against his attorney for malpractice. The attorney was not up to date on the relevant law in question, as evidenced by his comments to the Bargain Basement attorney. The attorney's ignorance of the new law almost certainly caused prejudicial harm to Verne's claim against Bargain Basement. It is true that courts disfavor engaging in complex speculation about what "could have" and "should have" happened — particularly in the context of a malpractice action. Yet it is difficult to imagine that Verne would have any trouble demonstrating that he recovered less than he would have without his attorney's error.

14. **Desperate for Music.** No. In some cases, the common law defense of coercion will protect parties who are desperate at the time they enter a contract. For coercion to serve as a defense, however, courts typically require some sort of improper threat of harm. (If Verne had promised this customer a violin for his daughter's concert, for example, and then extorted more money when the customer came to pick it up, that action would be duress.) Here, Verne has made no threat. Any pressure the customer is feeling is the customer's fault, not Verne's. Verne is free to take advantage of the extraordinarily favorable market conditions that just fell into his lap without running afoul of the prohibition against coercion.

Similarly, the common law doctrine of unconscionability offers little protection to the customer. Courts declare contracts to be unconscionable (and therefore refuse to enforce them) when the contracts were (1) procedurally unconscionable (the product of a tainted bargaining), or (2) substantively unconscionable (demonstrating an inappropriate disparity in the benefit of the bargain). The deal between Verne and the customer looks like it is tilted significantly toward Verne. But nothing in the bargaining between Verne and the customer rises to the level of procedural unconscionability. Verne did not bury the terms of the sale in illegible fine print. Verne did not create an untenable circumstance for the customer and then exploit it. Verne did not include onerous provisions in the deal in ways the customer would not have expected. Instead, Verne found an opportunity to charge a premium for a violin, and the customer was willing to pay the premium for a violin. The customer knew the price, and nothing in the law of unconscionability will prevent Verne from enforcing his agreement with the customer.

CHAPTER 3

An Introduction to Mediation

§3.1 INTRODUCTION: DEFINITION(S) OF MEDIATION

Two former business partners in a dispute with each other hire an expert
to come in and try to help them work out a resolution to the problem.
A middle-school child on the playground intervenes to help two fourth-
graders talk about the differences that led them to start fighting. A diplomat
from a third country is called in to convene meetings between the heads of
two warring countries. A retired judge is asked to help resolve a lawsuit
between disputants who are about to file costly cross-appeals. A psycholo-
gist helps a divorced couple work through challenging issues regarding their
children.

Each of these scenarios is *probably* an example of mediation. We say
"probably" because no single, uniform, accepted definition of mediation
exists. It's not that various people haven't suggested definitions. Instead, this
lack of uniformity stems from the reality that mediation can mean many
different things, in many different contexts. Some definitions are narrow,
and therefore often underinclusive. That is, they describe mediation so
narrowly that one or more of the scenarios described above would be
excluded. Other definitions are broad, and therefore often unhelpfully
vague. That is, they describe mediation in such broad terms that everything
seemingly fits, even things that probably should not belong under the
"mediation" umbrella.

The good news is that, because the field has yet to settle on an accepted
definition, you surely do not need to have a precise definition in your head.

Still, having at least *some* definition from which to work, even if it is one that needs refinement or further explanation, is useful. The Uniform Mediation Act (UMA) §2(1) declares that mediation is "a process in which [an individual] facilitates communication and negotiation between parties to assist them in reaching a voluntary agreement regarding their dispute."

That doesn't really tell us very much about what a mediator actually does. What kinds of things serve to "facilitate" communication or negotiation? Does a mediator act like a diplomat? Like a therapist? Like a schoolyard peacemaker? Like a judge? Like a trusted sounding board? Like an expert? The UMA definition (probably appropriately) leaves out answers to these questions. But of course, their absence from the formal definition does not mean these questions do not matter. They are, in fact, at the heart of mediation practice.

§3.2 MEDIATORS' APPROACHES OR STYLES

As you might imagine, because mediation has no universally accepted definition, no description could possibly capture exactly what happens in all mediations. Various efforts have been made to describe the steps or stages that commonly appear in mediation. Some of these descriptions are helpful (despite their lack of precision or uniformity) because they provide a sense of the kinds of things that might happen in a mediation. For example, some authors have suggested that mediation typically includes stages such as the mediator's introduction, opening remarks by parties, information gathering, issue identification, option generation, bargaining and negotiation, and then agreement. Other descriptions articulate one or more of these stages differently. Still others envision an entirely different "typical" sequence.

A far more important question than merely which steps a mediator might take, and in what order, is the question of the mediator's general approach. What is the mediator's fundamental approach to the mediation? How does the mediator conceive of her role? These questions capture the greatest differences among mediators.

Scholars and researchers have developed taxonomies of styles as a means of describing and comparing approaches in mediation. The models of mediation described by those taxonomies bear out the fact that there are recurring patterns of mediation practice. Those models are often used in mediation literature as a kind of shorthand to describe styles that combine key characteristics. The purpose of these models is to highlight the relevant and recurring patterns that are found in mediation practice by stripping away all but the very essence of those patterns. Models certainly do not capture all the subtle variations that can and do exist. Moreover, the classification schemes that appear in most textbooks are not all-inclusive, but instead serve to contrast one style against perhaps one or two others.

In the next section, we describe three of the most commonly articulated styles — facilitative, evaluative, and transformative. Your textbook probably lists one or two other styles, and the professional literature includes many other articulations of mediator styles. We highlight these three because they are among the most commonly taught and because these three provide a good basis for comparing many mediators' choices.

One final note before diving into the different styles of mediation: While mediators may consider themselves (or be considered by others) as followers of a particular style of mediation, that ideology usually reflects a preference or tendency to generally follow a particular set of practices. That does not mean, however, that a mediator always adopts that style in each mediation session to the exclusion of any other style. One of the key benefits of mediation is its flexibility, and it is common for mediators to apply different styles depending on the situation or even to switch styles during the mediation. This flexibility allows the mediator to use the most effective tools available in helping the parties reach their goal of conflict resolution.

§3.2.1 Facilitative Mediation

The historical roots of facilitative mediation in this country stem primarily from the community justice centers and alternative dispute resolution clinics of the 1960s and 1970s. In these centers, volunteer mediators aimed to facilitate communication between disputants in an impartial manner. The volunteers' training focused on communication skills and processes, rather than on the law or on particular industries.

Facilitative mediators continue in that spirit. With impartiality or neutrality as a prominent principle informing their practice, facilitative mediators take great pains to maintain distance from the positions of the parties as well as the likely outcomes if a settlement cannot be reached and the dispute goes to litigation. The facilitator's neutral position is motivated by three considerations. First, facilitative mediators see the parties as being the best-situated to determine which outcome(s) best meets their needs. Second, facilitative mediators see a neutral stance as more likely to engender the parties' trust. Finally, facilitative mediators believe that their approach maximizes the effectiveness of the mediator's interventions because the mediator is not simultaneously focused on other things (like the law, the merits of various options, etc.).

An idealized vision of facilitative mediation unfolds something like this: The facilitative mediator establishes a process by which the parties can gain an understanding of both their own interests and those of their counterpart that may underlie their respective stated positions. Through asking questions, understanding and reframing the perspectives of each party, and reframing issues, the mediator helps the parties discover shared interests and opportunities for mutually beneficial solutions. The mediator may accomplish this in a combination of joint sessions and private caucuses. During the process, the facilitative mediator resists crafting or assessing options and leaves those substantive decisions to the parties.

A variation on facilitative mediation, labeled "understanding-based" mediation, shares facilitative mediation's focus on mediator neutrality. In fact, understanding-based mediators shun even the idea of meeting privately with one of the disputants, out of the concern that information that emerges in private might affect the mediator's neutrality at the expense of the parties' mutual understanding of the situation. As with facilitative mediation, understanding-based mediators encourage parties to establish their own standards for assessing the merits of possible outcomes. In other words, the parties need not resolve their dispute on the basis of what a court would do.

§3.2.2 Evaluative Mediation

Modeled at least in part on judicial settlement conferences, evaluative mediations have a very different focus than facilitative mediations. While facilitative mediations aim at exploring parties' interests and exploring the possibility of creative settlement options, evaluative mediations focus primarily on the parties' alternatives to settlement.

At the heart of the theory underlying evaluative mediation is the idea that the mediators support parties' informed decision making. If, for example, one or both of the parties is overestimating how attractive litigation would be, then it makes sense that the parties would be having a difficult time finding a settlement. A service the evaluative mediator can provide to such parties, therefore, is helping the parties to assess more accurately the risks and opportunities each faces in litigation.

As you might imagine, this different stance often suggests a different personal or professional profile for evaluative mediators (as compared with facilitative mediators). An evaluative mediator typically comes to the mediation with expertise in the law or the particular substantive area of the dispute. The disputants may choose a particular mediator for her specific knowledge in a given industry. Those parties want and expect the mediator to apply her expertise to their dispute and provide guidance on their respective positions based on regulations and standards of practice in that particular field.

An idealized evaluative mediation is one in which the mediator (having assured herself that the parties have obstructive mismatching perceptions of their litigation alternatives) works with each of the parties to unpack the multifaceted prospect of *not* reaching settlement. By working with the parties to see the risks in their positions, the holes in their arguments, and the costs embedded in their litigation strategies, the evaluative mediator aims to make the prospect of settlement more attractive. In some cases, after enough information has been exchanged, the parties may even ask the evaluative mediator to make her own assessment or evaluation of the range (or even the precise figure) that the mediator believes represents the value of the claim in question. This *evaluative* process is how an evaluative mediator earns her title.

A variation on evaluative mediation — one often associated with evaluation, though not always — is *directive* mediation. Evaluative mediators focus on the prospect of nonsettlement. In effect, they focus on each party's perception of its BATNA. (See Chapter 1 for a reminder about the concept of a BATNA.) Directive mediators, by contrast, focus their energies toward promoting a particular settlement option. An evaluative mediator might say, in essence, "Your alternative is much worse than you think." A directive mediator might say, in essence, "This settlement option is a great idea." And the two can be done in tandem, of course. "Because your alternative to settlement is so terrible, I think this option would be a great idea for you. . . ."

§3.2.3 Riskin's Grid

Professor Leonard Riskin proposed a graphical representation of some of the variations between mediators — with a particular focus on the distinction between facilitative and evaluative approaches. The following is drawn from his article, *Understanding Mediators' Orientations, Strategies and Techniques: A Grid for the Perplexed*[1] (an excerpt of which probably appears in your textbook).

Riskin presented the idea that mediators' styles of mediation could best be understood as points along a continuum rather than putting mediators into specific stylistic buckets. Riskin placed the facilitative and evaluative styles on opposite poles of a vertical axis that represent the role of the mediator (recognizing that many mediators adopt traits from both of those styles). He juxtaposed a vertical axis with a horizontal axis, representing the scope of the problem to be mediated, where a narrow scope limited the mediation to the immediate dispute (legal and financial issues), and a broad scope allowed for exploring a wider range of issues and solutions (including community, social, personal, and broader business issues). He divided the axes into four quadrants, hypothesizing that a mediator's style

---

1. Leonard Riskin, *Understanding Mediators' Orientations, Strategies and Techniques: A Grid for the Perplexed*, 1 Harv. Negot. L. Rev. 7, 35 (1996).

Role of Mediator
EVALUATIVE

Urges/pushes parties to accept narrow (position-based) settlement **Proposes** narrow (position-based) agreement **Predicts** court or other outcomes **Assesses** strengths and weaknesses of each side's case	**Urges/pushes** parties to accept broad (interest-based) settlement **Develops and proposes** broad (interest-based) agreement **Predicts** impact (on interests) of not settling **Educates self** about parties' interests
Helps parties evaluate proposals **Helps parties** develop & exchange narrow (position-based) proposals **Asks** about consequences of not settling **Asks** about likely court or other outcomes **Asks** about strengths and weaknesses of each side's case	**Helps parties** evaluate proposals **Helps parties** develop & exchange broad (interest-based) proposals **Helps parties** develop options that respond to interests **Helps parties** understand interests

Problem Definition **NARROW** (left)   Problem Definition **BROAD** (right)

Role of Mediator
FACILITATIVE

could be characterized as an XY coordinate falling within one of four fundamental classifications.

Riskin suggested that while mediators will adopt a number of styles based on the needs of a particular situation, each mediator has a predominant style that falls within one of the four quadrants as evaluative-narrow, evaluative-broad, facilitative-narrow, or facilitative-broad. An evaluative-narrow orientation indicates a mediator that will assess the merits and deficiencies of each disputant's case, will push the parties to settle, and will limit the debate to the immediate dispute. An evaluative-broad mediator may be more likely to look for the interests underlying each party's position and look for shared interests beyond the immediate dispute, but will counsel the parties on the relative merits of their positions. A facilitative-narrow orientation suggests that the mediator will ask probing questions of the parties to help them develop an understanding of their positions, and will allow the parties to create a solution targeted at resolving the dispute at hand. Facilitative-broad mediators will work with the parties to uncover underlying interests beyond the formal parameters of this particular dispute and to explore options for settlement that serve those larger interests. Clearly, the grid is not all-inclusive — there are other key characteristics that can be analyzed in counterpoint. However, it has been well received and remains a useful model of mediator styles.

§3.2.4 Transformative Mediation

The "transformative" model, associated primarily with the works of Joseph Folger and Robert Baruch Bush, has perhaps the most idealistic objectives of any of the mediator approaches discussed here. Both facilitative and evaluative mediation have as their focus the resolution of a particular dispute. In some cases, the dispute may be quite narrow; and in others, it may be broad. But in the end, both approaches are simply means of finding resolution. Transformative mediation, by contrast, focuses on the disputants themselves and on their interactions, rather than on the specifics of a particular dispute (no matter how broadly defined). In the words of Bush and Folger, transformative mediation seeks to enable "moral growth" for the participants.

Underlying transformative mediation is the idea that conflict tends to cause disputants simultaneously to act badly and to feel as though they have lost some measure of control over their circumstances and their reactions. Transformative mediation seeks to empower individuals to pull themselves out of that negative spiral and to develop an ability to recognize the perspectives of someone on the other end of a conflict.

An idealized vision of transformative mediation is one in which the parties and the mediator are primarily in joint sessions. The mediator will take the participants through exercises that allow them to recognize themselves as decent, moral persons with their own intrinsic strengths and capacity to be compassionate. When the individual feels empowered, confidence grows, and the individual is able to listen, trust, respect the other party more, and potentially build a more productive relationship. Therefore, empowerment gives a party the ability to recognize and appreciate the values and perspectives of its counterparts. These two components, empowerment and recognition, are central to transformative mediation.

Transformative mediators focus primarily on the self-determination aspects of mediation. In transformative mediation, the participants are the sole owners of the process. The mediator not only refrains from pushing a particular substantive outcome, but also refrains from imposing a particular mediation process or agenda on the parties. Because success in transformative mediation is measured by the effect on the parties and their ability to deal with each other more effectively, transformative mediation treats the resolution of the immediate dispute as a second-order outcome instead of the primary goal.

At the risk of oversimplifying each of these categories, we offer the following table. You will see that each of these basic approaches to mediation has an internal logic. And, if you believe that different parties in different contexts face a range of different negotiation challenges, then it starts to make sense that there should be a range of different approaches to mediation to address those particular challenges.

	Facilitative	Evaluative	Transformative
Primary Goal	Settlement	Settlement	Improve the quality of parties' interactions
Likely Processes	Joint sessions and private caucuses	Primarily private caucuses	Primarily joint sessions
Negotiation Challenges Targeted	• Misunderstood or unexplored interests • Too few creative options • Bad communication	• Parties have unrealistic expectations about litigation alternatives • Parties need a "nudge" toward reasonable options	• Parties unable to resolve problems on their own • Bad working relationship • Neither understands the other well
Mediator Role(s)	• Ask open questions • Keep parties' conversations on track • Set agendas	• Assess the merits of each side's case • Explore possible alternatives to settlement • Urge particular outcomes	• Highlight opportunities for "empowerment" (parties taking charge) and "recognition" (parties seeing each other's perspective)
Typical Mediator Statements	• "Can you tell me more about your perception of what happened?" • "Why are you asking for . . . ?" • "What interests you about a resolution?" • "Do you have ideas about ways to address this set of interests?"	• "As I see it, you face the following risks and opportunities in litigation . . ." • "At trial, how do you plan to deal with the problematic fact that . . . ?" • "What would be wrong with a settlement like . . . ?"	• "How do you think we should spend our time together today?" • "What would be useful now?" • "What would you like to understand better about what they're saying?"
Primary Mediation Principle	Impartiality or neutrality	Informed consent	Self-determination

§3.3 BASIC PRINCIPLES OF MEDIATION

Just as it would be hard to understand the shape of modern litigation without recognizing its underlying assumptions — for example, the utility of adversarial perspectives, an impartial fact finder, and the application of broadly applicable laws to specific facts — certain basic assumptions underlie the practice of mediation.

Model Standards of Conduct for Mediators

I. Self-Determination

A. A mediator shall conduct a mediation based on the principle of party self-determination. Self-determination is the act of coming to a voluntary, uncoerced decision in which each party makes free and informed choices as to process and outcome. Parties may exercise self-determination at any stage of a mediation, including mediator selection, process design, participation in or withdrawal from the process, and outcomes. . . .

2. A mediator cannot personally ensure that each party has made free and informed choices to reach particular decisions, but, where appropriate, a mediator should make the parties aware of the importance of consulting other professionals to help them make informed choices.

II. Impartiality

A. A mediator shall decline a mediation if the mediator cannot conduct it in an impartial manner. Impartiality means freedom from favoritism, bias or prejudice.

B. A mediator shall conduct a mediation in an impartial manner and avoid conduct that gives the appearance of partiality. . . .

III. Conflicts of Interest

A. A mediator shall avoid a conflict of interest or the appearance of a conflict of interest during and after a mediation. A conflict of interest can arise from involvement by a mediator with the subject matter of the dispute or from any relationship between a mediator and any mediation participant, whether past or present, personal or professional, that reasonably raises a question of a mediator's impartiality. . . .

As you might expect, given the potential inadequacy of any single definition of mediation, no single articulation of mediation's bedrock principles has gained universal acceptance. One prominent articulation of mediation's fundamental values is the Model Standards of Conduct for Mediators, jointly produced by the American Arbitration Association, the American Bar Association, and the Association for Conflict Resolution. We have produced an excerpt here in a sidebar, and the full text appears in Appendix 2.

The Model Standards articulate a broad range of different principles. For our purposes, we think four are critical to understand. We explore three in this chapter — impartiality, self-determination, and informed consent — and the fourth (confidentiality) has its own chapter later in this book.

§3.3.1 Impartiality or Neutrality

The academic literature regarding mediation almost always includes some mention of the idea that the mediator is a third party who is impartial or neutral. Some use the terms "impartial" and "neutral" interchangeably. Others see the two terms as distinct and argue for one or the other as more accurately capturing this fundamental principle of mediation.

The basic idea is that mediators ought not to have an interest in the substance or outcome of the dispute. In some ways, this concept parallels the principle that judges must not have any interests in the dispute and must not have any relationship with any of the parties that would cast doubt on the legitimacy of the judge's decisions. Although a mediator's function is different from a judge's, the two share this principle of neutrality.

It may be easier to describe the concept of impartiality or neutrality by giving some examples of circumstances in which the principle would be violated. Impartiality would be violated if a mediator secretly owned stock in one of the companies participating in the mediation. Impartiality might be compromised if the mediator had a prior, or ongoing, relationship with one of the parties and failed to disclose it to the other parties. Similarly, impartiality might be threatened if a mediator stood to gain or lose financially, depending on the terms of the agreement the disputants reached in mediation. In all of these circumstances, we would fear that the mediator's conduct in the mediation might be motivated by the mediator's personal interests, rather than by the mediator's professional obligations to the disputants.

Why does impartiality matter? One of the driving ideas behind mediation, reflected in the definition offered above, is that mediation is a form of facilitated negotiation. If the mediator has an interest in the outcome of the negotiations, the mediator essentially becomes a *party* to the negotiations, rather than serving the facilitator function.

Impartiality or neutrality comes in at least two different forms, each of which is significant in the context of mediation and both of which are reflected in the Model Standards of Conduct for Mediators. (See Model Standards II and III.) One form is **externally perceived partiality**. This principle asks whether the circumstances would cause others to view the mediator as biased in some way. It does not ask whether the mediator is actually biased, just whether it appears as though the mediator might be. Conflict of interest rules address this concern. This externally perceived neutrality is important to the legitimacy of the mediation process, and, by extension, to the legitimacy of the outcomes mediation produces. The other form is **internally perceived partiality**, sometimes called "actual bias." This asks the more direct (though more difficult to measure objectively) question of whether the mediator holds biases or has preexisting incentives that affect the way the mediator will conduct the mediation.

In its strongest articulation, the mediation principle of impartiality or neutrality encompasses both of these forms. The ideal mediation, therefore, is one in which the mediator is free from any actual or perceived biases.

§3.3.2 Self-Determination

Self-determination — the idea that parties voluntarily determine the elements of an agreement — is a hallmark of mediation in virtually all of the articulations of mediation's foundational principles. This autonomy is also one of mediation's primary attractions. The most fundamental distinction between mediation and arbitration (to overstate it only mildly) is that in mediation, parties still retain the authority to decide whether to resolve the dispute and on what terms. By contrast, in arbitration and other adjudicative processes, parties cede the decision-making power to a third party. Self-determination is at the heart of this distinction.

A process lacking in self-determination may produce a settlement, but it will not be consistent with this fundamental principle of mediation. For example, a mediator with sufficient authority could threaten the parties so credibly as to force the parties to settle a case. ("I will leak horrible things about you and your company to the media if you do not agree to these terms," or "I know you haven't eaten in 18 hours, but you're not leaving this room until you agree to these terms.") Similarly, a mediator might be able to extract a commitment from a party if the party is incapacitated in some way (for example, if a party is a minor or is intoxicated). In all of these events, the mediator might be performing one aspect of the job (settling the case) but does so at the expense of one of the core principles underlying the process.

Why does self-determination matter? The first part of the answer rests in mediation's profoundly informal nature. Mediation involves few, if any, pre-set rules. It routinely involves free-wheeling conversation, unconstrained by structures like the Rules of Evidence. There are no formal motions and no record of the proceedings. Witnesses and other evidence are rarely involved to the same degree one would expect to find in court. All of this is what makes mediation attractive, at least to some. This informality is part of mediation's strength — provided the parties are still the ones making the decision of how the case will be resolved. If, instead, the mediator is the one rendering the decision, then informality, ex parte communications, unstructured conversation, and the other trappings of mediation become troublesome. We would never permit a judge to render decisions in those circumstances. Without self-determination, the mediator might be doing essentially the same thing.

A second reason for self-determination is that, by having the parties retain the ability to make choices about the terms of the outcome, mediation may maximize the opportunity for value-creating outcomes. In short, the parties know best what they care about, what is good for them, and what they can live with. If a mediator — even a mediator with good intentions — takes this decision-making power away, the mediator strips mediation of one of its most attractive promises.

Self-determination has at least two different forms, both of which are important in mediation and both of which appear in the Model Standards of Conduct for Mediators. (See Model Standards I and VI.) The first is that the parties in the mediation should be able to make decisions for themselves, *without improper interference from the mediator*. This does not mean the mediator cannot make suggestions or point out potential implications of different outcomes. But at the end of the day, the mediator must permit the parties to make the final decision.

The second form of self-determination is that the parties must be free to make decisions for themselves, *free of improper influence from others*. This principle is part of what makes the idea of mediating in the context of domestic violence so troubling, for example. Part of the very nature of the cycle of domestic violence can cause the battered spouse to be impaired in (or even incapable of) making decisions for herself or himself. In its purest form, mediation involves all of the relevant parties to a dispute, and each has the unimpaired capacity to make an independent decision about the substantive outcome of the mediation.

§3.3.3 Informed Consent

The third of these fundamental principles of mediation is that the parties' decisions must be adequately informed. At the heart of any voluntary process is the idea of choice. But for that choice to be meaningful, it must be adequately informed.

Not all processes that lead to agreement necessarily involve informed consent. Railroading a party into a particular process or into a particular agreement is anathema to the idea of informed consent. For example, if a mediator precluded the parties from having a meaningful opportunity to review the terms of a potential settlement, informed consent would be threatened. ("I've put together a possible settlement package, involving multiple, complex pieces. You have five minutes to decide. . ..")

Why does informed consent matter in mediation? Virtually all of the benefits mediation touts depend on the idea that the parties, at the end of the process, make good decisions. If the parties are unable to make high-quality decisions for themselves in mediation, then litigation or some other adjudicative process might be more appropriate. Mediation depends on parties making good decisions, and good decisions depend on the parties having adequate information.

Like the first two principles we mention above, informed consent involves at least two different components, both of which appear in the Model Standards of Conduct for Mediators. (See Model Standards I and VI.) The first component suggests that parties should make informed choices as to the mediation *process*. Parties enter into mediations through a variety of mechanisms. In some contexts, the parties initiate mediation independently, and in others, court systems encourage or even require parties to attempt mediation. Even in those circumstances in which mediation is mandatory, no disputant is forced to settle the case. They are forced merely to try mediation. And in order to try mediation, they must understand at least the fundamental aspects of the mediation process, including the role of the mediator. The second component of informed consent is that parties should be informed as to the *substance* of any possible agreement. A decision is only informed if the party understands the implications of the deal.

In its ideal form, each of the parties to a mediation understands and agrees to try mediation as a dispute resolution process. Each party understands what the alternatives to settlement are, and each party understands the implications of any settlement reached in the mediation.

In the chart below, we have summarized these important mediation principles. Recall, of course, that these are not the only three principles one might find in an articulation of mediation's goals. They are, however, the three most likely to be implicated in difficult or important ethical dilemmas in mediation practice.

Impartiality or Neutrality	Self-Determination	Informed Consent
External Impartiality	*Mediator Influence*	*Process Decisions*
Mediator is perceived as having no stake in the outcome	Each party can decide free from interference by the mediator	Each party understands and agrees to the mediation process
Internal Impartiality	*Other Influence*	*Substantive Decisions*
Mediator does not feel biased for or against either party	Each party can decide free from outside interference	Each party understands the substantive implications of possible outcomes

Three Principles of Mediation[2]

§3.4 QUALITY CONTROL IN MEDIATION

Unlike attorneys or doctors (or manicurists, for that matter), mediators require no license to provide their services. Doctors have a monopoly on providing certain medical services. Lawyers have a monopoly on providing legal advice to clients. But there are no general restrictions on who can be a mediator, and therefore, no restrictions on who can provide mediation (or mediation-like) services.

Of course, as a practical matter, not everyone can make a living as a mediator. Hanging a shingle announcing one's availability does not guarantee clients. In theory, one must be good (or at least appear good) in order to get customers.

Still, the question remains: How can we be assured that those who are providing their services as mediators do so competently? Because no monopoly exists, we cannot rely on a quality-linked barrier to entry into the market. Doctors must pass Boards. Lawyers must pass the Bar. Mediators have no equivalent.

Below we examine three potential avenues for assuring the quality of mediator services. As you will see, none of these is foolproof or sufficient to guarantee quality on its own. But these three avenues are not mutually exclusive, and for the moment at least, they represent the bulk of the formal mechanisms available to help mediation consumers know that they will receive quality services.

---

2. This construction of foundational mediation principles is drawn from Jamie Henikoff and Michael Moffitt, *Remodeling the Model Standards of Conduct for Mediators*, 2 Harv. Negot. L. Rev. 87 (1997).

§3.4.1 Certification or Credentialing

Because mediation is not a practice for which a monopoly has been established, no license is required. But that does not mean that the basic instinct behind licensure — identifying a pool of people deemed qualified and appropriate to practice — has no place in mediation. Certification or credentialing systems are potential vehicles for accomplishing these goals. There are two fundamental types of certification or credentialing systems: those linked to organizational affiliation and those linked to the institutions that receive mediation cases. We describe each briefly below.

Organizational affiliation credentials are established, as the name suggests, by organizations with whom potential mediators theoretically want to be affiliated. For example, a particular professional mediators' association might require its members to meet certain standards (perhaps a certain level of experience, a certain kind of education, or even performance on a certain kind of assessment mechanism). The idea is that practicing mediators might want to be members of these organizations because they provide direct benefits to their members in terms of conferences, resources, or referrals, or because the market of mediation consumers recognizes and values membership ("I am more likely to get hired because I can put this group's name on my website."). Of course, not all organizations' membership requirements are actual proxies for any definition of mediator quality. Some professional organizations' membership requirements begin and end with an annual dues check that doesn't bounce. Still, recognizing that the state is not in a position to monitor the behaviors of thousands of mediators, one avenue is to rely on private mediation organizations to do some initial screening by establishing membership standards.

Case source credentials represent another form of quality control through an initial screening mechanism of some sort by the institutions that receive mediation cases and assign them to a mediator. Much like organizational credentials, the basis for exclusion and inclusion is almost entirely in the discretion of the organization (including court programs) setting the standards. They could look to experience, to professional training, or to whatever else they want in determining who receives the "stamp of approval." The difference is that these organizations are the source of potential cases. These are the places from which practicing mediators draw some part of their business. And, as a result, we might expect that it would be that much more attractive for a mediator to strive to attain whatever standards the organization sets for its membership.

For example, a court-affiliated mediation program could be the source of cases for mediators. And the thousands of court mediation programs around the country do set certain standards (although there is considerable variation between the programs on just what they want to see in a mediator). A mediator who fails to meet these standards cannot receive cases through that particular source. Many sources of cases are governmental — court systems, social service agencies, and the like, though some are private or quasi-private. The United States Postal Service, for example, sets standards for the large cadre of mediators it employs to deal with employee disputes.

§3.4.2 Ethics Codes

We have already described some of the provisions of the Model Standards of Conduct for Mediators, the most widely recognized set of mediator ethics codes. Many other ethics codes exist as well. Some are specific to a particular type of mediation practice, for example, the Standards of Practice for Family and Divorce Mediation promulgated by the Association of Family and Conciliation Courts (AFCC). Others are specific to organizations. For example, the International Institute for Conflict Prevention & Resolution's Model Rule of Professional Conduct for the Lawyer as Third Party Neutral theoretically governs all of the mediators on its rosters.

One of the benefits of having ethics codes for the purpose of quality control is that they treat the question of mediators' *practices* rather than merely looking at their initial qualifications. Well-trained, experienced mediators can make mistakes. If the only quality control mechanism were credentialing, those mistakes would go entirely unaddressed.

For mediator ethics codes, particularly as they have been formulated currently, the major challenges are interpretation and enforcement. Lawyers tend to have a better sense than mediators of the true application of the ethics codes of the legal practice. This is, in part, because the Bar regularly hears complaints and publishes what amount to explanations of legal ethics rules. Few equivalents exist in mediation, although some states have grievance procedures for certain kinds of mediator misconduct. Further, legal ethics have enforcement mechanisms that make it unlikely a practitioner would ignore their provisions. If you violate legal ethics, you can be disbarred. If you violate mediation ethics provisions, however, the threat is more nebulous: Perhaps you'll be kicked out of the organization that promulgated the ethical rules. But because no mediation monopoly exists, you can continue to mediate (if you can continue to attract clients).

Despite these challenges associated with mediation ethics codes, their provisions are important to understand. In addition to the three fundamental principles described above, which appear in some form in virtually all ethics codes, most codes also include a set of rules that roughly parallel legal ethics topics (like conflicts of interest, advertising, and the boundaries on representation). A look at the headings of the Model Standards is informative.

Model Standards of Conduct for Mediators

Table of Contents

  I. Self-Determination
 II. Impartiality
III. Conflicts of Interest
 IV. Competence
  V. Confidentiality
 VI. Quality of the Process
VII. Advertising and Solicitation
VIII. Fees and Other Charges
 IX. Advancement of Mediation Practice

Mediators who are also lawyers must be aware that some provisions of legal ethics codes touch on the practice of mediation. Most prominently, Model Rule 2.4(b) provides that, "A lawyer serving as a third-party neutral shall inform unrepresented parties that the lawyer is not representing them. When the lawyer knows or reasonably should know that a party does not understand the lawyer's role in the matter, the lawyer shall explain the difference between the lawyer's role as a third-party neutral and a lawyer's role as one who represents a client." Giving bad legal advice in the course of a mediation, for example, could expose a lawyer to sanctions based on the giving of advice (if to one party, but not the other), the practice of law (if the lawyer is not authorized in that jurisdiction anyway), and the quality of advice (if following it harms the client, the client could sue for malpractice).

§3.4.3 Private Liability

With most kinds of professional services — even those for which no professional monopoly exists — if a consumer receives a substandard product, the consumer may be able to file a civil lawsuit against the service provider. Private liability for malpractice is a threat hanging over the head of most service providers. In theory, the same should be true of mediators. The reality in practice, however, is that most mediators operate without any significant exposure to malpractice liability. At least three factors contribute to this dynamic — mediator immunity, vague standards of care, and lack of proof for causation and damages.

§3.4.3.1 Immunity

At least some mediators operate without any fear of private liability for their actions as mediators because they enjoy immunity. This immunity can come in one of three forms. First, **quasi-judicial immunity** is a common law form of immunity that shields mediators from suits alleging harm. The theory behind quasi-judicial immunity is that we want judges (and people like judges) to perform their job without fear that one of their decisions might offend a party enough that the party would sue the judge. The theory behind extending quasi-judicial immunity to mediators is, as the name suggests, that mediators operate in a quasi-judicial capacity and therefore need the same kind of protections against lawsuits as judges. The most prominent case on this point is *Wagshal v. Foster*, 28 F.3d 1249 (D.C. Cir. 1994). In that case, the court appointed Foster to serve as a "neutral case evaluator" to try to settle Wagshal's claim. After a failed effort at settlement, Foster wrote the presiding judge a letter indicating that the case "can and should be settled if the parties are willing to act reasonably," and recommended that the judge order Wagshal, in particular, to mediate "in good faith." Wagshal subsequently settled his original claim, but then sued Foster, claiming that the letter to the judge had violated Wagshal's rights and had forced him to settle improperly. The court found that Foster's functions were sufficiently comparable to a judge's to extend quasi-judicial immunity. And, without much explanation, the court in *Wagshal* extended this logic to mediators as well as case evaluators. In some jurisdictions, therefore, mediators enjoy this common law immunity.

Second, some jurisdictions have established statutory **qualified immunity** for mediators. As the name suggests, qualified immunity is limited (or "qualified"), but typically, it only excludes liability for injuries resulting from egregious acts like intentional torts. A mediator with qualified immunity, therefore, operates largely free of the threat of private liability.

A third source of immunity can come in the form of a **contractual waiver**. Each jurisdiction handles the enforceability of such provisions differently, and it is beyond the scope of this text to survey those variations. You should know, however, that some mediator contracts include language that at least *purports* to serve the function of shielding the mediator from liability for any mediation conduct.

§3.4.3.2 Standards of Care

Most mediators' contracts contain such vague commitments about exactly what the mediator will and will not be doing that they would rarely serve as the basis for a complaint against a mediator. Instead, most complaints against a mediator would likely more closely resemble tort-based malpractice claims, of the sort filed against other kinds of service providers.

As with a negligence-based malpractice case against any other kind of service provider, a plaintiff alleging mediator malpractice must show that the mediator's conduct failed to meet the normal standard of care for professionals in that area. A doctor who mistakenly leaves a surgical instrument in a patient, or a lawyer who misses filing deadlines causing a case to be dismissed each clearly violate this standard. But what could a mediator do that would clearly violate mediation's standards of practice?

Some potential actions by a mediator, of course, would fall below a generally accepted standard of care: A mediator who shows up intoxicated, a mediator who forgets to show up at all, or a mediator who violates the specific terms of the mediation agreement. In these kinds of cases, an aggrieved party would have little difficulty demonstrating that the mediator's conduct fell short of that which is required. Similarly, if a mediator fails to disclose a known conflict of interest and the state has adopted a version of the Uniform Mediation Act (which explicitly requires such disclosures), the mediator will have breached an established duty of care.

But, consistent with the variations in approach or style we described in §3.2, mediation has fewer "generally accepted" practices than one might imagine. One might evaluate the merits of a legal dispute (evaluative mediation) or not (facilitative mediation). One might try to move the parties toward settlement (evaluative or facilitative mediation) or not (transformative mediation). One might ask open-ended questions or not. One might keep the parties together, or meet with them separately. In short, an unhappy mediation party will have a challenge in demonstrating that the mediator's actions were seen as unacceptable among the community of people who practice mediation, given the great variety of actions endorsed by that community.

§3.4.3.3 Causation and Damages

Proving that a mediator breached a duty of care is worthwhile (in practical terms) only if an unhappy mediation consumer can show that the mediator's actions also caused compensable injury. At the lowest level, this may not be difficult. ("The mediator never showed up to our scheduled meeting, causing me to lose the entire day and incur the following expenses.") But the prospect of serious damages is most likely to arise because the mediator's conduct allegedly affected the settlement of the case for which the mediator was hired. For example, "We didn't settle, but with a competent mediator we would have." Or "We settled, but I now believe I could have done better, and it's the mediator's fault."

An unhappy mediation party in either of those circumstances faces challenges demonstrating causation and damages. How can you prove that a different mediator's action would have produced a settlement or a different settlement? How can the plaintiff get around the fact that it was the plaintiff who signed the agreement, not the mediator? How can the plaintiff establish the difference between what the other party was willing to do in the mediation that took place (as opposed to during the mediation the plaintiff wishes had taken place)? The highly speculative nature of these inquiries explains, in part, why successful malpractice actions against mediators are so uncommon.

Examples

The State of the Estate

Following the untimely death of their parents, three brothers (Greg, Peter, and Bobby) find themselves locked in a bitter dispute over the division of the estate. During the decade prior to his parents' death, Bobby was largely estranged from the family. Greg, perpetually cash-strapped, had spent most of those years caring for his parents. Peter's acting career had delivered him some fame and even greater fortune.

Their parents' will suggested an unorthodox division of the estate, in a manner that may make the will vulnerable to a legal challenge. The three brothers met briefly to discuss whether they could agree on a division of the assets, without resorting to litigation. During that meeting, Greg insisted that "a court would give basically all of it to me." Bobby laughed and lobbed personal insults at both of his older brothers and Peter chided both of them for "inventing things to fight about." When Peter suggested that this might be about something more than the money, Greg and Bobby rolled their eyes, and the meeting quickly ended.

Assume that mediators in their area accurately describe themselves as adopting one of the three styles or approaches (facilitative, evaluative, transformative) described above. In the context of this dispute, what potential benefits might the parties see if they select a mediator who is

1a. facilitative in her approach?

1b. evaluative in her approach?

1c. transformative in her approach?

The Discriminating Palate

The owner of an upscale restaurant named The Discriminating Palate, Henri Leduc, has a notorious temper and an impeccable record as an entrepreneur. Recently, he created a new maitre d' position. Leduc hired an employee from outside of the restaurant, rather than promoting someone from within. Cecilia Cervantes, a long-time employee at The Discriminating Palate, had applied for the position and was deeply disappointed not to have been given the promotion. Cervantes spoke with Leduc shortly after the decision was announced, and the conversation only seemed to make Cervantes angrier. She has indicated an intention to file a lawsuit against Leduc and The Discriminating Palate, alleging gender discrimination.

Pursuant to the restaurant's employee handbook, Cervantes and Leduc are obligated to "attempt" mediation first. They agree on a mediator, and submit an initial brief outlining the facts above. At the outset of the mediation, therefore, the mediator knows only a limited amount of information about the case and the parties.

What kinds of questions might the mediator ask at the outset, if the mediator is

2a. facilitative in her approach?

2b. evaluative in her approach?

2c. transformative in her approach?

A Mediation Disaster, Yes, But What *Kind* of Disaster?

Romeo and Juliet are recent immigrants, neither of whom speaks English very well. After just under two years of marriage, they conclude that divorce is the only viable option for their troubled relationship. Each hires an attorney, and through those attorneys, agrees to try mediation.

At the mediation session, which takes place in English, Juliet's attorney indicates that she will be speaking on behalf of Juliet, and Juliet sits in a corner and begins to read a book. Meanwhile, Romeo's attorney fails to show up. After waiting for several minutes, the mediator says to Romeo, "Look, either we start now, or I'll report to the judge that you reneged on your promise to try mediation. And that's not going to look good for you." Romeo protests that he is not prepared "for to making law arguments," but eventually agrees to follow the mediator and others into the mediation room.

As the mediation unfolds, Juliet's attorney does virtually all of the talking. She lays out the basics of her legal case, and each time Romeo attempts to interject a point, she talks over him. The mediator, meanwhile, sits back and periodically nods at Juliet's attorney's statements.

After almost an hour of this, Romeo's attorney walks into the conference room. Upon seeing the mediator, Romeo's attorney's eyes light up and she laughs. She and the mediator rush to each other, hug, and begin talking about how "it's been too long since we've gone fishing."

At that point, both Romeo and Juliet sit back and watch the lawyers haggle, not understanding much of what was being discussed. At one point, the mediator produced a coin from his pocket, flipped it, and announced the result. One attorney shrugged and the other looked pleased. Shortly after, the three announced that a final agreement had been reached, and the lawyers told their clients to sign it.

3. **Problems to Explore.** With reference to the basic principles of mediation, describe the potential problems with this sequence of events.

A Mediation Dilemma?

Two former business partners, Cagney and Lacey, have a dispute involving the noncompete clause appearing in their partnership agreement. They agree to try mediation early in the life of the dispute, on the theory that it might be possible to resolve things before attorneys' fees become astronomical.

Cagney appears at the mediation with her lawyer. At the outset, Lacey speaks with the mediator privately and says, "I didn't know she was going to bring an attorney. I haven't hired one. I thought this was supposed to be informal. Should I go ahead with the mediation?" The mediator assures Lacey that she is not required to have an attorney in order to participate, but that she is free to consult one at any point. Lacey agrees to go ahead with the mediation session.

During the mediation session, Cagney's attorney takes an aggressive posture toward Lacey, outlining what he describes as the "airtight" nature of the noncompete clause. He also asserts that Cagney would be entitled to a vast range of different remedial options, including not only indefinite injunctive relief, but also punitive damages. Lacey appears shaken by the news, but after about an hour, seems convinced and appears on the verge of agreeing to drop the matter altogether.

The mediator, an attorney with extensive practice experience in employment law in this jurisdiction, is virtually positive that Cagney's lawyer has dramatically misstated the law in this case. The mediator knows that no court in the state has ever granted punitive damages in such a case, that no court in the state has granted an indefinite injunction in such a case, and that the liquidated damages figure claimed by Cagney would almost certainly be stricken under the relevant state standards. But Lacey appears to know none of this.

4a. **Doing Nothing.** If the mediator facilitated the discussions through to conclusion, such that Lacey signed Cagney's attorney's proposed settlement, what principle(s) of mediation might be implicated?

4b. **Providing Legal Advice.** If the mediator met privately with Lacey and advised her that Cagney's lawyer's assessment of the case is flawed, what principle(s) of mediation might be implicated?

4c. **Recommending Legal Advice.** If the mediator met privately with Lacey and advised her to seek legal advice before accepting Cagney's lawyer's proposal, what principle(s) of mediation might be implicated?

The Trouble with "Working It Out"

The parties in a relatively simple slip-and-fall case mutually consent to having their dispute referred to a court-affiliated mediator. The mediator gathers the disputants into a conference room and asks them, jointly, "Why can't you work this out?" Each party carefully describes the facts underlying the dispute, highlighting the major points of their disagreement. The mediator responds by saying, "OK, but why can't you work this out?" The parties explain further their prior efforts at settlement, indicating that they feel stuck. This repeats itself twice more, and after more than an hour, the mediator says, "As I see it, you all really should be working it out." The parties storm out of the mediation, furious at having wasted their time. They agree jointly to file a complaint against the mediator.

5. **Likely Trouble?** Is the mediator likely to get in trouble, and if so, what kind of trouble?

Neighborly Love

Two neighbors, Fred and Barney, have had a multiyear feud over issues ranging from noise and yard maintenance to property boundaries and easements. One day, after a tense conversation in their shared driveway, they agreed that they should hire a mediator to try to resolve "everything." They do some research, and ultimately agree to hire Morton, a mediator whose business card and website includes the slogan, "Pushy But Effective Mediation."

During the mediation, to which neither party brought an attorney, Fred and Barney outlined the substance of their various grievances against each other. They made considerable progress, and began drafting what they called an "omnibus settlement agreement." Barney was lobbying to include a revision to the language regarding an easement involving both properties. Fred opposed the revision to the language, and the entire mediation appeared on the brink of derailing.

Morton pulled Barney into a private caucus and said, "Listen, Barney. Give it up. The easement language you're pushing for is utterly unenforceable. There's a city ordinance directly on point, and the courts have weighed in as well. It's time to end this now." Barney expressed surprise, indicating that he had drawn the language from a contract given to him by a lawyer friend. Morton said, "Look, so far, I haven't told Fred about the enforceability problem. I'll stay silent if you go back in there and tell him you'll drop the easement request if he'll give you the language you want about shrubbery. That should end the whole thing. Otherwise, I'll tell Fred about the law, and you'll get neither." Barney reluctantly agrees, and the mediation quickly produces a settlement on the terms Morton outlined.

A few days after the agreement was finalized, Barney learned from a lawyer friend of his that Morton's legal opinion was completely unfounded. No city ordinance exists, and there have been no recent court cases involving easements of the sort Barney was proposing. Barney is livid, and wants to go after Morton.

6. **Exposure.** What, if any, exposure does Morton face for his conduct during the mediation?

Explanations
The State of the Estate

1a. Facilitative. A mediator who adopts a facilitative approach to the mediation often focuses on promoting understanding of each side's interests and the prospect of creative problem solving as a means of resolving the dispute. Each of the brothers comes to the dispute with different resources, and each probably has different interests and different priorities. As described in Chapter 1, these kinds of differences often lend themselves to crafting value-creating settlement options. A facilitative mediator, by unearthing each party's interests and by improving the parties' communication about possible options, might help them discover a more elegant solution to the problem than they might otherwise find.

1b. Evaluative. If everyone agreed on how the matter would be resolved in court, the dispute might be less challenging to resolve. In this case, however, Greg believes he would get "basically all of it" in court, and the others apparently disagree. An evaluative mediator might be able to address the brothers' assessments of their alternatives to an agreement. Using the terminology from Chapter 1, the evaluative mediator would help them assess the strengths of their BATNAs. Extended litigation on the matter risks burning through the assets of the estate, and an evaluative mediator may help to hasten the parties' discovery of an acceptable settlement option.

1c. Transformative. None of the brothers is immune to the costs of their difficult relationship. These brothers act as though they dislike each other, and they are apparently not skilled at solving problems together. Even so, they are going to remain brothers forever. So there is some reason to think that they would benefit from improving their relationship. With her focus on giving the parties an opportunity to (re)craft their interactions and to find opportunities to demonstrate that they recognize each other's experiences, a transformative mediator might help in that relationship-mending process.

The Discriminating Palate

2a. A mediator with a **facilitative** approach would be most inclined toward exploring opportunities for improving the parties' communication and finding problem-solving opportunities. To that end, a facilitative mediator would probably want to explore each party's perception of the events that led to the dispute underlying the mediation — for purposes of understanding what might motivate the disputants in their search for a settlement. Follow-up questions would most likely involve an exploration of each party's interests, their relative priorities among issues, and their ideas about possible avenues for settlement. What is most important to Cervantes? What kind of relationship would Leduc want with Cervantes in the future?

2b. A mediator with an **evaluative** approach would be most inclined toward exploring each party's perceptions of what a court might do in this case. To that end, like a facilitative mediator, an evaluative mediator would probably want to explore each party's perception of the events that led to the dispute underlying the mediation. But unlike the facilitative mediator, the evaluative mediator would likely explore these perceptions for the purpose of assessing the extent to which the facts establish a right to relief or a defense under the relevant law. Follow-up questions would most likely involve an exploration of whichever aspects of the legal case the mediator deems to be most important to assess accurately the risks and opportunities this case would present in litigation. Maybe the case will hinge on what Leduc told Cervantes. Maybe it will hinge on Cervantes' qualifications. Maybe the dispute over damages will be informed by Cervantes' experiences in the job market. In other words, the evaluative mediator will focus on whatever information he or she needs to collect in order to conduct a thorough assessment.

2c. A mediator with a **transformative** approach would be most inclined to invite the parties to suggest an agenda or sequence of topics for discussion in the mediation. The mediator might invite — but not force — conversation about each party's perception of the events that led to the dispute underlying the mediation. The aim of doing so, however, would not necessarily be the resolution of the narrow dispute in question. Instead, quite conceivably, the mediator's focus would be largely or entirely on the parties themselves or on their relationship. How well does Leduc genuinely recognize Cervantes' experience of their interactions? How well does she understand his? Are there ways of helping one or both of the parties to see more opportunities to make decisions for themselves about the mediation process and any eventual decisions that might emerge from that process? The mediator's role, in short, will be to help the parties to discover opportunities to expand their understanding of each other and of their own capacity to manage their differences.

A Mediation Disaster, Yes, But What *Kind* of Disaster?

3. **Problems to Explore**. This is a debacle of a mediation, by many measures. Each of the three primary principles of mediation was potentially offended by one or more of these events.

Impartiality. Two events during this sequence suggest at least the prospect of an impartiality problem. The first, and most glaring, is the hug exchanged between the mediator and one of the parties' attorneys. Neither the Model Standards of Conduct for Mediators nor any other mediation ethics codes of which we are aware prohibits a mediator from knowing one or more of the mediation participants, or even from having a relationship with them. The Model Standards demand, however, impartiality and freedom from conflicts of interest. As to the mediator's perception of his own bias, Model Standard II provides, "If at any time, a mediator is unable to conduct a mediation in an impartial manner, the mediator shall withdraw." It defines impartiality as "freedom from favoritism, bias or prejudice." Because the mediator continued with the mediation, we are left to presume that the mediator believed he could mediate without any **actual partiality or bias**. The Model Standards do not stop there, however. Model Standard III provides, "A mediator shall disclose, as soon as practicable all actual and potential conflicts of interest that are reasonably known to the mediator and could reasonably be seen as raising a question about the mediator's impartiality." (Model Standard III(C).) Here, the obvious prior relationship creates a **risk of perceived partiality or bias**. Perhaps the mediator thought the hug substituted for disclosure, but the question of the mediator's partiality is clearly appropriate. The mediator should have explained the context of the relationship between him and Romeo's attorney and received Juliet's approval before continuing with the mediation.

A second occurrence could — but probably does not — raise questions about impartiality in this case. As Juliet's attorney spoke, the mediator is said to have been "nodding." Clearly, there is some point at which a mediator might be so wholly and evidently favoring one side's arguments over the other's that the principle of impartiality would be implicated. At the same time, a mediator need not sit idly, stone-faced, unmoved or unaffected by any of the things the parties are saying during a mediation. Here, the mediator's responses could, in context, be an example of bias, or they could be an example of good listening. We don't have enough information here to condemn the mediator for partiality.

Informed consent. At the outset, Romeo appears not even to understand the basic nature of the mediation process to which he is being invited. To the extent he is **inadequately informed about the process**, we should be concerned about whether he could reasonably offer informed consent to participate in the mediation at all.

Because both parties have limited ability to speak English, we would question the degree to which either could have **adequate information about the substance of the agreement** to consent to it knowingly. If the parties were unrepresented, then this would clearly be an issue. Here, however, because of the presence of counsel, we *might* assume that the attorneys serve to cleanse the process and the agreement of any flaws. But it would at least implicate the principle of informed consent.

Self-determination. The mediator's threat to Romeo regarding the commencement of the mediation at least potentially implicates Romeo's self-determination in the process. To the extent the mediator's (improper) threat served to coerce Romeo or to strip him of his ability to choose appropriately for himself, the mediator impaired his self-determination. This does not mean that every time a mediator helps a party to understand the consequences of one decision or another, the mediator is impairing self-determination. But here, particularly because the threat was improper, the mediator acted improperly at the outset.

The other event that might give the appearance of threatening party self-determination is the manner in which the parties themselves were excluded from the process. Self-determination certainly does not mean that a party cannot turn over some aspects of the dispute to her attorney to handle. Concerns emerge, however, if a party *cannot* participate, as opposed to merely *chooses not to*. The fact that both remained inactive in the corner may (or may not) be evidence of impropriety here. The fact of the coin flipping, although unorthodox, is not per se evidence that the parties' self-determination was violated. Disputants can choose almost any method for resolving their differences in the unstructured, informal process that is mediation. Provided we are comfortable imagining that the attorneys were acting on their clients' behalf and that they were doing so with authority, the coin flip is the least of the problems in this sequence of events!

A Mediation Dilemma?

4a. Doing Nothing. A mediator cannot always avoid ethical problems by simply staying silent. To be certain, there are more ways to get in trouble if you actually *do* something as a mediator. But in this circumstance, like some others, a mediator who does not intervene may be overseeing a mediation that runs afoul of one or more of mediation's fundamental principles.

In this case, Lacey appears strongly at risk of making a decision without adequate information. In other words, her **informed consent** is in jeopardy. Her conversation with the mediator before the mediation began was not problematic, in the sense that the mediator gave her the choice of whether to continue and assured her that she was not required to have an attorney. Lacey understood mediation well enough that we would probably deem her consent informed as to the process. And it is not that Lacey fails to understand what Cagney's attorney's offer means. Instead, what is troubling here is that Lacey clearly misunderstands (as far as the mediator knows) what her alternatives to settling look like. In that sense, we might have concerns that her consent is not adequately informed.

There is a limit to this line of reasoning, of course. It cannot be the mediator's responsibility to assure that disputants have full and complete information both about the implications of possible deals and about their litigation alternatives. Such a level of information is almost surely unattainable, even if there were not impartiality and other constraints on what the mediator could do to achieve it. In addition, we really have no idea what is actually important to Lacey. What if the case — or the particular outcome she was seeking — was not actually very important to her? Still, particularly where one of the disputants is unrepresented, a mediator who sits silently while a party makes a decision based on plainly erroneous assumptions cannot be said to have fully protected that party's informed decision making. Model Standard I(A)(1) provides: "Although party self-determination for process design is a fundamental principle of mediation practice, a mediator may need to balance such party self-determination with a mediator's duty to conduct a quality process in accordance with these Standards."

Unfortunately, as the analysis of each of the two subsequent options suggests, a mediator who wants to take steps toward ameliorating Lacey's level of information is in a difficult position. To improve the degree to which the mediation is consistent with the principle of informed consent, the mediator risks doing damage to another of mediation's important principles. In this way, the three principles articulated in this section often interact with each other.

4b. Providing Legal Advice. In brief, neither legal ethics nor mediation ethics would permit the mediator to provide legal advice to Lacey.

Legal ethics prevent an attorney serving as a mediator from representing one of the parties. (See ABA Model Rule of Professional Conduct 2.4.) The idea behind this prohibition is that a mediator necessarily is providing a service when two or more parties have at least potentially conflicting (and often very conflicting) interests. And one of the fundamental ideas behind having a lawyer represent you is that you are hiring the lawyer to advocate for *you*, not for someone else. If the lawyer-mediator in this case were to provide legal advice to Lacey, he would be doing so at the expense of Cagney's interests — something legal ethics do not permit.

Mediation ethics also prohibit the mediator from providing legal advice to Lacey. The principle of **impartiality** is certainly implicated if a mediator begins to dispense legal advice. This is not merely a case of the lawyer providing a legal assessment of some sort to both parties (a practice we describe in the section below, and about which there is some controversy). Instead, this would be the mediator providing legal advice to one party, *but not to the other*. The Model Standards anticipate these dilemmas, and in Standard VI(A)(5) provide: "The role of a mediator differs substantially from other professional roles. Mixing the role of a mediator and the role of another profession is problematic and thus, a mediator should distinguish between the roles. A mediator may provide information that the mediator is qualified by training or experience to provide, only if the mediator can do so consistent with these Standards." In light of the Model Standards' insistence that mediators conduct mediations "in an impartial manner" and the legal ethics prohibition against providing legal advice to only one of the mediator's parties, the mediator would not be permitted to do so in this case.

This is not to say that a mediator would be wholly unjustified to at least think about this as a possible course of action. After all, among the principles we described above, **informed consent** is critical. And it is easy to imagine that the mediator might worry that Lacey is about to sign an agreement without adequately understanding its implications and the alternatives she might encounter in litigation. But this particular avenue for addressing that dilemma appears barred.

4c. Recommending Legal Advice. If the mediator met privately with Lacey and advised her to seek legal advice before accepting Cagney's lawyer's proposal, the mediator would be increasing the degree to which the mediation is consistent with the principle of informed consent. Lacey would, at a minimum, be informed that there are relevant legal principles of which she should be aware. And, theoretically, if she consults an attorney, she will be in a position to understand the tradeoffs involved between the proposed settlement and the prospect of litigation.

This matches the Model Standards' vision of an ideal mediation — one "in which each party makes free and informed choices as to process and outcome." (Model Standard IA.) In fact, the Model Standards specifically suggest that a mediator take actions like this: "A mediator cannot personally ensure that each party has made free and informed choices to reach particular decisions, but, where appropriate, a mediator should make the parties aware of the importance of consulting other professionals to help them make informed choices." (Model Standard I(A)(2).) This also supports the principle of self-determination, because the mediator is not forcing Lacey to do anything. Instead, the mediator is inviting Lacey to seek additional information in a way that enhances both her informed consent and self-determination.

The potential complication with this approach stems from the principle of impartiality. If the mediator had a standard policy of advising all clients to seek legal counsel before signing an agreement, impartiality would likely not be implicated. But here, the mediator is contemplating this intervention specifically because she believes Cagney's attorney is misstating the relevant law. Even if the mediator does not feel biased, Cagney and her attorney would likely be disappointed, to say the least, that the mediator was offering Lacey this suggestion. Of course, Cagney may never learn of the mediator's advice to Lacey because it may take place in private. But that practical consideration ("If they don't see me do it, it's not wrong.") does not answer the question of whether the practice is consistent with mediation's fundamental principles.

The drafters of the Model Standards clearly recognized that a mediator in this circumstance would necessarily need to balance multiple considerations. As a result, instead of a requirement or even a blanket endorsement of the idea of sending parties to lawyers, the Model Standards include the caveat that mediators should do so "where appropriate," without any further explanation of when it might and might not be appropriate.

The Trouble with "Working It Out"

5. **Likely Trouble?** Although the mediator in this case does not appear to have done anything helpful, the mediator's exposure to serious sanction is quite limited.

The first reason the mediator's exposure in this case is limited has to do with the difficulty of demonstrating that the mediator's behaviors were, in fact, substandard. In this case, the disputants were clearly unhappy with the mediator. And the mediation did not produce a settlement. But neither of those two facts is sufficient to demonstrate malpractice by a mediator. Not all parties are happy, and not all cases settle, even when the mediator does a perfectly respectable job. Here, the parties would have to demonstrate that the mediator's actions fell below the level of competence demanded by practitioners in the area. And a challenge in proving that will be that mediators do an extraordinary variety of things. Even this mediator's persistent, vague question is not utterly indefensible. True, the approach does not fit perfectly within the orthodoxy of any of the three major approaches to mediation. But mediators do any number of creative things, and most are entirely acceptable — or at least not facially malpractice.

The second reason that the mediator is not liable stems from the mediator's position as an official court-affiliated mediator. Whatever court program administers these mediations may have some sanction available for dealing with terrible mediators, but the sanction is likely limited to simply removing the offending mediator from the roster of mediators the program will call in the future. Even more significantly, because the mediator was acting through the court system, the mediator likely enjoys some form of immunity from liability. The court in *Wagshal v. Foster* held that mediators were sufficiently judge-like in their function to warrant the common law extension of quasi-judicial immunity to mediators. Even if this jurisdiction does not go that far, it is very likely that court-affiliated mediators would be protected in all but the most egregious cases. As unimpressive as this mediator's performance was, it does not rise to the level of intentionally harmful behavior for which a mediator might be found liable.

Neighborly Love

6. **Exposure.** Morton faces three possible kinds of trouble, if Barney wants to bring a complaint against him.

First, the mere fact that Morton provided legal advice to Barney exposes Morton to sanction. If Morton is an attorney, he may have violated his legal professional ethics by providing legal counsel to one client (Barney) to the detriment of another client (Fred). What precise sanction Morton faces depends on the particulars of the state Bar in question, and could range from a letter of reprimand to disbarment, though the most serious sanctions are quite unlikely. And if Morton is not an attorney, the fact that he gave legal advice very likely violates state restrictions against the unauthorized practice of law, violations of which are typically prosecuted through the state Bar.

Second, Morton not only gave legal advice, but also gave *bad* legal advice. As with any attorney who offers erroneous legal advice, Morton may face a legal malpractice action. Barney may face some challenges in proving that Morton represented him, that he provided bad legal advice, and that Barney relied on that bad legal advice to his detriment. But given the clarity of Morton's assertion, and because those assertions were demonstrably false, Barney has a chance of recovering some level of damages against Morton for legal malpractice.

Finally, Morton *might* be subject to some sort of sanction specific to his role as a mediator. For example, Morton's conduct violates most articulations of mediation ethics regarding the prospect of a mediator providing legal advice to one party. The sanctions for violating these ethics codes are generally limited by the power of whatever organization promulgated them. So, for example, if Morton violates the ethics code of the Association for Conflict Resolution, the Association might revoke Morton's membership. That, of course, might concern Morton, but it does not accomplish much for Barney.

Could Barney sue Morton successfully for mediator malpractice? As a privately contracted mediator (as opposed to a court-affiliated mediator), Morton is not likely to enjoy any form of immunity. Barney may have little problem demonstrating that Morton's conduct fell below the standard of care or practice reasonably expected of a mediator. But as with most forms of alleged mediator misconduct, Barney will have considerable challenges in proving that Morton's conduct caused a demonstrable injury. True, Morton gave bad advice, and that might be enough for Barney to avoid paying Morton's fees. But to recover anything more substantial, Barney would have to overcome hurdles such as proving that he would have succeeded in convincing Fred to agree to the easement but for Morton's advice. As a result, Barney is more likely to have success in pursuing an action against Morton by focusing on legal malpractice (the bad advice) than on the mediation-specific (violating impartiality) aspects of his conduct.

CHAPTER 4

Keeping Secrets: Confidentiality in Negotiation and Mediation

§4.1 INTRODUCTION

Litigation is presumptively public. We hear about big cases in the media, and we study judicial decisions to learn about the law. By contrast, many of the alternatives we discuss in this book offer at least some degree of confidentiality — both about the terms of the resolution and about the process that led to the resolution. The fact that ADR (Alternative Dispute Resolution) frequently takes place outside of the public eye represents one of its major attractions to some disputants.

Is confidentiality in ADR a good thing? It depends. The very best rationales for privacy point out (accurately) that some kinds of conversations can only take place out of the public eye. For example, it is far easier for diplomats to discuss delicate compromises in the confines of a secret conversation than it would be if the world were watching. Similarly, confidential conversations tend to lead to greater information disclosure, which in turn presents greater opportunities to develop mutually beneficial, creative options. Further, certain kinds of relationships depend on candid exchanges in order to flourish. For example, we protect the confidentiality of conversations between spouses, in part because we recognize the importance of that relationship and its dependence on candor. Similarly, in clergy-parishioner, doctor-patient, and lawyer-client relationships, confidentiality serves the function of promoting the kind of candid exchange upon which the relationship is built; therefore, we assign communications within these relationships protection from the outside world.

This same logic underlies the confidentiality that attaches to mediation. The mediator-disputant relationship may not be as important as a marriage or a doctor-patient relationship, but society generally considers the benefits resulting from those conversations sufficiently worthwhile to safeguard. Most people think that confidentiality encourages parties to be candid with the mediator. ("Why should I tell you anything if you're just going to go tell others?") Many have suggested that mediators can function effectively only if the disputants are at least somewhat candid with the mediator. ("How am I supposed to help solve this problem if I don't even know the real issues?") Most people also believe that disputants' perceptions of a mediator's neutrality are important to the success of mediation — a perception put at risk by the prospect of the mediator as an adverse witness. ("How can the mediator be neutral if he is called to testify about what happened, since inevitably his testimony will favor one side or the other?") Finally, confidentiality protects against certain ways in which disputants might abuse the mediation process. ("Tell me everything, and then I'll decide what to use against you in a subsequent legal proceeding.")

But some important public concerns weigh against the extension of confidentiality. Confidentiality prevents a fact finder from hearing information related to the dispute in question, and we generally favor judicial proceedings in which "every man's evidence" is available. Further, the public derives a benefit from the transparency that normally characterizes litigation because, at least theoretically, it permits "the whole truth" to come out. In some cases, this transparency can be essential both to deter misbehavior and to prevent further harm.

Confidentiality in ADR is potentially troublesome for two reasons — one that focuses on the ADR process itself and one that focuses on its results. A first potential cost associated with confidentiality is the degree to which it shields misbehavior *during the ADR process* from public view and public sanction. If a litigant crosses the preestablished "line" during the course of a lawsuit, there is a clear opportunity for correction. A misbehaving witness is subject to perjury charges. An attorney risks Bar sanction. A judge's decision is subject to reversal. A party's case is at risk of being dismissed. And so on. But in an ADR process, if confidentiality fully attaches, any of the participants may be able to engage in shenanigans that threaten the legitimacy of the process. (For more on the challenges of quality control in mediation, for example, see Chapter 3.)

Second, if the *substance* of the dispute and its resolution are confidential, the public may never learn about information it wants or needs. A company might *want* to keep disputes with its employees or consumers out of the news. A manufacturer of a defective product might *want* to shield its name and brand from the publicity associated with the defect. Two prominent Hollywood stars divorcing might *want* to keep the sordid details of the collapse of their marriage out of the public eye. Judging by media coverage, the last of these scenarios represents the kind of information in which the public is apparently most keenly interested. But confidentiality in the earlier two may actually prevent the public from learning important information that would otherwise be available through the mechanism of a trial.

The combination of these considerations for and against confidentiality in ADR has resulted in a complex compromise. Society has neither granted absolute confidentiality to ADR processes, nor has it insisted on complete transparency. Instead, a patchwork of protections may (or may not) exist in a given context.

Although confidentiality is sometimes treated as a single topic with respect to dispute resolution, we think the topic raises two distinct categories of questions. First, under what circumstances can disputants be assured that their *conversations* will be kept confidential? Second, under what circumstances can disputants be assured that the *substantive terms* of their settlements will be kept confidential?

§4.2 PROTECTING THE CONFIDENTIALITY OF WHAT WAS SAID

A combination of four basic mechanisms provides confidentiality protections in the context of dispute resolution.

1. evidentiary exclusions ("If the only place you heard it was during our settlement efforts, you can't use it in court.")
2. contract ("We have a deal to keep our mouths shut.")
3. privilege ("You can't make me testify. You can't even make me produce information in discovery.")
4. protective order ("Under penalty of contempt, you have to keep your mouth shut.")

Each of these mechanisms *sometimes* assures disputants that their conversations in negotiations or mediations will remain confidential. We examine each below.

§4.2.1 Statements in Contemplation of Settlement

The law establishes certain confidentiality protections for negotiations between two disputants. In order to encourage both candor and flexibility in the negotiations, the common law and, more recently, the Federal Rules of Evidence, protect these conversations from being used against a party if the dispute does not settle and proceeds to litigation.

Federal Rule of Evidence 408 prohibits one party from introducing evidence that the opposing party made a settlement offer or discussed the merits of a claim during negotiations, if the purpose of introducing this evidence is to show liability, the invalidity of the claim, or the amount being claimed. In other words, one cannot get on the stand and say, "They offered to pay me $300,000 for my injuries, so you know they are liable." Similarly, one cannot say, "They were willing to accept a measly $10,000, so their claim is clearly bogus." This protection includes conduct and other statements during the settlement talks as well as any documents prepared for settlement talks.

Rule 408. Compromise and Offers to Compromise

(a) Prohibited uses. — Evidence of the following is not admissible on behalf of any party, when offered to prove liability for, invalidity of, or amount of a claim that was disputed as to validity or amount, or to impeach through a prior inconsistent statement or contradiction:

    (1) furnishing or offering or promising to furnish or accepting or offering or promising to accept a valuable consideration in compromising or attempting to compromise the claim; and

    (2) conduct or statements made in compromise negotiations regarding the claim, except when offered in a criminal case and the negotiations related to a claim by a public office or agency in the exercise of regulatory, investigative, or enforcement authority.

Permitted uses. This rule does not require exclusion if the evidence is offered for purposes not prohibited by subdivision (a). Examples of permissible purposes include proving a witness's bias or prejudice; negating a contention of undue delay; and proving an effort to obstruct a criminal investigation or prosecution.

An offer of settlement does not necessarily say anything about the offering party's perspective on the merits of the underlying claim. A plaintiff may have an immediate need for cash, and might therefore be willing to settle for far less than the amount he would expect to recover at the conclusion of protracted litigation. A defendant may believe that it is entirely without fault, but might prefer to settle the case quickly as a means of minimizing costs and headaches. The purpose of this evidentiary exclusion is to promote settlement efforts, and the policy assumption underlying this rule is that settlement discussions will be promoted if both parties are comfortable letting their guard down without fear that their efforts will come back to haunt them in the event of a nonsettlement.

This protection does not mean, though, that everything that happens in a negotiation stays in the negotiation. Rule 408 does not require exclusion of evidence that is otherwise discoverable. For example, say you have a videotape of the plaintiff waterskiing the day after his allegedly crippling injury occurred, and you discuss it in settlement talks. The fact that you discussed it in settlement talks may be inadmissible, but you will still be able to introduce the videotape itself. Further, under Rule 408, if the evidence is being offered for a purpose other than to demonstrate liability or validity or to impeach a witness, the evidence can be admitted. This includes, for example, introducing evidence to show bias or prejudice of a witness or to prove a material matter other than liability.

Disputants have even more potential mechanisms for protecting the confidentiality of conversations that take place within the context of a mediation, as opposed to those that are merely part of a negotiation. Federal Rule of Evidence 408 still applies to mediation conversations because most of the endeavor in mediation is considered an attempt to settle (or in the words of the FRE, to "compromise" a claim). But a range of other confidentiality-protecting options may be available to mediation participants, depending on the context. Below, we consider three: contracts, protective orders, and privilege. The last of these is the most significant and the most complex, so we will spend most of our time there. But we will start with a survey of contracts and protective orders.

§4.2.2 Contracts: I Promise Not to Talk

Mediators typically include confidentiality clauses in the mediation agreements parties are required to sign at the outset of a mediation. These agreements often provide that the parties agree not to discuss what happens in the mediation (and in some cases, even the fact that there was a mediation). The clauses also commonly include an agreement that neither party will testify and that neither will seek the testimony from anyone else about the proceedings. The confidentiality agreement can also include provisions that prevent the use of documents or other statements in future litigation (and depending on the terms, may even provide protections broader than Rule 408). Confidentiality agreements typically provide (1) that the mediator will not discuss the mediation with anyone without the permission of the parties or as required by law and (2) that the parties will not subpoena the mediator to testify in a future case. Some confidentiality agreements even provide that the parties will pay for all costs should the mediator be subpoenaed.

It is easy to see why mediators might ask parties to sign these agreements, but the question is whether courts uphold the agreements. After all, you and a drug dealer may sign an agreement not to squeal on each other.

Neither of you, however, is going to prevail in a contract action against the other if one of you reneges on that agreement. Do courts uphold confidentiality clauses in mediation agreements? For the most part, yes. A classic example is found in *Simrin v. Simrin*, 233 Cal. App. 2d 90 (1965), in which a court upheld a confidentiality agreement signed during a marriage counseling session by Mr. and Mrs. Simrin. This agreement prevented either of them from compelling their rabbi, who acted as their marriage counselor, to testify. The court reasoned that, like mediation, marriage counseling would no longer be helpful if the parties knew that their conversations could be revealed at a later date. Most courts since *Simrin* have followed this general prohibition, but there have been exceptions.

Courts enforce confidentiality agreements in the same way they enforce any other contract. Consequently, if one of the participants breaches the agreement, that participant is liable to the other for any claims or damages. As you learned in your first-year Contracts course, courts have many different remedial options in breach of contract cases, and these same remedies are available for breach of a confidentiality agreement. Courts have dismissed the case, ordered new trials, and ordered costs in breaches of confidentiality agreements. In one particularly well-known case, *Toon v. Wackenhut Corrections Corp.*, 250 F.3d 950 (5th Cir. 2001), three plaintiffs entered a settlement agreement with a defendant. The settlement agreement included a strict confidentiality clause prohibiting any disclosure of the terms of the agreement. When the defendant failed to make the payment required by the terms of the agreement, the plaintiffs' attorney filed a motion in court seeking to have the agreement enforced. However, the plaintiffs' attorney did not file the motion under seal, and as a result, the terms of the agreement became public. At the request of the defendant, the court sanctioned plaintiffs' counsel by reducing his contingency fee, ordering him to pay a $15,000 sanction to the court, and preventing him from representing any other plaintiff in related claims without the court's permission. Clearly, courts take breaches of confidentiality agreements very seriously.

As with any other contract, a court can also refuse to enforce a confidentiality agreement if it violates public policy. A confidentiality agreement can violate public policy, for example, if it prevents parties from sharing information that a party could independently discover outside of the mediation. This also mirrors the provision in Rule 408.

§4.2.3 Protective Orders: Using the Court to Keep It Secret

Parties can also use protective orders to prevent specified information (like trade secrets or negotiated settlements) from discovery. Federal Rule of Civil Procedure 26(c) provides that parties can make a motion showing that a protective order is necessary to "protect a party or person from annoyance, embarrassment, oppression, or undue burden or expense." Since third parties to a mediation who have not signed the confidentiality agreement are not bound by it, some parties seek a protective order rather than (or in addition to) a confidentiality agreement. Although protective orders are attractive because they carry the weight of a court's potential sanction, they must be approved by the court before they come into effect. Therefore, as a matter of practicality (it takes time to get an order) and strategy (a court is more likely to uphold contractual confidentiality than to grant a protective order), protective orders are not the only mechanism disputants rely on.

§4.2.4 Privilege: This Relationship Is Special

As we mentioned earlier, parties may hold a privilege in the context of certain special relationships in which candid communication is critical. Drawing an analogy to the doctor-patient and lawyer-client relationship, many courts and legislatures have protected the conversations that occur in mediation under the same theory — that the process cannot be effective unless parties have confidence that the information candidly shared with the mediator will remain confidential.

One of the mechanisms by which a mediation privilege has been created is through common law extension. As the U.S. Supreme Court explained in *Jaffe v. Redmond*, 518 U.S. 1 (1996), under Federal Rule of Evidence 501, a federal judge can create a privilege if it is based on an interpretation of "common law principles . . . in the light of reason and experience." Some courts in states with similar rules of evidence have created a common law privilege for mediation, adopting the same reasoning. Other courts, however, have held that the creation of a mediation privilege is the province of the legislature, not of a court. Therefore, it is important to know what your specific jurisdiction's law provides.

Statutory provisions represent the other mechanism by which a privilege is sometimes created. The precise content of these mediation confidentiality statutes varies enormously from one state to another. Most state statutes prohibit participants from compelling a mediator to testify in a post-mediation hearing. State statutes often protect communications such as documents prepared by the participants and the mediator for the purposes of the mediation. Some states base their privilege on Federal Rule of Evidence 408, and require that any records created during mediation be kept confidential if they are relevant to any judicial proceeding. (In these states, if the communications are not relevant to a particular dispute, the documents are not protected by the privilege.) Some states do not provide specific exceptions for public policy arguments, while other states permit testimony related to criminal acts and mediation malpractice. Others provide that participants can compel mediator testimony if public policy calls for it.

Responding to this patchwork of state confidentiality statutes, in an effort to promote uniformity among states, the American Bar Association and the National Conference of Commissioners on Uniform State Laws proposed the Uniform Mediation Act (UMA) in 2001. Only a handful of states have adopted the UMA as of the date of this publication. Nevertheless, most of our analyses below rely on the UMA because it illustrates one relatively straightforward mechanism for creating a mediation privilege. If you understand how the UMA works, you will understand the mechanism (though not necessarily the details) of virtually all state-created privileges. We therefore discuss some of the key aspects of the UMA below.

§4.2.4.1 Who Holds a Mediation Privilege?

The first issue surrounding the question of a mediation privilege is who exactly holds the privilege, because this determines the level of protection for those involved in a mediation. If the privilege belongs to the parties, can they compel the mediator to testify? If the privilege belongs to the mediator, can the mediator prevent the parties from communicating? Under the UMA, the mediation privilege belongs to both the parties and the mediator. Even nonparty participants (such as experts, relatives, etc.) are granted a form of a mediation privilege. UMA §4(b) reads:

> In a proceeding, the following privileges apply:
>
> 1. A mediation party may refuse to disclose, and may prevent any other person from disclosing, a mediation communication.
> 2. A mediator may refuse to disclose a mediation communication, and may prevent any other person from disclosing a mediation communication of the mediator.
> 3. A nonparty participant may refuse to disclose, and may prevent any other person from disclosing, a mediation communication of the nonparty participant.

Essentially, each participant in mediation holds a privilege that protects his or her own mediation communications from disclosure. In addition, mediation parties have a broader privilege, permitting them to prevent disclosure of all mediation communications. The UMA defines a "mediation communication" as a "statement, whether oral or in a record or verbal or nonverbal, that occurs during a mediation or is made for purposes of considering, conducting, participating in, initiating, continuing, or reconvening a mediation or retaining a mediator." Under this definition, the privilege can be rather expansive for the parties and the mediator.

The functioning of a mediation privilege is probably easiest to understand with an illustration. Consider the case of *Folb v. Motion Picture Industry Pension & Health Plans*, 16 F. Supp. 2d 1164 (D. Cal. 1998). Scott Folb, who worked at MPIPHP, reported certain practices of his employers to government regulators, alleging that the practices were illegal. MPIPHP subsequently fired Folb. Folb sued his former employer, alleging that his termination was an illegal response to Folb's whistleblowing. In its defense, MPIPHP asserted that Folb was fired because he allegedly sexually harassed another employee, Vivian Vasquez. Meanwhile, Vasquez filed a lawsuit against MPIPHP alleging sexual harassment. Vasquez and MPIPHP attempted to settle the claim in mediation. No settlement resulted during the mediation, but not long after the mediation, Vasquez and MPIPHP settled the claim for undisclosed terms. Folb sought evidence about MPIPHP's contentions in the context of the Vasquez lawsuit, because Folb asserted that MPIPHP was taking inconsistent positions in the two related pieces of litigation (saying that Folb *had* sexually harassed Vasquez in the Folb lawsuit, and denying that he had sexually harassed her in the Vasquez lawsuit). The case raised the question of whether Folb could have access to information about what happened in the Vasquez mediation.

How would the UMA resolve the questions this case raises? Under the UMA, both Vasquez and MPIPHP would hold a privilege about any "mediation communication" that took place in their mediation. Undoubtedly, the information Folb sought would fall within the scope of the broad term "mediation communication." So under the terms of the UMA, Folb would have access to this information only if both of the parties holding a privilege agreed to waive the privilege. In this case, whatever Vasquez's disposition toward the privilege might be, it is highly unlikely that MPIPHP would agree to waive its privilege. Under the UMA, therefore, Folb would have to proceed through his litigation without the benefit of testimony about MPIPHP's stance in the Vasquez settlement efforts.

The *Folb* case arose in federal court before the adoption of the UMA, but found privilege elsewhere. As an initial matter, the federal court hearing the *Folb* case determined that any question of the existence of a privilege in this case would be governed by federal common law because the case was before the court on federal question jurisdiction. (If this Civil Procedure reference gives you unpleasant flashbacks, just recall that in some cases, a federal court would apply state law to determine this question, and in others, it would refer to federal common law.) The court then analyzed the policy arguments for and against privilege, relying heavily on the *Jaffee* case described above. The court concluded, "that encouraging mediation by adopting a federal mediation privilege . . . will provide a public good transcending the normally predominant principle of utilizing all rational means for ascertaining the truth." Folb, therefore, had no access to the mediation conversations that led to the settlement of Vasquez's sexual harassment claim.

§4.2.4.2 What if I Don't Want the Privilege (or Want to Waive It)?

The existence of a privilege does not mean that the covered information can never be disclosed. A privilege simply means that the information cannot be disclosed without the consent of the party who holds a privilege. This implies, correctly, that there is a mechanism for signaling consent for the discovery or the testimony to proceed. In short, a privilege holder can waive his or her privilege.

Imagine, for example, that in the *Folb* case described above, MPIPHP admitted that Folb had sexually harassed Vasquez. In that event, both MPIPHP and Vasquez *might* decide to waive their privileges, permitting Folb to have access to information about the mediation. (MPIPHP might waive in order to rebut Folb's assertion that the harassment claim was a pretext for the firing. Vasquez might waive simply to make Folb's life more difficult.) UMA §5 states "a privilege under Section 4 may be waived . . . if it is expressly waived by all parties to the mediation."

Mediators and nonparties also hold privileges that, if not waived, restrict the scope of information about which testimony can occur. For example, even if both of the parties wanted to testify about what happened in mediation, they would not be permitted to testify about "a mediation communication of the mediator," absent a waiver from the mediator. If MPIPHP wanted the mediator to testify about what happened in the mediation between MPIPHP and Vasquez, Vasquez, MPIPHP, *and* the mediator would all have to waive their respective privileges — an extremely unlikely situation. The same kind of three-way waiver requirement also applies to any nonparty participants — the parties and the nonparty participant *all* must waive their privilege for the nonparty participant to testify. Note how the UMA grants a separate privilege to the mediator. (Remember in other privileged relationships, the client can waive the lawyer-client privilege and the patient can waive the doctor-patient privilege because it is a client-held or patient-held privilege. Only in the mediation privilege do parties on all sides of this relationship hold a privilege.) This additional provision gives independent power to the mediator (or another privilege holder) to prevent him or her from being subpoenaed.

§4.2.4.3 Are There Any Exceptions to Privileges?

No privilege is absolute, and the mediation privilege has at least as many exceptions as exist in other privileged relationships. UMA §6 spells out exceptions to the mediation privilege, and you should review it in detail. In broad terms, UMA §6(a) spells out certain categories of information about which no privilege attaches. For example, the UMA provides no privilege regarding the planned commission of a crime or an intention to inflict bodily injury. Similarly, the UMA does not protect information about which disclosure is otherwise required, like public records laws or mandatory reporting of child abuse. And the UMA does not protect information about malpractice by attorneys or mediators during the course of a mediation.

The UMA also sets up a category of circumstances in which a mediation privilege *might* not exist, depending on the particular circumstance. For example, under UMA §6(b), in a court proceeding involving a crime or enforcement of the settlement agreement, if a court determines that the evidence is not available through another source and that the need for the evidence substantially outweighs the interest in protecting confidentiality, a mediation party will not be able to assert a privilege against the discovery of the information.

Again, the provisions of the UMA spell out, in detail, the circumstances in which a privilege will (and will not) exist. We recommend that you review its contents with care, as its logic is likely to govern most confidentiality questions.

§4.3 PROTECTING THE CONFIDENTIALITY OF WHAT WAS AGREED TO

The sections above focused on the degree to which the outside world can have access to information revealed during the *process* by which disputants arrived at (or attempted to arrive at) a resolution of the dispute. This section focuses instead on the degree to which outsiders have access to the *substantive terms* of the resolution reached by the disputants.

Most disputes, although desperately important to those immediately involved, simply are not interesting to the outside world. And if the world did not even care to know that two people were in a dispute, it is unlikely that the world is going to care about the terms of an agreement those two reached in order to resolve the dispute. As a matter of practice, therefore, many settlement terms remain out of the public eye for the simple reason that even if the public had access to the terms, the public would not care. But not all disputes, and not all disputants, are of such little interest to the outside world.

In many circumstances, disputants have a presumptive right to keep the terms of their settlement agreements private. If you and your neighbor get in a fight about appropriate hedge-trimming protocols and eventually resolve your fight, it is unlikely that some outside person could come in and insist upon knowing how you resolved your fight. In the context of disputes that have proceeded to litigation, the procedural rules in effect in most states have a provision permitting a plaintiff simply to dismiss her or his complaint voluntarily. If two disputants settle a case, therefore, part of the settlement almost always includes an agreement that the plaintiff will cease pursuing the legal claim, and the case would be dismissed. And, if the only thing that appears in the court record is an indication that the plaintiff voluntarily dismissed its claim, the outside world would again have little ability to access the terms of that settlement agreement.

Outsiders have a greater opportunity for access to settlement terms when disputants file the contents of their agreement with the court. (Parties might opt to file the terms with the court, for example, in order to have the court enter the agreement as a judgment, thereby making it easier to enforce in the event of a breach.) You will see examples of such circumstances in some of the cases described below. In some jurisdictions, filing a settlement with the court may not threaten the confidentiality of the deal's terms. But many jurisdictions have passed "open records" or "sunshine laws," providing public access to court records, including settlements, unless there is some substantial interest that outweighs this presumption of openness.

A disputant may attempt to achieve a degree of secrecy by simply filing only part of the settlement with the court. However, the court's judgment (which is now public) must generally reflect any private side agreements, so that it is accurate. In Janus Films, Inc. v. Miller, 801 F.2d 578 (2d Cir. 1986), Janus Films and Miller reached a settlement after Janus sued Miller for copyright infringement. The settlement, as stated by counsel for Janus, included the defendant conceding liability and a judgment for $100,000 in addition to a separate confidential agreement regarding the terms of the judgment. It turned out that the side agreement basically allowed the defendant to pay considerably less than $100,000 to the plaintiff in installments over an extended period of time. When Janus crowed about its litigation success to a Hollywood trade publication, Miller protested. The court refused to set aside the parties' settlement, but it did order that the judgment of the court be revised to reflect accurately all of the terms of the settlement.

Who are the people that might want to learn about settlement terms? Three major categories of outsiders might want access to the terms of certain settlement agreements: the government, interested parties in related disputes, and the media. The ability of each of these parties to break through the default assumption of privacy is different, and so we treat them in separate sections below.

§4.3.1 Hiding Settlement Terms from the Government

In certain contexts, the government has an affirmative interest in knowing about the terms of a privately negotiated agreement. Perhaps the easiest illustration of this is the set of circumstances in which the agreement itself is evidence in a civil or criminal investigation. For example, if the state is prosecuting you for dealing drugs illegally, and they want to present a signed contract for heroin between you and one of your "business associates," you will not be able to stand up in court and say, "Hey, wait a minute. That's a private deal!" In that same vein, if the government is investigating allegations of price fixing and antitrust activity, it will have an affirmative interest in knowing the terms of otherwise private agreements between the otherwise private businesses. Of course, a typical drug deal does not involve a signed contract. And a typical case of price fixing does not involve a written covenant to collude. But to the extent such agreements exist, the government will have unfettered access to those agreements. In addition, the government, under state "sunshine" laws, may be able to access certain settlements it perceives as affecting public safety. For example, if the agreement implicates public health or the environment, the state agency tasked with protecting the public may be able to request production of certain terms of the settlement that would otherwise hide certain hazards.

In other contexts, the government not only wants to know about the terms of an agreement, but also take responsibility for approving the terms of those private settlements. As we described above, the normal presumption is that private litigants have complete control and autonomy over the shape and nature of claims and their settlements. But in certain circumstances, the law reverses this presumption and requires courts to examine the terms of an agreement before it is given effect.

One example of this governmental supervision arises in the context of class action lawsuits. Once a suit is certified as a class action, the named plaintiff (now the named representative of all of the members of the class, however the class might be defined) is no longer fully free to settle the case whenever or however he or she wants. Instead, under Federal Rule of Civil Procedure 23 (and its state equivalents), any proposed settlement of a certified class action must typically be approved by the court before taking effect. In some cases, the proposed settlement must also be presented to the absent class members, providing them an opportunity to "opt out" of the settlement, thus preserving their right to litigate whatever the claim in question may be. When reviewing a potential class settlement, the court is charged with safeguarding against deals that inadequately protect the interests of class members. For example, a court would refuse to endorse a so-called sweetheart deal, in which the named plaintiff receives a large payout but the other class members receive little or nothing. Similarly, a court would guard against a settlement that protects class attorneys at the expense of class members (for example, by allocating all of the defendant's payment to plaintiff's counsel, rather than to payouts to class members). Class action litigation has been the focus of considerable legislative and judicial attention in recent years, and our purpose is not to provide a comprehensive survey of its procedural mechanics. Instead, our purpose is to point out that class actions are one instance in which the government (through the courts) takes an affirmative interest in knowing the terms of an otherwise private settlement.

Another example comes from family law, where judges are routinely charged with reviewing the terms of agreements — particularly those affecting the welfare of children. For example, two divorcing parents may agree on the terms of asset division, child custody, and support. Before the terms of their agreement will take effect, in most jurisdictions, a judge will review the terms of the proposed decree for fairness before entering it as a judgment. Again, this represents an example of an instance when the state examines the terms of agreements struck between private actors.

§4.3.2 Hiding Settlement Terms from Interested Parties in Related Disputes

An agreement settling a dispute is typically of little interest to anyone other than the parties. But sometimes, as in the *Folb* case discussed above, one dispute is so related to another that the settlement of one will be of interest in the other. In those circumstances, parties who were not part of the settlement might be very interested to learn the contents of the settlement. Imagine that multiple former employees of the same company have now brought separate lawsuits against their former employer, each alleging that she was the victim of sexual harassment while on the job. If one plaintiff settles her claim, the remaining plaintiffs would probably have a strong interest in learning the terms of the settlement — both because of what it might suggest about the possible settlement value of their cases and because it might indicate something about the nature of their claims.

Sometimes, the terms of the settlement agreement are relatively easy for an outsider to access. For example, one of the remaining plaintiffs might be able simply to call up her former colleague and ask about the terms of the settlement. If the former employee has no contrary obligations (as in, she did not sign a confidentiality agreement), she will be free to discuss the settlement. Even if the parties who settle are now not inclined to volunteer information about the settlement, the remaining litigants may be able to compel the disclosure of the settlement through the civil discovery process if the terms of the settlement really are relevant to the remaining dispute. A subpoena can do wonders to someone's willingness to spill the beans!

Recognizing this possibility, some disputants enter into complex confidentiality agreements, and some even go to court to have the terms of their agreement filed with the court under seal. Doing so *may* shield the settlement terms from the outside world, but not necessarily.

The case of *Bank of America v. Hotel Rittenhouse Assocs.*, 800 F.2d 339 (3d Cir. 1986), provides an illustration of a case in which filing the agreement with the court eventually permitted a nonparty access to its terms. In *Rittenhouse*, a bank and a developer reached a settlement in a dispute over financing for the construction of a hotel. To ensure the enforcement of the agreement, the bank and the developer filed their settlement under seal with the district court. And indeed, shortly after the settlement agreement was entered, the parties called upon the court to resolve a dispute about the terms of the settlement (which the court did). A concrete contractor on the project filed suit against the bank seeking direct payment for the concrete work conducted on the same project that had been the subject of the lawsuit between the bank and the developer. The concrete contractor then made a motion to unseal the settlement between the bank and the developer, claiming that its contents would support a claim of conspiracy. The court acknowledged "the strong public interest in encouraging settlement of private litigation," but ordered the settlement terms to be unsealed. The court wrote, "Having undertaken to utilize the judicial process to interpret the settlement and to enforce it, the parties are no longer entitled to invoke the confidentiality ordinarily accorded settlement agreements. Once a settlement is filed in the district court, it becomes a judicial record, and subject to the access accorded such records." Not all agreements filed under seal would be subject to such an order, but the existence of a seal does not guarantee secrecy.

§4.3.3 Hiding Settlement Terms from the Media, the Public, and Other Busybodies

In some circumstances, the public will be denied access to the terms of private agreements, even if it is keenly interested in those agreements. Imagine that two Hollywood stars get into an altercation outside of a hip nightclub, one sues the other, and the parties subsequently announce that they "have reached an undisclosed mutual agreement fully resolving the matter." The tabloids, the entertainment shows, and many fans would love to have access to the terms of the agreement. But unless the disputants submitted their agreement to be entered as an order of the court, or unless one filed a claim on the basis of the agreement, the terms of that agreement are entirely private. The media can ask all they want about the terms of the agreement, but the media cannot force either party to share a copy of the settlement any more than they can force one of the stars to sit down for a tell-all interview.

If one of the disputants is a public governmental entity, however, the typical presumption is in favor of access. For example, if the local teachers' union and the local school board have a dispute, the public will probably have far greater access to the process(es) by which the dispute is resolved and to the terms of its resolution. With only some exceptions, open-meetings laws in many states provide the public with access to decision-making processes of governmental units like the school board. And any agreement to which the school board is a party is generally a matter of public record. In these cases, therefore, the public can have access to the outcome.

A final example of public access involves processes that are quasi-judicial. As a baseline matter, absent a special court order to the contrary, court proceedings and papers are public records. Anyone can access them. But what if a case starts in court, but is resolved through a court-affiliated, nonlitigation alternative? In *Cincinnati Gas & Elec. Co. v. General Electric Co.*, 854 F.2d 900 (6th Cir. 1988), multiple parties were in a dispute over the construction of a nuclear power plant. At the outset of their litigation, the parties to this dispute negotiated a comprehensive protective order for documents the parties classified as "confidential." Later in the course of litigation, the court ordered the parties into a summary jury trial, which was closed to the press and public. Two months after the summary jury trial, the parties reached a settlement. When the settlement was filed with the court, the gag order regarding the summary jury trial and the sealing of all documents and transcripts related to the summary jury trial was ordered to remain in effect. Several newspapers filed a joint motion to intervene in the litigation for the purpose of challenging the closure of the summary jury trial. The newspapers argued that there was a public right to know what happened in the summary jury trial, in part because the summary jury trial is structurally similar to a civil jury trial. (See Chapter 9 on court-connected ADR processes.) The Sixth Circuit held that there was no right to observe *any* negotiations leading to the settlement of a case and that summary jury trial is another example of a process used to promote settlement. As a result, the newspapers had no access to these quasi-judicial (but ultimately, private) proceedings.

Examples

The Clearwater Creek Catastrophe

One morning, Paula discovered that chemicals had washed up onto her property on the shores of the legendarily pristine Clearwater Creek. She concluded that one or both of the companies located upstream must be responsible for the pollution, and she filed a lawsuit against both of them. Neither Mountain Manufacturing nor Valley Vehicles had any history of environmental trouble, and both launched vigorous defense efforts against Paula's claims.

Early in the life of the lawsuit, Paula, Mountain Manufacturing, and Valley Vehicles agreed to try mediation. They hired Michelle to conduct the mediation. The parties met, but no settlement resulted. Eventually, the three parties fired Michelle and the mediation ceased.

The local newspaper ran a story the day after the end of the mediation. The columnist who wrote the story included considerable detail about what allegedly took place during the failed mediation. The story described both Mountain Manufacturing and Valley Vehicles in very negative (and perhaps even libelous) terms. Nowhere in the story did the reporter indicate the source of his information about what happened in the mediation.

After further pretrial litigation, Paula, Mountain Manufacturing, and Valley Vehicles agreed to try mediation a second time. They hired Miranda to conduct the mediation. During the course of the mediation, at the invitation of the parties and Miranda, Paula's neighbor Nancy Norton came in and provided "testimony" about what she saw the morning the pollution first appeared. During the rest of the mediation with Miranda, the attorney for Mountain Manufacturing struck a conciliatory tone, and Paula and Mountain Manufacturing quickly settled. The attorney for Valley Vehicles, however, refused to consider any payment to Paula, and eventually, the mediation ceased and Paula continued with her lawsuit against Valley Vehicles.

Assume that the jurisdiction within which all of the above actions took place has adopted a state version of the Uniform Mediation Act.

Paula Versus Valley Vehicles

1.a. In the context of Paula's ongoing lawsuit against Valley Vehicles, Valley Vehicles believes that some of the information that came out in each of the mediation sessions would be helpful to its defense. Could Valley Vehicles compel Mountain Manufacturing to testify about what occurred during the mediation sessions?

1.b. If, in the context of the litigation between Paula and Valley Vehicles, Mountain Manufacturing volunteered to help out Valley Vehicles by agreeing to testify about what transpired in the mediation sessions, would Mountain Manufacturing be permitted to testify?

1.c. Could Valley Vehicles compel either of the mediators to testify about what occurred during the mediation sessions?

1.d. Could Valley Vehicles compel Nancy Norton to testify about what occurred during the mediation session when she was present?

1.e. Assume that Paula and Mountain Manufacturing included a broad confidentiality clause in the terms of their mediated settlement, which purported to cover not only the discussions leading up to the settlement, but also the terms of the settlement. Could Valley Vehicles compel production of the terms of the settlement between Paula and Mountain Manufacturing?

1.f. Encouraged by the number of readers who responded positively to the local newspaper's story about the first mediation, one of its reporters wants to attend any subsequent mediation efforts between Valley Vehicles and Paula. If the parties do not mutually consent to the reporter's presence, is there any way for the reporter to force her way into the sessions?

Everyone Versus Michelle

2.a. Paula, Mountain Manufacturing, and Valley Vehicles all agree that the first mediation effort was a complete waste of time. They believe the mediation failed because of malpractice on the part of Michelle, and they all bring a lawsuit against her. In the context of that lawsuit, could Paula, Mountain Manufacturing, and Valley Vehicles compel Michelle to testify about what happened during the mediation?

2.b. Alternatively, in the context of their suit against Michelle, could Paula, Mountain Manufacturing, and Valley Vehicles prevent Michelle from testifying about what happened during the mediation?

Manufacturers Versus the Media

3.a. Mountain Manufacturing and Valley Vehicles jointly file a lawsuit against the local newspaper and the reporter who wrote the story, alleging that their story about the mediation was libelous. Could Mountain Manufacturing and Valley Vehicles compel the reporter to testify about who leaked information about what transpired in the first mediation session?

3.b. The local newspaper and the reporter defend their story, claiming it is true and therefore not libelous. Could they compel Paula to testify about what happened in the first mediation session?

3.c. In the context of their lawsuit against the newspaper and the reporter, could Mountain Manufacturing and Valley Vehicles testify about what occurred in the first mediation?

Valley Vehicles Versus Its Lawyer

4.a. After seeing that Mountain Manufacturing easily settled with Paula, Valley Vehicles became convinced that the only reason it did not arrive at a settlement as well was the fault of its attorney. Valley Vehicles files a legal malpractice claim against its attorney, citing the attorney's unnecessarily aggressive and standoffish attitude during the second mediation. Valley Vehicles alleges that, but for the attorney's conduct, Paula would have offered Valley Vehicles the same attractive settlement terms that she offered to Mountain Manufacturing. Could Valley Vehicles compel Paula to testify about the mediation in which the alleged malpractice took place?

4.b. Could Valley Vehicles compel Miranda to testify about her observations of the behavior of Valley Vehicles's attorney during the second mediation?

The State Versus Mountain Manufacturing

5.a. The state agency charged with enforcing environmental laws brings an action against Mountain Manufacturing. As part of its defense, Mountain Manufacturing wants to present evidence that during the mediation sessions, Valley Vehicles accepted fault for the pollution. Can Mountain Manufacturing testify about statements Valley Vehicles made?

5.b. Could the state agency compel either of the mediators to testify about either of the companies' statements during mediation?

5.c. Could the state agency charged with enforcing environmental laws compel production of the terms of the settlement agreement between Mountain Manufacturing and Paula?

Explanations

Paula Versus Valley Vehicles

1.a. No. The UMA provides certain actors connected with mediations with a set of privileges for "mediation communications." When such privileges attach, they have the effect of making the material in question "not subject to discovery or admissible in evidence" unless the privilege is waived or a specific exception applies. See UMA §4(a). In this case, because Mountain Manufacturing is a mediation party, it clearly holds a privilege regarding the mediation communications in question. Mountain Manufacturing's privilege provides that it "may refuse to disclose, and may prevent any other person from disclosing, a mediation communication." §4(b)(1). Assuming Valley Vehicles is trying to compel Mountain Manufacturing to testify about something that would qualify as a "mediation communication," Mountain Manufacturing will be able successfully to resist providing that information.

1.b. Maybe. The UMA does not *prohibit* all testimony about what occurs within a mediation session. Instead, it provides specific actors with privileges, which they can then exercise or waive. In this case, Mountain Manufacturing holds a privilege as a mediation party. §4(b)(1). Clearly, if it sought to resist testifying about what happened at the mediation, it could do so. (This is the question immediately above.) Here, however, the facts state that Mountain Manufacturing would prefer to testify. We can assume, therefore, that Mountain Manufacturing would be willing to waive its privilege. Similarly, we can assume that Valley Vehicles, also a mediation party and also a holder of the same privilege, would be willing to waive it. But that answers only two-thirds of the question. One mediation party remains — Paula. Under UMA §5(a), a privilege is waived "if it is expressly waived by all parties to the mediation." Therefore, only if Paula is also willing to waive her privilege will Mountain Manufacturing be free to testify about what transpired during the mediation sessions.

1.c. No. Under UMA §4(b)(2), a mediator "may refuse to disclose a mediation communication, and may prevent any other person from disclosing a mediation communication of the mediator." Each of the mediators, therefore, holds a privilege that they could exercise. Even if all of the parties waived their privileges under UMA §5(a), it is unlikely that either of the mediators would be willing to waive their privileges. The mediators would probably see little to gain from waiving their privileges and testifying. (Other than as expert witnesses, perhaps, there's not much of a living to be made as a witness.) And the mediators would probably see plenty to lose from testifying about what transpired in the mediation. Inevitably, the mediator's testimony would be seen as more favorable to one party than to another, and the mediator's understandable interest in preserving a reputation for impartiality would risk being tarnished. As a practical matter, therefore, it is extraordinarily unlikely that Valley Vehicles could compel either of the mediators to testify.

1.d. Probably not. The UMA provides a special privilege for "nonparty participants," and Norton appears to qualify as one of those. (She is "a person, other than a party or mediator, that participate[d] in a mediation." UMA §2(4).) Under UMA §4(b)(3), a nonparty participant holds a privilege permitting the nonparty participant to prevent the disclosure of the nonparty participant's mediation communications. Most likely, therefore, if Valley Vehicles sought to compel Norton to testify about Norton's role in the mediation, Norton would invoke her privilege, and Valley Vehicles would fail.

Even if Norton was favorably disposed toward the idea of testifying about the mediation, recall that each of the mediation parties also holds a relevant (and much broader) privilege. Under UMA §5, every mediation party would also have to waive its privilege before Norton would be free to testify. And if Valley Vehicles wanted Norton's testimony to include anything about what the mediator said, the mediator would also hold a privilege under §4(b)(2). Valley Vehicles is extraordinarily unlikely to secure a waiver from both of the other parties, from the mediator, and from Norton. And therefore, it is not likely to have the benefit of Norton's testimony about the mediation. Remember though, Norton can still testify to the same substance of the testimony she gave in the mediation, as it is independently discoverable.

1.e. Probably not. The terms of the settlement agreement itself are not privileged under the UMA. Even if the settlement agreement contained one or more "mediation communications," those terms are explicitly excluded from coverage under UMA §6(a)(1). But the contractual confidentiality provision may not be easy for Valley Vehicles to thwart. Valley Vehicles would have two avenues for attacking the confidentiality clause. First, Valley Vehicles could argue, much like the concrete contractor in *Rittenhouse*, that access to the settlement is necessary in order to prevent prejudice to a third party. Here, however, the settlement does not appear to have been filed with the court, so a court would have no direct mechanism for unsealing that which was never filed or sealed. Second, Valley Vehicles could argue that the settlement hides important environmental information that is needed to protect public health. In some jurisdictions, confidentiality clauses in settlements of claims affecting public heath will be stricken as contrary to public policy, but this is a jurisdiction-by-jurisdiction analysis. If Valley Vehicles is in one such jurisdiction, and if Valley Vehicles can argue successfully that the "goop" under dispute constitutes a threat to public health, it will be in luck. Otherwise, Valley Vehicles is unlikely to have access to the settlement terms between Mountain Manufacturing and Paula.

1.f. No. Mediation sessions between private disputants are private. If Valley Vehicles or Paula were a state agency, for example, state sunshine laws would almost certainly apply, and access would be more likely. But that is not the case here. This is a private corporation in a dispute with a private individual, contracting for a private third party to provide mediation services. Even if the mediation were ordered by the court (see Chapter 9 for more on these processes) the basic confidential nature of these proceedings would remain unchanged. Indeed, even if the subsequent dispute resolution effort by Valley Vehicles and Paula were more judicial in nature (for example, a summary jury trial), the logic of *Cincinnati Gas & Elec.* would still permit the parties to exclude the reporter from the process.

Everyone Versus Michelle

2.a. Yes. A mediator holds a privilege that would normally permit the mediator to block testimony about any of her mediation communications. See UMA §4(b)(2). However, the UMA specifically provides an exception to that privilege in the event that the testimony is "sought or offered to prove or disprove a claim or complaint of professional misconduct or malpractice filed against a mediator." UMA §6(a)(5). In the absence of such a privilege, the mediation parties will be able to compel testimony from Michelle.

2.b. No. It is true that each of the parties holds a privilege about what happened in the mediation, and Michelle has a mediator's privilege about her communications. UMA §4(b)(1) and §4(b)(2). However, if Michelle offers her testimony to disprove a claim of malpractice, the exception in §6(a)(5) applies, and the communication is not privileged. Even without this protection, the parties' claim against Michelle may also have the effect of waiving their privilege altogether under UMA §5(b). Under §5(b), the parties cannot assert a privilege that prevents Michelle from defending herself. Thus, under either section, the communication is not privileged, and the parties cannot prevent Michelle from testifying.

Even before the UMA, courts permitted mediators to testify in order to defend themselves against allegations of misconduct. For example, in *Allen v. Leal*, 27 F. Supp. 2d 945 (S.D. Tex. 1998), the mother of a child shot by a police officer was attempting to avoid the settlement agreement, which she claimed was coerced by the mediator. Faced with the question of whether the mediator could testify about what occurred in the mediation, the court held that the plaintiff " 'opened the door' by attacking the professionalism and integrity of the mediator and the mediation process, [and hence] the Court was compelled, in the interests of justice, to breach the veil of confidentiality."

Manufacturers Versus the Media

3.a. Maybe. Nothing in this question implicated the privileges created under the UMA. Notice that the reporter is not a party, a mediator, or a nonparty participant in the mediation. Those are the only holders of privileges under the UMA. And this makes sense in this case, because the conversation in question—the one between the reporter and the informant—did not actually take place in a mediation session.

The reporter will have to rely on a reporter's privilege to resist testifying about the source of his information. A full discussion of reporters' privileges is far beyond the scope of this chapter, or even this book. The quick summary is that some states offer reporters an absolute privilege against disclosure. Most, however, provide only a qualified privilege. Under this qualified privilege, a party seeking to compel disclosure must typically demonstrate that the reporter's information (1) is highly material and relevant to the claim; (2) is at the "heart of the claim," meaning that it is necessary or critical to maintaining the claim; and (3) cannot be obtained from alternate sources. In cases involving libel claims against reporters, most courts have found that the matter is "at the heart of the claim," and therefore do not recognize a reporter's privilege. Whether the companies can compel testimony from the reporter about the leak, therefore, depends on the jurisdiction's construction of reporters' privileges.

3.b. Probably not. Under §4(b)(1), a mediation party may refuse to testify about mediation communications. It is entirely likely that Paula would resist testifying altogether, and there would be little the newspaper and the reporter could do about it.

This could change if Paula were inclined to cooperate in the civil libel suit. Under normal circumstances, each of the other parties (and depending on the nature of the evidence being sought, potentially the mediator as well) would hold privileges in addition to Paula. Each of them would, therefore, have to waive those privileges expressly before Paula would be permitted to testify.

One potential wrinkle in this is that the newspaper and the reporter could argue that Mountain Manufacturing and Valley Vehicles *waived* their privileges by bringing this libel action. The argument would be that under UMA §5(b), "a person that discloses or makes a representation about a mediation communication which prejudices another person in a proceeding is precluded from asserting a privilege under Section 4, but only to the extent necessary for the person prejudiced to respond to the representation or disclosure." Here, the companies declared the newspaper account to be false. Whether that constitutes a representation about a mediation communication is arguable. If it is, however, the newspaper and reporter could clearly claim that they have been prejudiced by their claim of falsity, and they would assert the need to compel testimony about what was actually said in order to respond to that representation.

3.c. Probably not. If Mountain Manufacturing and Valley Vehicles want to testify, they would clearly be willing to waive the privilege they would otherwise hold, as mediation parties, under UMA §4(b)(1). However, under the terms of UMA §4(a), mediation communications are privileged unless waived, and under the terms of UMA §5, "all parties" to the mediation must waive in order for a waiver to be effective. Therefore, Mountain Manufacturing and Valley Vehicles will only be able to testify if they secure a waiver from Paula. And, given the reality of the other litigation pending between these parties, such a waiver seems unlikely. In short, Paula would have little incentive to be helpful (by waiving the privilege in this case) to someone occupying an adverse position in another piece of litigation.

Valley Vehicles Versus Its Lawyer

4.a. Yes. For many purposes, as we have illustrated above, both Paula and Mountain Manufacturing would hold privileges that would prevent testimony about the kinds of mediation communications that are likely to be at the heart of Valley Vehicles's claims. But this is an exception to those general circumstances. Under UMA §6(a)(6), no privilege exists if the information is being sought "to prove or disprove a claim or complaint of professional misconduct or malpractice filed against a mediation party, nonparty participant, or representative of a party based on conduct occurring during a mediation." Valley Vehicles's claim against its attorney centers on the attorney's conduct during the mediation. Therefore, this information is not privileged, and Valley Vehicles will be able to compel Paula's testimony.

4.b. No. As we described in the answer immediately above, UMA §6(a)(6) makes the information in question *not* the subject of a privilege. However, UMA §6(a)(6) is further modified by UMA §6(c), which provides that "a mediator may not be compelled to provide evidence of a mediation communication referred to in" §6(a)(6). As a result, Valley Vehicles could succeed in compelling testimony from other parties — whether they were co-parties or opposing parties — but could not compel testimony from the mediator who was present.

The State Versus Mountain Manufacturing

5.a. It depends, but probably not. The communication in the mediation would generally be protected unless it falls under one of the exceptions in §6 of the UMA. Two exceptions might be relevant to this case. First, there is no privilege for communication that is used to conceal "ongoing criminal activity." (UMA §6(a)(4).) So Mountain Manufacturing might be able to argue that Valley Vehicles's statements are evidence of ongoing criminal activity violating environmental laws. Second, under §6(b)(1), there is no privilege if a court or administrative agency finds, after a hearing in *camera*, that the evidence is not otherwise available, there is a need for the evidence, and this is a court proceeding involving a felony or misdemeanor. If the action brought against Mountain Manufacturing is a criminal action versus a civil action, there is a good argument that Mountain Manufacturing is entitled to have all evidence in its defense available to it. Mountain Manufacturing would need to run through the process outlined in the UMA but, after a hearing, the judge could determine that Valley Vehicles's statements are relevant and not subject to privilege.

5.b. Maybe. It most likely depends on whether the state agency's action against Mountain Manufacturing is part of a felony prosecution. If the environmental claim in this case is serious enough to constitute a felony, UMA §6(b)(1) will apply. Under its terms,

> there is no privilege under Section 4 if a court, administrative agency, or arbitrator finds, after a hearing in camera, that the party seeking discovery or the proponent of the evidence has shown that the evidence is not otherwise available, that there is a need for the evidence that substantially outweighs the interest in protecting confidentiality, and that the mediation communication is sought or offered in . . . a court proceeding involving a felony.

The state agency would, therefore, be able to compel testimony about the relevant mediation communications. (Note that it can even compel mediators' testimony because the mediator shield under UMA §6(c) does not apply to §6(b)(1) cases.) If, however, the agency's action is merely a minor one (for example, a misdemeanor), §6(b)(1) may not apply and the standard privilege will protect a mediator from having to testify.

If the manufacturers' behavior could be characterized as an ongoing crime or an effort to conceal an ongoing crime, the exception under UMA §6(a)(4) would apply. But in this case, the facts do not necessarily support such an assertion.

5.c. Probably yes. The terms of the settlement agreement are not the subject of a privilege under the UMA or under federal common law. The only thing protecting the confidentiality of the terms is the contractual agreement between Mountain Manufacturing and Paula. To the extent the environmental agency would be successful in arguing to a court that the settlement terms relate to the protection of public health in connection with its own enforcement action, it might be able to have the confidentiality clause stricken as contrary to public policy.

An Introduction to Arbitration: The Role of Courts in Enforcement

§5.1 INTRODUCTION

Most students arrive at law school with some idea of what a trial looks like. Their vision of a trial is often the product of television and movies, rather than actual experience, so their initial impressions are frequently mistaken. Still, having that basic model in mind can be helpful as students begin to navigate the details of procedure and law.

By contrast, very few students arrive at law school having any personal experience with arbitration, and virtually nothing interesting on TV even acknowledges arbitration, much less provides an accurate picture of it. As a result, students studying arbitration often find it difficult to find meaning in the various legal doctrines involved, in part because they have neither a background in nor a mental image of arbitration.

So, with some hesitation, we suggest the following initial mental image as you begin to study arbitration: litigation.

Arbitration, like litigation, is an adversarial proceeding in which competing parties make arguments and present evidence before a third party, who will render a decision. So far, this should sound like litigation. Arbitration has some important differences from litigation, however. Instead of picturing the formal litigation proceedings that take place in a courthouse, picture a fancy conference room in some office complex. Instead of a randomly appointed judge, picture someone with no robe and someone whom the parties had a hand in selecting. Imagine a more relaxed version of the Rules of Civil Procedure and the Rules of Evidence. Imagine that the arbitrator is not necessarily bound to follow the law that would govern the dispute if it were going through litigation, and might just as well examine business practices or the parties' common history as a basis for decision. Picture a timetable for resolving the dispute that could be more streamlined than litigation. And imagine that the party who loses will have very limited opportunities to file an appeal.

A final difference — and perhaps the most important one — between arbitration and litigation is that arbitration is fundamentally a creature of contract. Parties appear in binding arbitration because at some point they agreed to go to arbitration. And the arbitration itself will, for the most part, take on whatever shape or procedure the parties agreed it would have. If the parties *want* the Rules of Evidence to apply, they will apply. If the parties' contract spells out a set of procedures identical to litigation, those will govern the arbitration. If they *want* the arbitrator to wear a robe, that's probably fine as well. As Judge Posner colorfully put the matter in *Baravati v. Josephthal, Lyon & Ross, Inc.*, 28 F.3d 704, 709 (7th Cir. 1994), "short of authorizing trial by battle or ordeal or, more doubtfully, by a panel of three monkeys, parties can stipulate to whatever procedures they want to govern the arbitration of their disputes; parties are as free to specify idiosyncratic terms of arbitration as they are to specify any other terms in their contract." In many cases, parties opt not to adopt all of the formal trappings of litigation. But any effort to describe arbitration generically must be laden with caveats along the lines of "depending on what the parties' agreement says." This description is no exception. We have just described ONE version of arbitration, albeit a typical one. There are many others. Still, this is a starting point from which you can begin to appreciate the important legal and policy issues that arise in arbitration.

The most fundamental distinction between arbitration and most other forms of dispute resolution outside of court is that arbitrators *decide* the matters submitted to them. Arbitration — in all of its various forms — is an adjudicative process. And, in almost all forms of arbitration, arbitrators' decisions are binding on the disputants.

§5.1.1 Arbitration Is Not Mediation

In this respect, arbitration stands in stark contrast with mediation. A mediator might offer suggestions, might make predictions about what a court would do, might facilitate conversation between the disputants, and might engage in a wide variety of activities aimed at helping the disputants to find a mutually acceptable outcome. But a mediator does not render a binding decision. A mediation ends one of two ways: Either the parties reach a settlement with each other, or they don't reach a settlement with each other. An arbitration ends one way: The arbitrator makes a final decision. This is a modest overstatement, of course, because just as litigants can agree to settle on the courthouse steps, or while the jury is deliberating, parties to an arbitration can agree to settle even during the course of the arbitration. The important difference is that mediation is explicitly designed to promote settlement, whereas litigation and binding arbitration are designed to produce a judgment.

§5.1.2 Arbitration Is Not Litigation

Now that we've set up a mental image of arbitration as similar to litigation, it might be helpful to see how arbitration compares with litigation. In most of your law school classes, the chronological "life" of a dispute appears to begin with some unfortunate incident occurring between two or more parties. (You have surely noticed by now that if two people coexist happily, we are unlikely to study their interactions in law school.) Some time after the incident, the dispute finds its way to court. After adjudication in some form (for example, a dispositive motion or a verdict at trial), the court enters a judgment. And the court's judgment then takes effect. The simplified "timeline" of a litigated case, therefore, looks something like this:

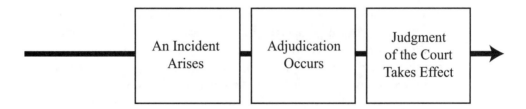

This simplified timeline omits, of course, the possibility that the parties had some relationship prior to the incident. In any contract claim or divorce, for example, one would expect to see a box before the incident — one in which the parties at least arguably entered into a relationship with each other.

This timeline also ignores the increasingly prominent role of ADR in modern litigation. ADR appears in the timeline of modern litigation in a number of possible places, depending on the type of ADR in question. For example, it would be perfectly normal (though perhaps surprising to students after their first year of law school) for one party to pick up the phone and call the other person following an incident. Perhaps the parties will work something out through fully private negotiation. Or perhaps they will engage the services of a mediator to explore the possibility of settlement before the dispute even ripens into a lawsuit.

Negotiation and mediation may also occur after a lawsuit has commenced. For example, as you have seen in other chapters of this book, some jurisdictions require litigants to pursue some form of ADR before they proceed to trial. Parties might, therefore, try mediation just before or just after discovery to see if they might prefer some settlement over further litigation. In some systems, opportunities for ADR extend even beyond the end of trial. For example, appellate mediation programs, which seek to promote post-verdict settlement before a matter appears before appellate courts, are increasingly common. At every step along the timeline pictured above, opportunities for negotiation and mediation arise.

Informal ADR methods like negotiation and mediation, therefore, can occur at any point along this basic timeline of litigation. Depending on the process, the lawsuit may proceed as if settlement efforts were not occurring. For example, the parties may continue with discovery. They may continue to file motions with the court. The clock on the court's deadlines may continue to tick along. These forms of ADR, in some important ways, function as supplements to litigation or even companions to it. They may resolve the dispute without resort to further litigation, but litigation is frequently hanging around as a "just in case" alternative to settlement.

§5.1.3 Arbitration Is a Contractual Substitute for Litigation

Arbitration is different. Arbitration, the most formal of the ADR methods you are likely to study, operates in most instances as a true substitute for litigation through the courts. Those in arbitration are not, for the most part, simultaneously pursuing litigation. As a binding[1] method of alternative dispute resolution, arbitration takes place in lieu of trial.

One way in which an arbitration's timeline differs from that of litigation is that binding arbitration only occurs if there was a preliminary step — one in which the parties agreed to arbitrate. (We discuss in later chapters the range of behaviors that are treated as "agreement" for purposes of enforcing arbitration clauses.) Notice the basic chronology of arbitration, produced below.

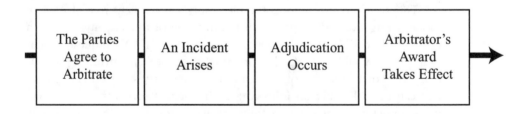

We should also note that in some cases, parties with no prior contractual relationship may find themselves in a dispute and may agree to take their

---

1. As you will see in Chapter 9, a nonbinding version of arbitration exists. For purposes of simplicity, when we refer to arbitration in this chapter, we speak of the version in which the arbitrator's decision is binding on the participants.

existing dispute to arbitration. In that event, the order of the first two of these boxes would be reversed. But the basic idea remains the same: Arbitration necessarily involves a step in which the parties in a dispute agree to submit the dispute to arbitration.

As you learned in your first-year Contracts course, parties enter into contractual relationships all the time. (A consumer buys a product. An employee takes a job. Two businesses set up a joint venture. A patient checks into a hospital. A union and a company enter a collectively bargained agreement. And so on.) In the process of entering that relationship, parties sometimes wisely anticipate that something could go wrong down the road. Though predicting future problems may not be the kind of thing one would normally expect at the blissful moment of entering into an exciting contract of some sort, few lawyers survive law school without noticing that a fair percentage of deals wind up going sour. Lawyers tend to be good at envisioning bad scenarios, and the best among them craft contracts that address those difficulties effectively.

One common approach to dealing with the possibility of a future dispute is to insert a clause describing *how* the parties will resolve future disputes. This clause might include, for example, choice of law and choice of forum provisions. Increasingly, this clause also calls for the parties to enter arbitration (rather than litigation) to resolve those future disputes.

To return to the major point of this section: Arbitration, in most of its forms, is entirely a creature of contract. If the parties agreed to arbitrate a dispute, they will be held to that agreement, and either party will be able to block the other from pursuing an action in court. The corollary is that if the parties did *not* agree to resolve their dispute through arbitration, they cannot be compelled to resolve their dispute through arbitration. As a preview of some of the materials we cover in Chapter 6, however, you should know that courts have been expansive in their assessment of what constitutes "agreeing" to arbitrate. In some circumstances, you are deemed to have agreed to arbitrate by accepting employment, by purchasing a product, or by paying for a service. It would be inaccurate to assume, therefore, that all of arbitration can be avoided if one simply prefers to litigate. (For example, if you bought this book through certain online vendors, you may have agreed to submit any disputes related to the purchase of this book to arbitration, whether you were aware of it or not. . . .)

§5.2 A BRIEF HISTORY OF THE LAW OF ARBITRATION

The idea of submitting a dispute to a third party and having that party render a decision is by no means a recent development. In one very common form, the third party is someone who has a degree of control over the disputants. Historically, the third party might be a ruler, a leader, or a king, for example. (Any parent with two or more children has seen this instinct to call in a higher authority — probably more times than the parent would prefer.) Perhaps the most famous maternity dispute in history involved two women, each claiming to be the mother of the child in question, who submitted the dispute to Solomon.[2] As the story is commonly told, we might imagine that the women chose Solomon because he was "wise." In fact, he was the king (although many also thought him to be wise).

The notion of submitting a dispute to someone in a position of general authority has considerable appeal. If the person rendering the decision is also capable of assuring compliance with that decision, the service is even more valuable. And this trend continues to this day. Many disputants take their disputes to judges (through the vehicle of litigation), because the state has a system of mechanisms for assuring that judges' decisions are binding.

For centuries, various forms of arbitration have been available to disputants who prefer not to submit their cases to the state's traditional dispute resolution mechanism (typically a court). Why might a disputant opt for a process other than litigation in court? Consider the example of merchants in medieval Europe. These businesspeople, particularly those engaged in the textile trade, commonly traveled to fairs all over Europe as a means of connecting with suppliers and customers. As can be expected in business relationships, disputes sometimes arose. But for these merchants, submitting a dispute to the courts that existed at that time meant paying considerable fees — including paying for the judge's services. Further, there was little reason to think that the judge would have any familiarity with the merchants' customs, reputations, or trade practices. And while the dispute was pending, the disputing merchant faced the prospect of having to stay in that (likely foreign) city, rather than moving on to the next fair and the next business opportunities.

In response to these conditions, an arbitration practice emerged among merchants. Disputants would mutually choose another member of the trade to whom they would submit their disputes for binding resolution. The chosen arbitrator would hear each party's perspective, examine whatever evidence the arbitrator wanted to consider, and render a decision. Compared with formal litigation, the process was faster, cheaper, and more likely to be based on the norms and practices that the merchants would expect to govern their interactions. This is still the same primary theory behind the bulk of international commercial arbitration.

---

2. Solomon decided that the baby should be split in two. One of the two claimants relented, agreeing that the other woman should have the baby. Solomon then deemed the woman who refused to permit the baby to be divided to be the true mother. The story is the origin of the commonly used phrase "to split the baby."

Evidence of arbitration in the United States dates to colonial times, but arbitration was used only modestly in most contexts until the twentieth century. Some labor disputes were resolved through binding arbitration more than one hundred years ago. There were also some well-known international arbitration cases between countries. For example, the United States and Great Britain arbitrated the *Alabama* Claims in 1871, stemming from the U.S. allegation that Great Britain violated its neutrality during the U.S. Civil War by aiding the Confederacy.[3]

Businesses who were engaged in regular commerce with one another also frequently sought the speed, efficiency, and expertise arbitration offered. But standing in the way of broad application of arbitration to resolve disputes was the courts' reluctance to enforce arbitral agreements. Arguing that arbitration agreements inappropriately "divested" the courts of their proper jurisdiction, many courts refused to give effect to arbitration agreements or the awards of arbitrators. That is, the courts saw arbitration as an illegitimate intrusion into their "turf." Without any assurance that an agreement to arbitrate a dispute would be enforced, parties saw little reason to include one in a contract. Similarly, unless parties were assured that an arbitrator's decision would be respected, they had little reason to submit a case to arbitration. As a result, for some time, arbitration enjoyed only moderate usage.

In 1925, responding to the business community's displeasure over courts' reluctance to give effect to arbitration agreements, Congress passed the Federal Arbitration Act (the FAA). The FAA, described in more detail in Chapter 8, essentially commands courts to treat arbitration clauses in contracts the same way that they treat all other clauses in contracts. As a result, arbitration came to be commonplace in resolving contract disputes among repeat-player businesses (those who frequently do business with each other). Arbitration also enjoyed a prominent role in resolving labor disputes, and many of the most significant arbitration decisions of the U.S. Supreme Court in the mid-twentieth century arose in the context of labor arbitrations.

Beginning in the 1970s and 1980s, arbitration started to expand to other categories of disputes. It was no longer just sophisticated businesses and those with ongoing commercial relationships who were entering arbitration agreements. Instead, arbitration clauses began to appear in employment contracts and in consumer sales as businesses took advantage of the efficiencies, cost savings, and control offered by arbitration. The expansion of arbitration into these realms has added a layer of complexity to arbitration, and the courts continue to sort out the boundaries of this expansion. Unlike the attitude from one hundred years ago, however, the general trend has been for courts to embrace arbitration agreements in a wide variety of

---

3. *See* Frank Warren Hackett, *Reminiscences of the Geneva Tribunal of Arbitration 1872: The Alabama Claims* (Houghton Mifflin, 1911).

settings, supporting what they perceive as "a federal policy favoring arbitration."

---

§5.3 MAKING THEM PLAY: HOW COURTS COMPEL PARTICIPATION IN ARBITRATION

The usefulness of arbitration agreements hinges significantly on the ability of each party to hold the other to the terms of the arbitration agreement. After all, what good is an agreement to arbitrate if you are unable to compel the other side to arbitrate? What good is winning a case before an arbitrator, if the arbitrator's judgment cannot be enforced? What makes arbitration agreements and arbitral awards worth something more than just the pieces of paper they appear on? These questions overstate the issue somewhat. There are ways in which an agreement or an award could have some utility, even if they were unenforceable. But the bulk of the attraction of arbitration clauses is that parties can bind themselves (or more accurately, that they can bind the other side) into arbitration in an enforceable way.

To give arbitration this certainty and finality requires a particular relationship with the courts, because courts are the ones with the established power of the state to compel or prohibit certain behavior. This relationship between the private actions of parties and arbitrators, and the public machinery of the courts, is at the heart of the rest of this chapter.

In its most simplistic form, arbitration is entirely private. Two parties enter a contract together (a wholly private act), and they include an arbitration clause in the contract. Then they get into some kind of dispute. (This is still private, assuming neither one called the police or involved the state in some way.) They mutually recognize that they anticipated this possibility in their contract, so they agree (privately) to hire a private arbitrator. They engage in the arbitration (still no state involvement), and the arbitrator rules in favor of one party over the other. The loser does whatever the arbitrator orders, and the matter is resolved completely privately. In fact, most arbitrations are conducted without the state being involved in any way.

In contrast, in its most simplistic form, litigation is largely public. Two parties get into a dispute, and one drags the other into court through the vehicle of a lawsuit, a public filing. The court follows prescribed procedures in adjudicating the dispute in open court, and at the end, enters judgment in the public record in favor of one of the disputants. That judgment is enforceable through the machinery of the judiciary, ensuring compliance.

Potential complications arise when the private and the public processes bump into each other during the course of a dispute. What happens when the theoretically private process of arbitration calls on the machinery of the public judiciary? What happens when, during the course of litigation, it emerges that the parties may have entered an agreement to arbitrate the dispute in question? The answers to these questions give shape to the complex relationship between arbitration and the courts.

The Federal Arbitration Act provides the statutory framework for the relationship between courts and arbitration. However, as you will see in Chapter 8, various state laws also shape this relationship, and in some cases, federal and state laws differ. As to the subject of this chapter, however, both federal and state laws adopt virtually identical mechanisms for governing the relationship between arbitration and the courts.

§5.3.1 Motions to Stay the Litigation

What happens if a plaintiff files a complaint in federal court, and the defendant believes that the matter is properly the subject of an agreement to arbitrate? Under the authority of §3 of the Federal Arbitration Act, the defendant would file a *motion to stay the litigation* in court.

In a simple case, therefore, the defendant seeking to have the claim heard in arbitration would file a motion to stay with the court, would show the court the written arbitration agreement, and would demonstrate that the subject of the lawsuit is covered by the arbitration agreement. Upon satisfaction of these conditions, the court would grant the stay, and no further litigation would be permitted until the arbitration had run its course. Assuming the arbitration clause was sufficiently broad to cover everything that would have appeared in the litigation, nothing will be left for the court to do upon the conclusion of the arbitration. In short, an order staying litigation under FAA §3 can effectively end the dispute's life in court.

Now, you are probably already thinking of the many ways in which this sequence might be more complicated in practice. In later chapters, we take up such questions as: "What if it's not clear that the contract containing the arbitration clause is enforceable?" (Chapter 6). "What if it's not clear whether the arbitration agreement covers the subject of the plaintiff's complaint?" (Chapter 7). And "What if state and federal laws clash over the answer to any of these questions?" (Chapter 8). For now, you should simply understand that if a party believes that a claim should be heard in arbitration rather than in litigation, the party can file a motion to stay the litigation, pending the outcome of the arbitration.

§5.3.2 Motions to Compel Arbitration

What if one party believes that arbitration is required, but the other party refuses to participate in arbitration? Again, the party seeking to enforce an arbitration agreement can call upon the machinery of the courts, this time by seeking an order to *compel* arbitration of the matter. The federal statutory basis for such an order appears in §4 of the Federal Arbitration Act, under which parties can compel arbitration if they are "aggrieved by the alleged failure, neglect, or refusal of another to arbitrate under a written agreement for arbitration."

As with motions to stay the litigation, before granting a motion to compel arbitration, a court must be satisfied that a contract containing a relevant arbitration clause exists. This raises all kinds of possible legal wrinkles that we will cover in the next three chapters. But the big picture is that a party can use the coercive powers of the court to give effect to an agreement to arbitrate.

In some cases, a party might file both a §3 motion to stay the litigation and a §5 motion to compel arbitration. For example, a defendant against whom a plaintiff has filed a lawsuit, but who believes that arbitration is called for, might go to the court and say, "Stop this litigation, please, and send that ne'er-do-well plaintiff to arbitration, where he agreed to go in the event of a dispute." In practical terms, this could be overkill, because success with the first would necessarily bring about the desired effect from the second. Still, you should be aware that many of the important cases we discuss in these chapters, concerning the relationship between arbitration and the courts, arose in contexts in which one party sought both to stay the litigation and to compel arbitration.

§5.3.3 Defaults in Arbitration

What if a party files an arbitration claim and the defendant refuses to show up? As you may recall from Civil Procedure, if someone sues you in court and you fail to show up, you are at great risk of having the court declare you to be in default. In fact, the procedural rules in virtually every jurisdiction provide for the entry of default and (quickly thereafter) entry of default judgment against you (the absent defendant). And then that default judgment, like any judgment of a court, can be enforced against you. For example, the plaintiff can get the assistance of local law enforcement to seize your property to satisfy the judgment if you refuse to pay it. Assuming the court's jurisdiction over you is proper and you received proper notice, it is going to be a losing strategy for you to simply not show up for litigation in which you are the named defendant.

The picture is not all that different in arbitration, though the mechanisms vary depending on the jurisdiction and the terms of the arbitration agreement itself. Under a variety of laws — many states' arbitration laws, the Uniform Arbitration Act, the new Revised Uniform Arbitration Act, and the Federal Arbitration Act — an arbitrator may enter a default judgment against an absent party, provided the party had adequate notice of the hearing. Arbitrations that are administered under some organizations' rules handle absent parties differently. For example, under the rules of the American Arbitration Association or the International Chamber of Commerce, an arbitrator cannot enter a judgment by default. The arbitrator must still hear the claim of the party who is present and render a decision. Of course, as you might imagine, if you don't even show up, it's going to be hard for you to win.

As a practical matter, therefore, the capacity to compel the participation of an absent party is not always central to the functioning of arbitration. But, as in litigation, we assume that parties will be concerned enough that they might be bound by a decision rendered in their absence that they will decide to show up.

§5.3.4 The Preclusive Effects of Arbitral Awards

Motions to stay or to compel represent one way to assure that a dispute is processed in the forum of the disputants' choosing. But what if the dispute goes to one place, gets resolved, and then one of the disputants tries to bring the case again in another forum? In most instances in litigation, disputants have only one bite at the apple. And the reason rests with the preclusion doctrines.

Preclusion is an umbrella term that encompasses two separate affirmative defenses. The first is the doctrine of res judicata, or claim preclusion. If res judicata applies, a plaintiff is precluded from bringing his or her entire claim on the theory that the plaintiff already litigated (or had a chance to litigate) this claim in a previous action. Res judicata acts like a sledgehammer, eradicating entire claims. By contrast, the second form of preclusion, collateral estoppel (also known as issue preclusion), only prevents the relitigation of certain issues that were already litigated in a previous action. If collateral estoppel applies, the rest of the claim may proceed through litigation, but some issues within that litigation will already be decided.

In the context of your Civil Procedure course, these doctrines probably appeared in the discussion of two sequential court actions. The first case went to court and was resolved in some way. Then a party filed a second action in court, and the other party sought to preclude the relitigation of some or all of what happened in the first lawsuit. But what if one or the other (or both) of the two cases instead appeared before an arbitrator? How do the preclusion doctrines affect arbitration?

If a party seeks to preclude an issue or a claim in court, citing a prior arbitration, the court must decide whether the preclusion doctrines apply to arbitral awards. Courts are split on this. The Supreme Court, in *McDonald v. City of West Branch*, 466 U.S. 284 (1984), held that an arbitration is not a "judicial proceeding," and therefore denied the application of the Full Faith and Credit Clause to its enforcement. For the same reasons, it held that the federal court in question should not give the arbitral award preclusive effect under the usual common law preclusion doctrines, either. In many cases, federal courts have some discretion about whether to give preclusive effect to arbitral awards. Some state courts, however, give full preclusive effects to arbitral awards, treating the awards as if they were court judgments. For example, the Connecticut Supreme Court, in *Corey v. Avco-Lycoming Div.*, 307 A.2d 155 (Conn. 1972), holding that a prior arbitration barred a subsequent lawsuit, wrote that it saw "[n]o satisfactory reason . . . why an award, which the parties have expressly stipulated should be final as to the subject submitted, should not be as conclusive as a court-rendered judgment."

The preclusion doctrines typically run smoothly in the other direction as well. What if the first case was in court and resulted in a final judgment on the merits, and the second one appeared before an arbitrator? Could the party who was victorious in the first (litigated) case succeed in avoiding having the claim or issue re-adjudicated in the second case (in arbitration)? In short, yes. The details of the enforcement of preclusion-based defenses is beyond the scope of this book, but the big picture is that a party who fails in court will not find, in arbitration, a refuge in which to try again.

However, all of the above analysis is often irrelevant in practice because many victorious arbitration parties seek (successfully) to have the arbitrator's award entered as a judgment of the court. And once it is given the status of a court's judgment, there is no question that it will be given preclusive effect. Courts play virtually no role in reviewing or supervising the entry of the award, yet this simple act gives the arbitrator's decision preclusive effect in subsequent actions.

§5.4 MAKING THEM PAY: HOW COURTS ENFORCE ARBITRAL AWARDS

The simplest progression of events related to arbitration looks like this: Two parties agree to arbitrate, a dispute arises, the parties bring their dispute before an arbitrator, the arbitrator rules in favor of one party, and the parties abide by the arbitrator's decision. Why do losing parties typically abide by the decisions of arbitrators? Perhaps it is because they do so out of a sense of fairness. ("After all, I agreed that I would abide by the arbitrator's decision.") And perhaps it is for the same reason that most people abide by an adverse judgment of the court — they know that they can be formally compelled to abide by it, so they go ahead and follow the order up front. Or perhaps it is a combination of these reasons.

The mechanisms by which a party can be compelled to give effect to an arbitral award vary somewhat depending on the nature of the arbitration. The most significant distinction is between domestic arbitrations and those involving international awards. We treat each briefly below.

§5.4.1 Disputes at Home: Entering Arbitral Awards as Judgments

Courts have certain coercive powers. If a court orders a litigant to do (or refrain from doing) something, the litigant must either appeal the order or abide by it. If the litigant simply refuses to follow the order, she is at risk of being found in contempt of court, and she may face the prospect of fines or imprisonment. Similarly, if a court enters judgment against a litigant, that judgment is given effect unless it is overturned on appeal or a jurisdictional defect is successfully raised in a collateral attack. So, as we outlined earlier, if the court enters a monetary judgment against a defendant and the defendant refuses to pay, the winning plaintiff can enlist the services of the sheriff to seize the defendant's property and sell it off in order to get the money to satisfy the judgment. Of course, the system includes safeguards and elaborate procedures around these coercive powers, but the basic idea is that when a court issues an order or a judgment, it can enlist a variety of the state's mechanisms to give effect to that order or judgment.

An arbitrator's award or order, by contrast, is not itself an order or a judgment of the court. The Federal Arbitration Act and its state equivalents, therefore, provide a formal mechanism by which an arbitrator's award is treated as a judgment of the court.

Parties' contractual agreements to arbitrate virtually always include language specifying that the decision of an arbitrator will be final and may be entered as judgment (commonly called *confirming the arbitral award*) in one or more courts. Under §9 of the FAA, "any party to the arbitration may apply to the court so specified [in the agreement to arbitrate] for an order confirming the award, and thereupon the court must grant such an order unless the award is vacated, modified, or corrected." In the event the parties did not specify a particular court, the FAA provides that application may be made to the court located where the arbitration award was made. And commonly, parties drafting arbitration clauses will include far more expansive language about the entry of judgment on the arbitrator's award. For example, the clause suggested by the American Arbitration Association provides that, "judgment on the award rendered by the arbitrator(s) may be entered in any court having jurisdiction thereof." In essence, under FAA §9, if the winning party succeeds in having the arbitrator's award confirmed by a court, the award is enforceable in the same way that any other judgment from that court would be enforceable.

You should notice that the court to whom an application to confirm an arbitral award is made has very little discretion. It must confirm the award (and therefore enter it as a judgment of the court) unless the award is "vacated, modified, or corrected." We return to the question of the circumstances in which a losing party can succeed in appealing or otherwise changing an arbitral award later in this chapter. For now, you should know that a losing party in arbitration is extremely unlikely to get out from under the arbitrator's award.

§5.4.2 Disputes Without Borders: International Arbitral Awards

Companies from different countries routinely do business together, and as a result, companies from different countries routinely get in disputes with one another. What happens when international parties get in a dispute? In some ways, their choices are similar to domestic disputes. They can negotiate, mediate, arbitrate, or go to court. Of course, if you are going to court, you'd prefer a "home field" advantage with your laws, your language, and your customs. But so would the other side. One explanation for the appeal of arbitration in the international business context is that arbitration offers international businesses an opportunity to negotiate over the forum and the governing law relevant to any future disagreements. Rather than either side necessarily securing a home field advantage, the contracting parties can agree to submit the dispute to a predetermined international arbitration provider whose location and rules are acceptable to both sides.

Enforceability of foreign arbitration awards, versus foreign court awards, is probably even more important to the selection of arbitration as the dispute resolution method of choice in international commerce. Unlike domestic court orders, orders from foreign courts are not automatically enforceable in a different country. Unless both of the relevant countries have a treaty regarding the enforcement of civil judgments across borders, enforcement is questionable at best. And only some such treaties exist. In arbitration, by contrast, virtually all countries are signatories to the New York Convention (the common name for the 1958 Convention on Recognition and Enforcement of Foreign Arbitral Awards), which makes the enforcement of arbitral awards extraordinarily easy — even in cross-border circumstances. So once parties determine to adjudicate their disputes (versus settle on their own), they frequently conclude that it makes much more sense to arbitrate than litigate.

Consider a Canadian company that has a dispute with a Brazilian company with whom it has been doing a joint venture in Mexico. If the parties have no contractual dispute resolution provisions, a dispute would quite possibly result in the sort of transnational choice-of-law mess law professors would enjoy (but businesspeople would hate). Now assume instead that the terms of their joint venture include an agreement to arbitrate disputes arising under the contract. Assume it sets forth the arbitration procedures and even specifies a venue (for example, London, Singapore, or New York). An arbitrator's decision in this case will be easily enforced not only in the venue in which the arbitration took place, but also (and more importantly) in the country where the losing company's assets are located. (In general, arbitration awards are easy to enforce, but one should confirm this in the country where the judgment will be enforced.) In short, arbitral awards are more portable internationally than court orders, making arbitration even more attractive as the international adjudication process of choice.

§5.5 GETTING YOUR WAY: HOW COURTS HANDLE APPEALS OF ARBITRATORS' DECISIONS

Arbitration is an adjudicative, adversarial process. In most cases, it produces winners and losers. What can a losing party do about the undesired outcome, beyond complain bitterly? Can the losing party appeal or somehow have the arbitrator's award vacated?

The short answer is probably not. One of the attractions of arbitration, at least to many parties, is its finality. In the words of the court in *Moncharsh v. Heily & Blasé*, 832 P.2d 899, 903 (Cal. 1992), "The arbitrator's decision should be the end, not the beginning, of the dispute." Arbitration, therefore, presents very few opportunities to succeed with an appeal. It may be an overstatement to say that a losing party in an arbitration should abandon hope. But only barely.

There are really two possible arguments you could make to avoid enforcement of an award an arbitrator issued at the conclusion of an arbitration: (1) "The arbitrator procedurally messed up the arbitration process, so it shouldn't be binding," and (2) "The arbitrator's award is so flawed substantively that it shouldn't be binding." We consider each below, but as you'll see, both of these are difficult arguments to win.

§5.5.1 Procedural Flaws as Grounds for Appeal

Section 10 of the FAA sets out four procedural grounds upon which a court can vacate an arbitrator's award. An unhappy arbitration party need only demonstrate one of the four grounds in order successfully to avoid the outcome of the arbitration. But the task is more difficult than it might seem. Each of the FAA's grounds for vacatur is crafted narrowly, and courts have construed these narrowly crafted grounds even more narrowly. We describe each below.

When you review the four FAA grounds for vacatur, notice that the party seeking to avoid the award does not need to demonstrate that the arbitrator made a poor decision. In fact, a court is unlikely to be willing even to hear such a complaint. This section is about *procedural flaws* — something that went wrong with the process that led to the outcome — not about the substantive outcome itself. Of course, if the party is seeking to avoid the award, it's certainly because the party is unhappy with the award. But vacatur is available under FAA §10 only when one of a limited number of procedural flaws led to the losing party's unhappiness.

(1) **"The arbitrator was duped!"** FAA §10(a)(1) provides that a court may make an order vacating an arbitral award "where the award was procured by corruption, fraud, or undue means." This is one of the FAA provisions that is concerned about the prospect that the arbitrator might have been influenced by something other than the appropriate considerations one would expect of a decision maker. In the case of §10(a)(1), the question is whether the arbitrator's decision was based on evidence that was corrupt or fraudulent.

A typical case involving §10(a)(1) involves an allegation that one of the witnesses committed perjury during the arbitration hearing. If the perjured testimony was central to the case and the arbitrator relied on it to make a decision, the losing party might convince a court to vacate the award on the basis of §10(a)(1). This was the outcome in *Bonar v. Dean Witter Reynolds, Inc.*, 835 F.2d 1378 (11th Cir. 1988). In *Bonar*, the plaintiffs presented an "expert" witness to testify in an arbitration hearing involving a dispute over securities. The expert claimed to have degrees in finance and accounting, as well as experience in the banking industry. The arbitrators heard the expert's testimony, and, consistent with the expert's testimony, imposed punitive damages against one of the named defendants. When the defendant against whom punitive damages were imposed learned that the "expert" had fabricated all of his credentials, it appealed to a federal court under FAA §10(a). The court held that §10(a)(1) requires that the appellant establish fraud by clear and convincing evidence, that the fraud in question must not have been discoverable before or during the arbitration, and that the fraud was material to the decision. In *Bonar*, the court found all three elements were met. Because the arbitration rules in *Bonar* did not permit prehearing exchanges of witness lists, there was no real opportunity for the defendant to discover the fraud. And the arbitrators would not have permitted "expert" testimony from the witness if they had known that the witness held no relevant credentials. As a result, a court vacated the arbitrators' imposition of punitive damages against the defendant and ordered a rehearing before a new panel of arbitrators.

(2) **"The arbitrator was on the take!"** FAA §10(a)(2) provides that a court may refuse to enforce an arbitrator's award if there was "evident partiality or corruption in the arbitrators." As with §10(a)(1), the complaining party does not need to demonstrate any error in the arbitrator's decision. It suffices to demonstrate that the arbitrator deviated so significantly from the presumption of impartiality that attaches to arbitration that it makes no sense to enforce the arbitrator's award. For example, if an arbitrator fails to disclose that his son is an executive in one of the organizations appearing in the arbitration, a court would very likely deem this to be evident partiality for purposes of FAA §10(a)(2). Citing §10(a)(2), the Supreme Court has held that if an arbitrator has a history of dealings that might create an impression of bias, the arbitrator must disclose those dealings. In *Commonwealth Coatings Corp. v. Continental Cas. Co.*, 393 U.S. 145 (1968), the Court wrote:

> It is true that arbitrators cannot sever all their ties with the business world, since they are not expected to get all their income from their work deciding cases, but we should, if anything, be even more scrupulous to safeguard the impartiality of arbitrators than judges, since the former have completely free rein to decide the law as well as the facts and are not subject to appellate review. We can perceive no way in which the effectiveness of the arbitration process will be hampered by the simple requirement that arbitrators disclose to the parties any dealings that might create an impression of possible bias.

In some cases, therefore, a court may refuse to enforce an arbitral award on the basis of §10(a)(2) even if there is no showing of actual bias, corruption, or partiality in the arbitrator.

(3) **"The arbitrator conducted a sham hearing!"** FAA §10(a)(3) provides that a court may refuse to enforce an arbitral award "[w]here the arbitrators were guilty of misconduct in refusing to postpone the hearing, upon sufficient cause shown, or in refusing to hear evidence pertinent and material to the controversy; or of any other misbehavior by which the rights of any party have been prejudiced." For example, in the case of *Tempo Shain Corp. v. Bertek, Inc.*, 120 F.3d 16 (2d Cir. 1997), arbitrators refused to postpone a hearing to permit the testimony of one of the executives of the defendant corporation, Bertek. The executive, who the defendants argued was at the center of the events giving rise to the arbitration claim and who would have offered testimony favorable to Bertek, was temporarily unable to testify because his wife had been diagnosed with cancer and he needed to attend to her. Based on a set of evidence that did not include the executive's testimony, the

arbitrators found against Bertek. But on appeal, the Second Circuit held that the arbitrators were guilty of misconduct under FAA §10(a)(3). Calling the proceeding "fundamentally unfair," the appellate court vacated the arbitrators' ruling against Bertek.

(4) "The arbitrator did something, but not what the contract told the arbitrator to do!" The final of the FAA §10 grounds for vacatur provides that a court may refuse to enforce "[w]here the arbitrators exceed their powers, or so imperfectly executed them that a mutual, final, and definite award upon the subject matter submitted was not made." Some parties have tried to stretch this ground into a broad opportunity for review of the substance of the award. (The logic goes, "We didn't contractually authorize the arbitrator to make an error of law, so this erroneous ruling exceeds the arbitrator's authority.") But this logic has not swayed courts. Instead, the logic of the opinion in *United Paperworkers Int'l Union v. Misco, Inc.*, 484 U.S. 29 (1987), prevails: "As long as the arbitrator is even arguably construing or applying the contract and acting within the scope of his authority, that a court is convinced he committed serious error does not suffice to overturn his decision."

FAA §10(a)(4) is reserved for the relatively rare instance in which the arbitrator's decision is flawed in a way that makes enforcement problematic. For example, an award will not be enforced if it is unintelligible. ("We can't figure out what the hell this decision means.") An award is also subject to vacatur if the scope of the arbitrator's award does not match the scope of the arbitrator's contractual mandate.

In some cases, an arbitrator does less than what the contract called for. For example, in *Escobar v. Shearson Lehman Hutton, Inc.*, 762 F. Supp. 461 (D.P.R. 1991), Andres Escobar and Pedro Escobar each held accounts with a brokerage firm, and each filed claims against the firm. The claims were consolidated for the arbitral hearing, the arbitrator took evidence about both accounts, and the dealer defended against both claims. The arbitrator ruled in favor of the claimants, but the arbitrator's award only made reference to one of the two disputed accounts. On motion for vacatur, the court held that this constituted an "imperfectly executed" award and refused to enforce it.

Similarly, an award is subject to vacatur if it clearly exceeds the boundaries of the question put before the arbitrator. ("We disagreed about the value of the defective widgets, so we submitted it to arbitration. But the arbitrator issued an award naming the value at $1.2 million, ordering me to do community service, and ordering the other party to return my dachshund. The arbitrator had no authority to order me to do community service, and we never agreed to arbitrate anything about the ownership of any dog.") As with all of the other FAA §10 grounds, however, you should assume that vacatur is unlikely except in the most extraordinary circumstances.

§5.5.2 Substantive Flaws in the Award as Grounds for Appeal

Each of the above grounds for challenging an arbitrator's award stems from the statutory language of the FAA. In addition to statutory grounds for appeal, many states have established common law bases for overturning an arbitrator's decision. (In Chapter 8 we will return to the question of the applicability of state laws relevant to arbitration, given the potential for federal preemption. For now, you should simply understand that potential avenues exist for parties who are dissatisfied with an arbitrator's decision.) These nonstatutory grounds examine the substance of an arbitrator's award more than the FAA, which purports to care only about unearthing and overturning flaws in the process leading to the arbitrator's award.

The most significant and most widely recognized of these additional grounds for appealing an arbitrator's decision is the *manifest disregard of the law* standard. (Other jurisdictions have overturned arbitral awards when they were "completely irrational" or "arbitrary and capricious," but the overwhelmingly dominant common law basis for attacking the substance of an arbitrator's decision remains the "manifest disregard" standard.) We treat the manifest disregard standard with some care below, but the headline you should remember is this: To succeed in appealing an arbitrator's decision under even the more expansive manifest disregard of the law standard, you need to demonstrate something more than merely saying, "The arbitrator got the law and the facts wrong." The manifest disregard standard does not reverse the presumption of finality in arbitration.

The manifest disregard argument has essentially two separate components, each of which must be met before a party challenging an arbitral award will be successful. First, the arbitrator must have made an error that is so profound as to be apparent (or "manifest") on the face of the award. This category does not, therefore, cover mistakes in procedure or errors in evidentiary rulings, for example. Instead, the law in the area must be so clear, and the arbitrator's decision must be so clearly contrary to that law, that the arbitrator's decision can be called "manifestly" contrary to that law.

Second, the arbitrator must have clearly "disregarded" the relevant law. It is not enough to demonstrate that the arbitrator was utterly ignorant of the law. It is not enough to demonstrate that the arbitrator made a mistake in applying the law. Instead, the party seeking to have the arbitral award vacated must demonstrate that the arbitrator *knew* the relevant law and *chose* to disregard it in rendering a decision.

The opportunity to vacate arbitral awards that are issued in "manifest disregard of the law," therefore, is more limited than might appear initially on the face of this common law doctrine. How often is an arbitrator going to make such an error as to be "manifest" in the decision, knowing that the decision goes against the dictates of the clearly relevant law (hence "disregarding" it)? The answer is: once in a great while. *Gas Aggregation Servs., Inc. v. Howard Avista Energy*, 319 F.3d 1060 (8th Cir. 2003), provides one example of a circumstance in which an award may be deemed sufficiently flawed so as to be unenforceable. In that case, a natural gas marketing company and a natural gas trading company went to arbitration over breach of contract, fraud, conversion, and other charges against the gas trading company. The arbitral panel ruled in favor of the natural gas marketing company, and awarded attorneys' fees and costs to the prevailing company. Under Minnesota law (the law the parties' contract specified would apply), however, attorneys' fees in such cases are available only to claimants who are consumers. Explaining that it was clear that neither of the companies was a "consumer" under the state statute, and that the arbitrators were presented with evidence of the state law's requirement during the arbitration hearing itself, an appeals court vacated that portion of the arbitrators' award. Your presumption, however, should be that a court will uphold the decisions of an arbitrator who conducted the arbitration properly and at least arguably construed the contract in question.

The manifest disregard argument is not the only common law basis for opposing the enforcement of an arbitrator's decision. For example, a party who loses in arbitration could make an argument that the arbitrator's award should not be upheld on the grounds that the award violates *public policy*. However, the Supreme Court has been consistent in narrowly construing the "public policy" basis for overturning an arbitrator's decisions.

For example, in *Eastern Associated Coal v. United Mine Workers Dist. 17*, 531 U.S. 57 (2000), the Court reviewed an arbitrator's award stemming from a dispute that arose in a collective bargaining context. The contract signed by the UMW on behalf of all employees stipulated that an employee could be fired only for "just cause." James Smith, a unionized driver with EAC, tested positive for marijuana use. When the company tried to dismiss Smith, the union filed a claim with an arbitrator. The arbitrator determined that this failed test did not constitute "just cause" for termination, and the arbitrator ordered Smith reinstated. Some time later, Smith tested positive for drugs again. Again the company fired Smith, and again the union appealed on Smith's behalf. The second arbitrator considered Smith's testimony about the second relapse, again judged the firing not to be "just cause," and ordered Smith both to undergo treatment and to submit a signed resignation letter for use in the event that Smith was ever caught again in the future. The employer sought to have the arbitrator's award vacated on the grounds that it violates public policy. The Court upheld the arbitrator's award, saying that the question is NOT whether the Court agrees with the arbitrator's decision. Instead, the Court instructs us to assume that the contract says and means whatever the arbitrator rules it says and means. The question then becomes, if the contract says and means *that*, is that contract unenforceable on the grounds that it violates public policy? And in this case, the Court found that there were competing interests at play here. On the one hand, we as society have a keen interest in assuring that the people who operate heavy, mobile machinery are not under the influence of drugs. On the other hand, we as society have a strong interest in providing rehabilitation to those who struggle with addiction. Both of these policies have statutory bases and both are legitimate. The Court noted that it would not have been able to prevent its enforcement on "public policy" grounds, even if the contract explicitly included the terms as interpreted by the arbitrator, given that the interpretation is up to the arbitrator. The Court, therefore, left the arbitrator's decision intact.

Both the statutory and nonstatutory grounds for contesting an arbitrator's decision are, therefore, extremely limited. But what if the parties mutually *want* to have greater post-arbitration opportunities for judicial scrutiny? Can parties *contractually expand* these bases for judicial review? Until 2008, courts were split on this question. In *Hall Street Assocs. v. Mattel, Inc.*, 552 U.S. 1396 (2008), the Supreme Court declared that the answer is no. Although the Court was closely divided, the majority held that the grounds listed in FAA §10 and §11 are, essentially, the "exclusive" grounds under the FAA. The Court left the door open for other statutory and common law bases for review outside of the FAA. (An example of such review might be the manifest disregard of the law analysis we described above.) But it closed the door on contractually expanded judicial review of arbitral awards under the FAA.

§5.6 HAVING YOUR SAY: CONFIDENTIALITY IN ARBITRATION

In addition to considerations of speed and efficiency, many parties also prefer arbitration to litigation because it often leads to resolution wholly outside of the public view. In arbitration, transcripts are not necessarily required, the arbitrator often issues a decision without any opinion explaining the reasoning underlying the decision, and the hearing itself is rarely open to public access. Further, because a dispute that finds itself in arbitration tends to stay in arbitration before the same arbitrator, there is rarely a reason for outside interest in the arbitration proceedings. The combination of these factors means that arbitration is usually characterized by relative secrecy.

Having said all of that, arbitration does not enjoy the same kind of confidentiality protection as negotiation or mediation. (See Chapter 4 for more on confidentiality in negotiation and mediation.) The reason for this distinction rests largely in the differences between those processes and arbitration. Recall that confidentiality in mediation and negotiation is justified, in large measure, because we want to provide an incentive for participants to engage fully. Engaging fully in mediation and negotiation might involve acknowledging the other side's perspective, suggesting compromise options, disclosing your own priorities, etc. In arbitration, by contrast, confidentiality is not needed in order to provide this incentive, because arbitration is an adversarial proceeding, akin to litigation. In adversarial proceedings, we imagine that both parties present the best evidence and make the best arguments they can. There is no reason for them to hold back on these arguments, even in the absence of formal confidentiality protections, because they want to win the case. Thus, courts and legislatures have not given arbitration parties the same array of confidentiality protections as negotiation and mediation.

Still, issues of confidentiality in arbitration do sometimes arise. The leading case on arbitration confidentiality is *United States v. Panhandle Eastern Corp.*, 118 F.R.D. 346 (D. Del. 1988). The United States, on behalf of the Maritime Administration, brought a civil action against Panhandle and its affiliates to protect its security interest as a guarantor of ship financing bonds. As part of discovery, the United States requested documents concerning an earlier arbitration conducted between Panhandle and Sonatrach (the Algerian National Oil and Gas Company). Panhandle made a motion for a protective order to prevent the disclosure of the Sonatrach documents, including the briefs filed by the parties in that arbitration. It argued that disclosure of the arbitration documents to third parties would severely prejudice its ongoing business relationship with Sonatrach and the Algerian government. The court found this argument unpersuasive, holding that Panhandle had failed to demonstrate good cause for the protective order. As a result, the arbitration documents were discoverable and admissible. Arbitration parties who would prefer additional confidentiality are only *sometimes* able to achieve it by including confidentiality clauses in their contracts.

Examples

Larry, Moe, and Curly enter a joint venture to produce blockbuster motion pictures. In the contract establishing their joint venture, they agree to arbitrate "any and all disputes related to the formation, performance, or breach of this agreement." At a recent meeting of the three partners, an arguably comical melee broke out when each came to believe that the other two had done none of the things required under the terms of the joint venture. None of the partners sustained injuries in the fisticuffs, but each was livid about the others' apparent breach of the joint venture agreement.

1. **A Race to Somewhere.** Each of the three venture partners consulted with separate legal counsel, contemplating possible legal actions against the other two. The first to act was Larry, who raced to the local courthouse and filed a complaint against Moe and Curly, alleging breach of contract and breach of fiduciary duty. The next day, Moe filed a claim against Larry and Curly with an arbitrator, pursuant to the procedures set forth in the joint venture agreement, alleging breach of contract. Curly, now confused, sat back and waited to figure out where he should bring his claim against his other two partners. What options does each party have for pursuing his claims in the forum of his choice?

2. **Where Is That Wise Guy?** Moe files an arbitration claim against Larry and Curly, pursuant to the procedures set forth in the joint venture agreement, alleging breach of contract. Curly appears in the arbitration, responding to Moe's allegations and filing a set of counterclaims against Moe. Larry, however, is nowhere to be found. The arbitration rules to which the three agreed do not permit the arbitrator to enter a judgment by default. Both Moe and Curly are eager to have Larry be part of the action because he has comparatively deep pockets and because they believe his breach was particularly egregious. What options do Moe and Curly have?

3. **Where Is That Wise Guy's Money?** With respect to the claims between Moe and Curly, the arbitrator ruled entirely in favor of Curly. The arbitrator found that Curly had met his obligations under the contract and that Moe had breached his. The arbitrator's award held that Moe owed Curly $100,000. Immediately upon receiving the award, Curly had the award confirmed in the local court. Weeks later, however, Moe has still not paid Curly. What could Curly do to try to collect from Moe, and what are his prospects of success?

4. **Slapping Larry Again.** Moe files a claim against Larry in arbitration, alleging breach of contract. Larry defends himself vigorously in the arbitration hearing, but the arbitrator finds for Moe in the amount of $50,000. Moe goes to court and has the award confirmed. Larry grumblingly pays the money to Moe. A month later, Moe files a lawsuit in federal court against Larry, seeking to recover additional money for the same injuries stemming from the same set of facts that gave rise to Moe's arbitration claim against Larry. What options does Larry have?

5. **Slapping Moe Again.** Curly files a claim against Moe in arbitration, alleging breach of contract. Moe defends himself vigorously in the arbitration hearing, but the arbitrator finds for Curly in the amount

of $50,000. Moe grumblingly pays the money to Curly. A month later, Curly files a lawsuit in federal court against Moe, seeking damages stemming from the same set of facts that gave rise to Curly's arbitration claim against Moe. What options does Moe have?

6. **You Call That an Expert?** Larry, Moe, and Curly appear in arbitration, and each party asserts a claim against each of the other two. The dispute hinges on whether any of the parties' conduct constituted a breach of their movie-making joint venture agreement. During the course of the arbitration hearing, Larry calls Willy Woopwoop as an "expert" witness. Moe and Curly object to Woopwoop's credentials as an expert. Woopwoop testifies that he has a degree in cinematography, an MBA, and ten years' experience in the movie business. On this basis, the arbitrator permits Woopwoop's testimony as an expert. Woopwoop tells the arbitrator that Larry was the only one of the three who made defensible business decisions. The arbitrator subsequently ruled for Larry on all claims. Moe and Curly, still angry about Woopwoop's testimony, hired an investigator to look into his background. A week later, the investigator produced evidence that Woopwoop never received even a college degree and that his only experience in the movie industry was as a frequent patron of a local cinema. Would Moe and Curly succeed in having a court vacate the arbitrator's award?

7. **One Hairy Hearing.** Larry and Curly appear before an arbitrator to resolve claims each of them has, alleging that the other attempted to embezzle money from the joint venture. About an hour into the rather heated hearing, Curly confronted Larry by saying, "That isn't even your real hair, is it? Remember that you're under oath." Larry angrily shouted, "Of course it's my real hair, you imbecile!" Animated fisticuffs ensued, and eventually the arbitrator declared that she had heard enough testimony. Not long afterwards, the arbitrator issued an award in favor of Larry. Not long after that, Curly came into possession of a videotape of Larry putting on a wig, along with sworn testimony from one of Larry's former employees, swearing that Larry has not had hair in years. If Curly seeks to have the arbitrator's award vacated on the basis of fraud, would he succeed?

8. **Curly's Perpetual Parade of Pals.** During an arbitration involving Larry and Curly, Larry presented two witnesses and rested his case. Curly began presenting his evidence by calling one of his friends to serve as a character witness. At the conclusion of that friend's testimony, the arbitrator asked if Curly had anyone else to call. "Soitenly!" replied Curly, who then called another friend as a character witness. At the conclusion of that friend's testimony, the arbitrator again asked if

Curly was finished yet. But Curly kept calling witnesses, one after the other, and each of them testified about Curly's unfailing veracity. Eventually, the arbitrator grew tired of the parade of witnesses, and refused to permit any further testimony from either party. If the arbitrator rules against Curly, what chance would Curly have of convincing a court to vacate the award?

9. **Shemp, Man of Reason.** In anticipation of an arbitration involving Larry, Moe, and Curly, a dispute arose about who would serve as arbitrator. The parties reviewed a list of candidates, and eventually settled on a man named Shemp. Shemp conducted the hearings in accordance with the procedures articulated in the parties' agreement, and he issued an award in favor of Larry against the other two. Later, Moe and Curly discovered that Shemp and Larry are business partners. Would Moe and Curly be likely to persuade a court to vacate the arbitral award issued against them?

10. **Arbitral Snoozing.** Larry and Moe submit their dispute to an arbitrator, according to the procedures specified in their contract. The arbitrator renders an award in favor of Larry. Moe seeks to have the award vacated, claiming that the arbitrator slept during most of the portion of the hearing when Moe was presenting his evidence. Is Moe likely to be successful in his efforts to resist the arbitrator's award?

11. **The Opinion of a Knucklehead.** Moe brings a claim against Larry in arbitration, alleging that Larry violated a noncompete clause in their contract. Moe introduces as evidence a signed employment contract between Larry and a competing film studio, timesheets signed by Larry, testimony from the competing studio's payroll officer, and a videotape of Larry handing out the competing studio's business cards at a film festival. Larry presents, as his defense, a copy of his bank account, showing that his earnings from the other film studio were not quite as significant as Moe had alleged. Larry also pleads, during the arbitration hearing, "I'm sorry, Moe. Please forgive me!" The arbitrator issues an award in favor of Larry, and writes in a reasoned opinion that he "found Larry's evidence more persuasive." What chances would Moe have of convincing a court to vacate the arbitrator's award?

12. **The Opinion of a Chowderhead.** Curly brings an arbitration action against Larry, alleging that Larry unlawfully discriminated against Curly on the basis of Curly's "follicularly challenged coiffure." Curly presented as evidence a document showing that bald members of the joint venture received less favorable benefits than those with "more lustrous locks." Larry argued vigorously that the law does not recognize any protected class on the basis of hair, noting that no discrimination claim could possibly survive if the plaintiff is not in some

way protected. In his opinion, the arbitrator wrote, "Discrimination isn't about just certain classes of people. I don't care what the law says. Anybody can feel badly if they're left out. And that's wrong." The arbitrator concluded by ruling in favor of Curly and awarded him $1 million in compensatory damages. What is the likelihood that Larry would succeed in having the award vacated?

13. **What's the Big Idea?** In the same dispute between Curly and Larry as was described in the example immediately above, would it make any difference if the arbitrator had merely found in favor of Curly, but had issued no written opinion at all?

Explanations

1. **A Race to Somewhere.** Moe filed his claim against the other two in arbitration. On the face of things, this appears to be consistent with the partners' agreement. Moe presumably prefers to have his claim heard by an arbitrator. And the only possible threat to this would be if Larry's court case were to proceed, because the result of the court case risks precluding Moe's claim in arbitration. As a result, the best course of action for Moe would be to file a motion to stay the litigation in court under FAA §3. The court would then need to satisfy itself that "the making of the agreement for arbitration or the failure to comply therewith is not in issue." Here, nothing suggests impropriety in the formation of the arbitration agreement. The agreement clearly covers the alleged claim, and Moe did everything required under the arbitration agreement. Therefore, the court would almost certainly grant Moe's motion to stay the litigation. If something remains of Larry's claim following the arbitration, Larry can return to court to have the court resolve the unresolved issues. But most likely, Moe will succeed in having the entire set of disputes related to the alleged breaches heard in arbitration.

The procedural option available to Larry to try to maintain the action in court would be to file a motion to stay the arbitration. Motions to stay arbitration will be granted in circumstances in which the court is satisfied that no arbitration agreement legitimately applies to a dispute, and an arbitrator's decision risks creating inappropriate preclusive effects or conflict with existing litigation. Here, however, for the reasons we described above, Larry appears to have a weak claim that this case belongs in court rather than in arbitration. His motion to stay the arbitration, therefore, has little chance of being granted.

Curly has not yet filed a claim in either forum. If the action were maintained in court, the joinder doctrines you encountered in Civil

Procedure would certainly permit Curly to add his claims against the other two. (Here, the joinder would take the form of a counterclaim and a cross-claim.) But as described above, the litigation is almost certain to be stayed, pending the outcome of the arbitration. The arbitration procedures to which the three parties agreed surely included procedures for adding claims — probably something akin to the Civil Procedure rules on this point. Curly will most likely figure out that arbitration is where the action will take place and therefore will join his claims in that forum.

2. **Where Is That Wise Guy?** Moe and Curly have two basic options. First, under FAA §5, Moe and Curly are "aggrieved by the alleged failure, neglect, or refusal of another to arbitrate under a written agreement for arbitration." They could, therefore, file a motion to compel Larry to arbitrate. Assuming the court sees this agreement to arbitrate as valid, binding, and applicable to this dispute, the court would grant the motion. If Larry subsequently failed to arbitrate, he not only would be in violation of his contractual duty, but also (and more seriously) would be in violation of a court order. And the court's contempt power to sanction parties who refuse to adhere to a court order make this an effective mechanism for compelling Larry's participation.

   The second option for Moe and Curly would be to proceed with the arbitration even in the absence of Larry. The arbitration agreement does not permit the arbitrator to enter a judgment by default. But nothing in the facts suggest that the arbitrator would not be permitted to hear the merits of the case and render a decision. If Larry is not there to present his case, the arbitrator is likely to render a decision that Larry will not like. Assuming Moe and Curly follow all of the procedures properly, the arbitrator's award would be binding against Larry.

3. **Where Is That Wise Guy's Money?** Because Curly had the arbitrator's award confirmed with the court (either under FAA §9 or a state equivalent), the award is treated the same as any judgment of the court. Each jurisdiction has its own specific procedures for the enforcement of judgments. But in most cases, Curly would be able to enlist the services of a local law enforcement officer (such as a sheriff) to enforce the court judgment. Enforcement might take the form of seizing Moe's property and selling it in order to satisfy the judgment. And again, because the award was confirmed by the local court, Curly could even enforce the award as a judgment in other states under the Full Faith and Credit Clause. Unless Moe is so poor as to be effectively judgment-proof, Curly's prospects for recovery are excellent.

4. **Slapping Larry Again.** Larry should assert the affirmative defense of res judicata. The complaint in court rests upon the same set of facts as those asserted in the prior arbitration. Res judicata acts to preclude claims that

were (or could have been) brought in the prior action, provided the prior action resulted in a valid, final judgment on the merits. Here, the arbitrator's award satisfies all of those requirements (unless there was something odd about the arbitrator's jurisdiction that would have prevented her from hearing one of Moe's claims arising out of those facts, in which case collateral estoppel might still apply, depending on the circumstances). And because Moe confirmed the arbitrator's award in court, there are none of the difficulties that sometimes arise about the preclusive effects of an arbitral award. Here, the award is treated as a judgment of the court. Larry will not have to face the prospect of a second dose of liability for the same wrongdoing.

5. **Slapping Moe Again.** This is exactly the same scenario as the question immediately above, except that this time, the prevailing party did not have the arbitrator's award confirmed in court. The Supreme Court, in *McDonald v. City of West Branch*, 466 U.S. 284 (1984), suggested that arbitration alone (without judicial confirmation) did not constitute a "judicial proceeding," and therefore carried no preclusive effect in subsequent litigation. By contrast, some state courts accord preclusive effect to unconfirmed arbitration awards.

In a case like this, where the losing party immediately paid the adverse arbitral award, the winning party would have no real reason to have the award confirmed. Moe already paid up, so what would Curly stand to gain by taking the award to court? To refuse Moe's assertion of res judicata on this matter would, in effect, punish Moe for living up to his promise to abide by the arbitrator's decision. Had he been a bad sport and refused to pay the award, Curly would have needed to go to court to have the award confirmed and enforced. And if that happened, res judicata would plainly be available to Moe. It is unlikely that a court would, in this circumstance, refuse the application of res judicata, but it is less clear than the example above.

6. **You Call That an Expert?** Probably yes. The standards for successfully challenging an arbitrator's decision are strict, but in this case, the court would probably find that the arbitrator's decision was based on fraudulent testimony from Woopwoop and thus subject to vacatur under FAA §10(a)(1). In *Bonar v. Dean Witter Reynolds, Inc.*, 835 F.2d 1378 (11th Cir. 1988), a purported expert witness deceived the arbitrator about his credentials, and a court subsequently vacated the arbitral award for fraud. The same would likely occur in this case, for the same reasons. The testimony of Woopwoop was material, and it was presented to the arbitrator only because of fraud. Assuming Moe and Curly had no reasonable opportunity to unearth and challenge the fraud before or during the course of the arbitration, FAA §10(a)(1) would permit vacatur.

7. **One Hairy Hearing.** No. It is true that FAA §10(a)(1) permits parties to avoid arbitral awards that were procured on the basis of fraud. Even if we assume, however, that Larry's testimony about his hair was knowingly false, it is difficult to imagine that an arbitrator would have based her decision on this testimony. And unless the testimony was material, it cannot be the basis of vacatur under §10(a)(1). Curly's best argument would be that if the arbitrator had known Larry's propensity for falsifying some things (like the true state of his hair), the arbitrator would have found it easier to believe that Larry would falsify other things (like the allegedly embezzled money). But the distance between Larry's locks and embezzlement are too remote to make vacatur likely.

8. **Curly's Perpetual Parade of Pals.** Curly would have little chance to convince a court to vacate the arbitrator's award if the only alleged defect in the hearing was the arbitrator's decision to cut off testimony from Curly's redundant parade of character witnesses. FAA §10(a)(3) does provide that courts may refuse to enforce arbitral awards when they were the product of a flawed process (for example, when the arbitrator "refus[ed] to hear evidence pertinent and material to the controversy" as in the *Tempo Shain Corp. v. Bertek, Inc.* case, in which the executive caring for his sick wife never got to testify, and the award was vacated). However, in this case, Curly was not prejudiced by the arbitrator's decision. There is no evidence that the arbitrator ignored all of the testimony that had come up to that point. And clearly, the arbitrator must have some discretion in controlling against a filibuster version of arbitration hearings. There is surely a gray area in the question of how much an arbitrator must permit. But this case is clearly beyond what is even arguably prejudicial. A motion to vacate would be denied.

9. **Shemp, Man of Reason.** Probably yes. FAA §10(a)(2) permits vacatur "where there was evident partiality" in the arbitrator. Even though there is no particular accusation that Shemp's conduct was inappropriate, his relationship with one of the arbitration parties creates such a substantial impression of impropriety and bias that a court might refuse to enforce his award. In the case of *Julius Erving v. Va. Squires Basketball Club*, 349 F. Supp. 716 (E.D.N.Y. 1972), the Virginia Squires sought an injunction preventing Erving (a.k.a. "Dr. J") from playing with any other basketball team. Part of Erving's contract included an arbitration clause, which specified that the arbitrator would be the Commissioner of the American Basketball Association (the league in which the Virginia Squires competed). In an order compelling arbitration, the court took notice of the fact that the newly appointed Commissioner was a named partner in the law firm representing the Virginia Squires. As a result, the court ordered arbitration but ordered that a different, "neutral" arbitrator be appointed. Even though the case involving Shemp is in

a different posture than the Julius Erving case, the fact that the partiality of the arbitrator was not evident until after the proceedings had concluded would probably lead a court to the conclusion that the arbitral award cannot stand.

10. **Arbitral Snoozing.** Moe's best shot at having the arbitrator's award vacated would be under FAA §10(a)(3), which permits a court to vacate an award where the arbitrator engaged in "misbehavior by which the rights of any party have been prejudiced." As incredible as these circumstances may sound, according to the party who was seeking to have an arbitral award vacated in *National Post Office Mailhandlers v. USPS*, 751 F.2d 834 (6th Cir. 1985), the arbitrator "dozed" during their presentation of evidence. The court hearing the motion to vacate held an evidentiary hearing, asking each party about its recollection of the arbitrator's apparent inattention. As you might imagine, each side recalled the arbitrator's conduct differently. The court eventually determined that whatever lack of arbitral attention occurred was not significant enough to constitute misbehavior under FAA §10(a)(3), holding that "the standard for judicial review of arbitration procedures is merely whether a party to arbitration has been denied a fundamentally fair hearing."

Moe's chances of having the arbitrator's award vacated, therefore, depend on whether Moe can actually demonstrate that (1) the arbitrator napped during the presentation of Moe's evidence, and (2) the arbitrator napped during such an important part of Moe's presentation of evidence that Moe's rights have been prejudiced. Given the uncertainties involved, however, Moe's better course of action would have been to waken the slumbering arbitrator and request a continuance or a caffeine break.

11. **The Opinion of a Knucklehead.** Moe's chances of having the award vacated are slim. Nothing in the facts suggest any defect in the arbitration proceeding itself, so nothing in the FAA is likely to support Moe's efforts. Nothing in the arbitrator's award comes near to constituting a violation of public policy. Moe's best chance for vacatur, therefore, would come from asserting that the arbitrator's decision constitutes "manifest disregard of the law." Moe's objection is that the arbitrator's award appears to be against the clear weight of the evidence. But courts generally refuse to second-guess the legal conclusions, much less the fact finding, of arbitrators. Nothing suggests that the arbitrator disregarded a clearly applicable law here. The arbitrator may have gotten it wrong, but a court is extraordinarily unlikely to disturb the award.

12. **The Opinion of a Chowderhead.** Larry has as good a chance of having this award vacated as any "manifest disregard" claim is likely to have.

In order for a manifest disregard assertion to succeed, the party contesting the arbitral award must show that "(1) the arbitrator knew of a governing legal principle yet refused to apply it or ignored it altogether, and (2) the law ignored by the arbitrator was well defined, explicit, and clearly applicable to the case." This is a high standard and, as we have discussed, is exceedingly rare. For instance, in *Montes v. Shearson Lehman Bros.*, 128 F.3d 1456 (11th Cir. 1997), a former employee charged Shearson Lehman with violating federal overtime laws. During the arbitration hearing, the attorney for the defendant urged the arbitrators to "ignore the law," and the arbitrators subsequently ruled in favor of the defendants. The Eleventh Circuit acknowledged that manifest disregard is an extremely narrow circumstance, but nonetheless vacated the award and sent the case back for a new arbitration. In Curly's action against Larry, given Larry's vigorous defense based solely on the sound legal principle that bald people do not belong to a protected class, and given the arbitrator's apparent understanding of this law, a court would be likely to view the arbitrator's award as being the product of manifest disregard of the law. Larry is, therefore, likely to succeed with his request that the award be vacated.

13. **What's the Big Idea?** Maybe. Courts are split over how to deal with the situation in which the arbitrator has written no reasoned opinion. Recall that arbitrators are under no obligation to explain their decisions, unless the parties' contract calls for a reasoned decision. Does silence make it virtually impossible to assess the arbitrator's thought process, and therefore make it virtually impossible to say what the arbitrator knew or disregarded? Or does silence invite the court to assume knowledge in a way that makes it more likely to overturn arbitral awards?

Both lines of logic find support. A federal judge in *Federated Dep't Stores v. JVB Indus.*, 894 F.2d 862, 871 (6th Cir. 1990) described the exercise of trying to determine whether an arbitrator manifestly disregarded the law, when the arbitrator issued no written opinion, as a "judicial snipe hunt." For example, in *DiRussa v. Dean Witter Reynolds*, 121 F.3d 818 (2d Cir. 1997), a former securities dealer, DiRussa, brought a claim against his former employer alleging age discrimination in violation of the Age Discrimination in Employment Act (ADEA). Consistent with the terms of DiRussa's employment contract, the case went to arbitration, where DiRussa sought compensatory damages, punitive damages, and attorneys' fees. The arbitrator found in favor of DiRussa and awarded him compensatory damages, but denied all other relief. Noting that the ADEA mandates that attorneys' fees be granted to successful claimants, DiRussa filed a motion to vacate or modify the award to include attorneys' fees on the basis that the arbitrator's refusal to award attorneys' fees constituted manifest disregard of the law. The court agreed that the ADEA does mandate attorneys' fees. But the court nonetheless upheld the arbitrator's award (without attorneys' fees) because there was no evidence that the arbitrators *knew* that the ADEA had this requirement. Absent this knowledge, the arbitrators could not be held to have disregarded the law.

By contrast, in *Halligan v. Piper Jaffray, Inc.*, 148 F.3d 197 (2d Cir. 1998), Halligan, a salesman, was fired from his job shortly before his retirement. Halligan alleged age discrimination, and during the arbitration hearing, his former employer admitted that Halligan was "basically qualified." Halligan presented evidence showing that he was among the top producing salespeople at the company, and presented witnesses who testified about Halligan having been "pushed out" of the job. The arbitrator ruled in favor of the company and issued no written opinion. In considering a motion to vacate, the court wrote, "when a reviewing court is inclined to hold that an arbitration panel manifestly disregarded the law, the failure of the arbitrators to explain the award can be taken into account. Having done so, we are left with the firm belief that the arbitrator here manifestly disregarded the law or the evidence or both."

It appears that the weight of cases leans in favor of the *DiRussa* logic — that an arbitrator's award that is silent about the arbitrator's logic cannot serve as the basis of a manifest disregard objection. Such awards may be subject to review and vacatur on other bases, but in most jurisdictions, the manifest disregard avenue is unavailable for these opinions.

CHAPTER 6

Is This Agreement to Arbitrate Enforceable?

---

§6.1 INTRODUCTION

Although some disputants like the idea of having their claims resolved through arbitration, some prefer to retain the option of litigating in court. Why might some disputants prefer court? Maybe they want the publicity associated with public adjudication. Maybe they love the idea of a jury deciding questions of fact. Maybe they like the formality a trial offers. Maybe their lawyers are simply more familiar with litigation. There are many legitimate reasons why some parties might prefer not to arbitrate.

The next two chapters examine the range of different avenues available to a disputant who seeks to avoid arbitration. It might seem counterintuitive that in a section of an ADR book devoted entirely to arbitration, we will spend the bulk of our time and space dealing with ways to *avoid arbitration*. But the reality is that much of modern law and litigation about arbitration relates precisely to the question of whether parties will be compelled to submit their disputes to arbitration.

As we mentioned in the first chapter in this section (with the exception of court-ordered, nonbinding arbitration, which we discuss in Chapter 9), arbitration is a creature of contract. From that basic observation, it stands to reason that the simplest way to prevent an arbitration agreement from being enforced is to attack it the way you would any other contract. So, for example, an arbitration agreement between two companies is unlikely to be enforceable if the contract was printed in 6 point font in ancient Sanskrit and the only signature on the contract is a block-letter crayon effort by the five-year-old daughter of one company's receptionist. We pledge not to force you to relive your entire Contracts class in this chapter, but we will give you a survey of some of the most common contract-based defenses parties raise in seeking to avoid arbitration.

Contract-based strategies for avoiding arbitration essentially boil down to one of two lines of attack. One avenue for avoiding arbitration is to assert that "there was no contractual agreement to arbitrate." The other is to assert that "there was a contractual agreement to arbitrate, but the contract is unenforceable." You will see that we have divided the range of contract-based challenges to arbitration into one of these two categories.

As we examine each of these basic defenses to arbitration, we will also talk about who *decides* each of these challenges (a court or an arbitrator). As you can imagine, a party who seeks to avoid arbitration would almost certainly prefer to have a court hear challenges to arbitration. ("After all, if I'm trying to avoid arbitration, it's because I don't want an arbitrator deciding things.") And a party who believes she entered a binding arbitration agreement wants to have that agreement take effect without going through the machinery of court. ("After all, what's the point of agreeing to arbitrate disputes if it all just winds up before a judge anyway?") As you will see, the test for resolving the question of *who* decides depends on the nature of the challenge being raised.

§6.2 OBJECTION #1: "THERE WAS NO CONTRACTUAL AGREEMENT TO ARBITRATE"

With the exception of certain court-annexed, nonbinding forms of arbitration (which we discuss in Chapter 9), arbitration occurs only when the parties entered a contractual agreement to send a dispute to arbitration. Perhaps the most obvious objection a party can raise to arbitration, therefore, would be that no such agreement was ever reached. A party who credibly demonstrates that it never agreed to arbitrate will not be compelled to arbitrate.

§6.2.1 Standards for Deciding if a Contract Exists

Entering into a contract is typically not a terribly complicated matter. It takes only a few things (offer, acceptance, and consideration), all of which are surely familiar from your first-year Contracts class. But just as you discovered in your Contracts class, disagreements sometimes arise about each of those seemingly straightforward concepts. Was there an offer? Was there an acceptance? Was there consideration? In the sections below, we provide a brief survey of the landscape of contract-based objections likely to arise in the context of arbitration.

§6.2.1.1 Mutual Assent

Among the most basic principles in contract law is that a contract is not enforceable unless there was **offer** and **acceptance**. An offer means showing a willingness to enter a bargain so that the other party has the power of acceptance. An acceptance means showing an agreement to the terms of the offer in the way invited or required by the offer. Of course, as you learned in your first-year Contracts class, nothing is quite so simple as that. What if a million different crazy things happen between the time the offer is extended and the time when the acceptance occurs? You likely spent weeks on this as a first-year law student. And at the end of it all, the basic proposition still stands: Unless there was an offer and acceptance, a contract is not enforceable.

Agreements to arbitrate are no different: They require offer and acceptance. Imagine that you are walking to school when a runaway delivery truck drives up onto the sidewalk, runs into you, and causes you some minor injuries. You file a tort claim against the driver of the truck in a local court. Could the driver convince that court to stay the litigation and order you to arbitrate your claim despite your preference to have your claim heard in court? No. You never agreed to arbitrate this claim against the truck driver, he never offered to arbitrate the claim, and you certainly never assented to the terms of an arbitration agreement. Absent that, no contract exists, and there is no basis for the court to send your claim to arbitration.

Some kinds of contracts must be in writing in order to be enforceable. (Recall the Statute of Frauds from your first-year Contracts course.) The Federal Arbitration Act includes a provision that limits its applicability to *written* arbitration agreements. "Acceptance," however, is governed by state contract law. In *Caley v. Gulfstream Aerospace Corp.*, 428 F.3d 1359, 1368 (11th Cir. 2005), for example, the court held that "[W]hile the FAA requires that the arbitration agreement be in writing, it does not require that it be signed by the parties." Arbitration clauses in unilateral contracts (ones in which acceptance is demonstrated by an action, not by a signature) meet the FAA's requirement that the arbitration agreement be "written."

Of course, an agreement to arbitrate does not necessarily have to precede the incidents giving rise to the claim in question. The truck driver, having run you over, could jump out of his truck, help you to your feet, apologize profusely, and then ask you if you would be willing to sign an agreement to arbitrate any and all claims arising out of the incident. If you assent to the arbitration agreement, but then file a claim in court, the court might very well send you off to arbitration. (We look at questions like consideration and duress in subsequent sections of this chapter.) As a basic matter, if you did not form a contract in which you agreed to arbitrate your claim, you cannot be compelled to arbitrate the claim. And you cannot form a contract without offer and acceptance.

§6.2.1.2 Consideration

For a contract to be binding, courts almost always also require adequate consideration. Examining consideration means focusing on parties' bargained-for exchanges. These bargained-for exchanges are only enforceable if the promisor (the person making the promise) gets a benefit of some sort or the promisee (the person to whom the promise is made) incurs a detriment of some sort. For example, your first-year casebook probably talked about *Hamer v. Sidway*, 27 N.E. 256 (N.Y. 1891), the case involving an uncle who promised his nephew a large sum of money on condition that the nephew forbear drinking, gambling, and swearing. The nephew apparently spent the requisite number of years not doing those things. When the time came for the nephew to collect, the uncle refused to pay. The nephew sought to enforce the promise as a contract, and the case turned on whether there was consideration. The court eventually said yes. There was a bargained-for exchange. It is not clear that the uncle incurred any particular benefit from the exchange, but the nephew incurred a detriment (for example, not swearing, something he would have otherwise had a right to do). The contract, therefore, was deemed to have been supported by adequate consideration.

In the arbitration context, a common and straightforward illustration of adequate consideration would be two companies planning the terms of a joint venture, both envisioning the possibility of a dispute arising during the course of the joint venture. They agree to include an arbitration clause in their contract, under which both agree to submit "any and all disputes" to a particular form of binding arbitration. In that case, each receives the benefit of having secured arbitration, and each incurs the detriment of having forgone the possibility of adjudicating subsequent contract claims in court. Another common scenario is when you purchase something, a laptop, for example, and the warranty of the laptop includes an arbitration provision. You received a benefit—a brand new computer—as part of an exchange that included handing over your money and agreeing to their arbitration clause.

Consideration becomes more complicated in the arbitration context when there was some prior relationship between parties, and then contractual terms were modified to include an arbitration agreement. For example, it is now common for employees to agree to a thick set of terms in their employee handbooks. The terms included in the handbook are (for the most part) going to be binding on the employee, assuming they are not outrageous. And there is no consideration problem because these were the terms the employee signed on to when the employee accepted the employment. Now, imagine that an employer sent out an e-mail notice to all employees saying, "Good morning, employees. The company intends to amend the Employee Handbook to include an arbitration clause. If you continue to work for us after next week, we will deem that acceptance of our new policy." Would the arbitration clause be binding? You might first analyze whether there was an offer (clearly yes) and acceptance (yes, courts consider it constructive acceptance if you keep working after notice like this). Consideration is also probably fine because in exchange for the detriment of the arbitration clause (to the extent you view that as a detriment), you receive the benefit of a paying job. That is plenty.

If the above scenario troubles you, that's probably good. You are probably imagining all kinds of potential abuses. What if the employer sneaks some terrible provisions into that new arbitration clause? What if the handbook is now crazily lopsided in its treatment of employees? What if the employees really don't have time to read or review the new clause? What if the employer keeps changing the terms around? Isn't there some limit? Yes. And we discuss those near the end of this section, when we talk about unconscionability.

§6.2.2 Who Decides Whether a Contract Exists?

If one party to a dispute seeks to compel arbitration and the other believes that it never agreed to arbitration, the "I never agreed to arbitrate anything" defense will be heard by a court. That probably sounds entirely intuitive. After all, to challenge the simple existence of a contract is to say, for example, "They never made a clear offer, so there was nothing to accept." Or "I don't care what they were offering, I never signed an agreement or did anything to signal acceptance." Or *Somebody* may have agreed to it, but it wasn't me." These are contract-related contentions with which the court is accustomed to dealing in contexts far beyond arbitration. And unless the court is satisfied that the parties entered into a contract containing an arbitration clause, it will not send the parties to have any disputes resolved by an arbitrator.

As a preview, however, courts do not resolve *all* contract-based defenses to arbitration. As you will see in the section below, if a court is satisfied that an agreement was entered and the agreement contains an arbitration clause, there is a decent likelihood that arguments about the enforceability of the agreement will be determined by an arbitrator.

§6.3 OBJECTION #2: "THERE WAS A CONTRACTUAL AGREEMENT TO ARBITRATE, BUT THE CONTRACT IS UNENFORCEABLE"

The section above focused on those circumstances in which the person seeking to avoid arbitration is arguing that no agreement to arbitrate ever existed. But that's not the only way a party can avoid arbitration. Much more commonly, the parties will have entered into an agreement of some sort, but the party seeking to avoid arbitration will argue that the portion of the contract containing an agreement to arbitrate should not be enforced.

§6.3.1 Avenues for Challenging a Contract's Enforceability

Your Contracts class surely provided you with a number of different ideas about circumstances in which a court might not treat an agreement as enforceable. Some of the most significant avenues you likely studied (indefiniteness, capacity to contract, illegality, and statute of frauds) do not commonly arise in the context of arbitration. Other contract defenses, however (fraud, public policy, duress, and unconscionability), are more typical avenues for opposing the enforcement of arbitration. Below we survey some of the most significant bases for challenging the enforceability of an agreement to arbitrate.

§6.3.1.1 Fraud

A contract is not enforceable if it was fraudulently induced. The elements of fraud commonly relevant to arbitration are not difficult to recite: Under contract law, a party can avoid a contract on the basis of fraud if the other side misrepresented a fact and either (1) the other side knew it was misrepresenting a material fact, or (2) the listener was reasonable and justified in relying on the misrepresented fact. As with almost every area of the law, each little component of that statement is subject to pages and pages of definition, clarification, application, exception, and refinement. But the basic idea stands. Contracts — including arbitration agreements — will not be enforced if they were the product of fraud.

Most of the time, when fraud is committed in the formation of a contract, the alleged material misrepresentation has to do with some aspect of the contract other than the arbitration clause that happens to be included in the overall contract. For example, the other side lies to you about the nature of the product being sold. ("This can opener also serves as a cellular phone in

Europe.") They misrepresent their assets. ("We own the patent on this device.") They fail to correct inaccurate assertions they made earlier about their prior performance. ("The report we gave you last week covered everything from the past three years.") And so on.

Of course, it is possible (but less common) that a lie will relate specifically to the arbitration clause itself. For example, a representative of a circus company could say, "I know that our proposal specifies that the arbitrations will take place under the rules of the ClownCo Arbitration Association. And I know their website is down right now. But don't worry, their procedures precisely mirror those of the American Arbitration Association," when, in fact, the procedures are nothing like those of the American Arbitration Association. If you can demonstrate that the claims a party is making are material and knowingly false, and that you reasonably relied on them to your detriment, the arbitration clause will not be enforced against you.

So why are we even bothering to distinguish between fraud about one part of the contract and fraud about some other part of the contract? The legal analysis of what constitutes fraud is the same with either. The difference is that the *subject* of the alleged fraud turns out to have an impact on the question of *who decides* whether it constitutes fraud. We cover this in detail in Chapter 7. For now, it is enough to know that a contractual agreement to arbitrate is unenforceable if it is the product of fraud, just like any other contract.

§6.3.1.2 "Public Policy" Objections

As a general matter, courts will not enforce contracts that are against public policy. For example, even if you and a drug dealer on the street corner execute an otherwise flawless heroin contract, the court will not entertain a civil lawsuit if one of you reneges on the agreement. (As a matter of criminal law, on the other hand, you might be able to attract some attention from the judicial system. . . .) Of course, the line between what is and is not consistent with public policy is not necessarily easily defined.

You might be thinking, "Wait, I thought there was a well-established policy *favoring* arbitration. What could possibly be the problem?" It is certainly true that courts have, in recent years, developed an expansive jurisprudence stemming from the basic proposition that courts should favor enforcing agreements to arbitrate. But this does not mean that courts will enforce any agreement to arbitrate under any circumstances. The agreement must still withstand a challenge that its enforcement would violate public policy.

For many years, courts applied the "public policy" doctrine to strike down arbitration agreements that purported to cover claims involving statutorily created rights. As you know, many legal claims derive from common law, rather than statutory, rights. But within the past several decades, statutorily created rights have become increasingly common, particularly at the federal level. For example, most antidiscrimination lawsuits are based not in the common law, but rather in a set of statutes. We refer to these, and other rights, as statutorily created rights. Agreements to arbitrate were not enforced in the context of many of these statutory rights for a long time. For example, in *Wilko v. Swan*, 346 U.S. 427 (1953), the U.S. Supreme Court pointed out that arbitrators are not required to have legal training, that arbitrators operate "without judicial instruction on the law," and that arbitrators are under no requirement to articulate their reasoning or to preserve a record of their proceedings. The combination of these factors, the Court concluded, made arbitration agreements relating to claims under the Securities Act unenforceable, despite the public policy generally favoring arbitration. The logic at the time was that arbitration would simply frustrate the public policy underlying statutes like the Securities Act, particularly when those acts create causes of action that aim to provide relief for consumers or others with relatively less sophistication or power.

During the 1980s, however, the Supreme Court took a different approach and eventually overruled *Wilko*, making statutory rights broadly amenable to arbitration. Under its modern decisions, the Supreme Court has said that an agreement to arbitrate statutory claims will only be unenforceable if arbitration is inherently inconsistent with the statute's underlying purpose. And the Court rejected what it called "generalized attacks on arbitration" as inherently unfair or biased. Instead, the Court has said that arbitration is not necessarily inconsistent with the vindication of statutory rights, even in circumstances in which arbitration procedures differ from court procedures.

The door is still open to the possibility that *some* arbitration agreement, in some form, will be so inconsistent with the statutory purposes underlying a particular claimant's cause of action that it will be stricken on the basis of public policy. An arbitration agreement that prohibited all access to discovery materials, restricted the scope of awards, and fundamentally stripped away a claimant's ability to prevail in a statutory claim would probably not be enforced. But it is an uphill battle for the party seeking to avoid arbitration on the basis that the contract providing for arbitration is contrary to public policy.

Of course, Congress is always able to prohibit arbitration of a statutory claim by expressly prohibiting it in the terms of the statute creating the cause of action. Many statutes creating causes of action were passed when *Wilko* was still good law (and therefore, there was no clear reason for Congress to have specified that arbitration would be an inappropriate forum for vindicating the statutory rights in question). In the years since *Wilko* was overturned, however, Congress has not amended the statutes. As a result, without an express congressional prohibition against arbitrating a statutorily based claim, the presumption is that arbitration is merely a different, but still entirely valid, forum for vindicating these rights. Proposals often surface in Congress to prohibit the arbitration of certain statutory rights, but to date, very few of these proposals have passed. One exception is the 2007 Defense Authorization Act, which now protects servicemembers from forced arbitration with their creditors.

§6.3.1.3 Duress

The agreement that results from an exchange beginning with the phrase, "your money or your life" and ending with the target of the phrase opting to relinquish his money is not an enforceable contract. The reason lies in the concept of duress. At one point in time, the defense of duress was limited to only those circumstances involving physical danger. In modern times, however, courts have recognized the concept of economic duress. Briefly, when one party wrongfully coerces the other into a circumstance in which there is no reasonable alternative but to accept, economic duress exists and the contract will not be enforceable. Traditionally, a party alleging economic duress must show (1) that he or she has been the victim of a wrongful or unlawful act or threat and (2) that the act or threat deprived the victim of free or unfettered will. In addition to economic duress, some courts have also recognized emotional duress (for example, demanding a prenuptial agreement on the eve of the wedding). But as with most contract law, this formulation varies from state to state. Still, high-pressured situations in which one party enjoys disproportionately greater influence may suggest the presence of duress.

§6.3.1.4 Unconscionability

A court will refuse to enforce a contract if it is convinced that the contract is unconscionable. Judge Skelly Wright, in the case of *Williams v. Walker-Thomas Furniture*, 350 F.2d 445 (D.C. Cir. 1965), articulated the concept of unconscionability this way: "Unconscionability has generally been recognized to include an absence of meaningful choice on the part of one of the parties together with contract terms which are unreasonably favorable to the other party."

Essentially, unconscionability includes two components: procedural unconscionability and substantive unconscionability. In most jurisdictions, a contract will be deemed unconscionable only if both of these are present, at least to some degree, but the analysis presents something of a sliding scale. (In a contract involving grotesque substantive unconscionability, for example, the party challenging the contract needs to show comparatively less procedural unconscionability.) But the question remains what each of these terms means.

6. Is This Agreement to Arbitrate Enforceable?

Procedural unconscionability asks about the process by which the agreement was reached. How lopsided was the bargaining? To what extent did each party have a meaningful choice? Any context involving contracts of adhesion, for example, are marked by an absence of meaningful choice. Similarly, if a party has vastly different bargaining power and wields that power in a way that creates surprise or oppression, it may be deemed procedurally unconscionable. In one of the early law review articles on this topic, issues of procedural unconscionability were described as "bargaining naughtiness."[1]

Substantive unconscionability asks about the terms of the contract in question. How lopsided are the terms of the deal? As you might imagine, there is no formulaic, bright-line test for determining whether a deal is substantively unconscionable. No single term is likely to be dispositive on its own. (If you really tried, you could probably draft a single provision in a contract that would be so offensive that it would independently surpass the boundaries of unconscionability. But most terms within an agreement are not so scandalously bad when they are viewed alone.) Rather, a court will examine the totality of the contract to determine whether it exceeds acceptable boundaries.

The question of unconscionability is a significant one in the realm of arbitration. Arbitration clauses now appear in a vast array of adhesion contracts — ranging from employment agreements to consumer sales to health care. You can be certain that attorneys for companies drafting arbitration clauses have been spending considerable time testing the limits. Common targets include placing limits on arbitrators' powers to award certain kinds of remedies. For example, many arbitration clauses specifically prohibit arbitrators from ordering injunctive relief or awarding punitive damages. Still others target the joinder doctrines, placing limits on the ability of parties to join together — for example, in a class action. Courts have been divided on whether a bar to class actions is unconscionable.

The party drafting an arbitration clause has an incentive to make it very favorably skewed toward its interests, *just barely* on the acceptable side of the line between enforceable and unconscionable. Whether a court will actually deem an arbitration agreement unconscionable depends not only on the particulars of the agreement and its formation, but also on the contract laws of the jurisdiction in which the arbitration agreement is under dispute.

A great example of an unconscionable arbitration agreement (at least "great" in the sense of providing a clear illustration) arose in the case of *Hooters of America, Inc. v. Phillips*, 173 F.3d 933 (4th Cir. 1999). In that case, a bartender who worked at a Hooters restaurant brought suit against her employer, alleging sexual harassment in violation of Title VII. Hooters

---

1. Arthur A. Leff, *Unconscionability and the Code — The Emperor's New Clause*, 115 U. Pa. L. Rev. 485, 487 (1967).

filed a motion to compel arbitration, citing the arbitration clause within an ADR policy the company had presented to employees two years earlier. The arbitration clause was a caricature of a biased procedure. It imposed pleadings and discovery burdens only on the employee. At the same time, Hooters reserved special privileges only for itself, such as dispositive motions, revocation, and fixing the composition of the pool of potential arbitrators. In the end, the court concluded that the Hooters rules were "so one-sided that their only possible purpose is to undermine the neutrality of the proceeding." It called the overall policy "a sham system unworthy even of the name of arbitration" and refused to enforce the arbitration clause. There are several examples of courts overturning arbitration agreements that restrict the identities of arbitrators. For example, in *Broemmer v. Abortion Services of Phoenix*, 840 P.2d 1013 (Ariz. 1992), the court refused to enforce an arbitration agreement that limited the arbitral panel to licensed obstetricians and gynecologists. Similarly, in *Graham v. Scissor-Tail, Inc.*, 623 P.2d 165 (Cal. 1981), a court refused to enforce a requirement that an arbitrator be a member of a particular musicians' union, when one of the disputants was a member of the same union.

Of course, most arbitration clauses do not overreach so dramatically. And as a result, the analysis involved in deciding whether a given set of arbitration terms is unconscionable demands far more balancing, judgment, and case-by-case analysis. What if the Hooters clause had merely contained one or two of these lopsided provisions, rather than an entire set of them? Or what if Hooters had provided more opportunity for its employees to read, consider, and even opt out of the arbitration agreement? A party seeking to avoid arbitration on the basis of unconscionability must demonstrate that the arbitration provisions were imposed in an unfair, adhesive manner (procedural unconscionability) and that they contain unreasonably burdensome terms (substantive unconscionability).

The Supreme Court considered an assertion that an arbitration clause was unconscionable in the case of *Green Tree Fin. Corp. Ala. v. Randolph*, 531 U.S. 79 (2000). In that case, Larketta Randolph bought a mobile home and financed the purchase through Green Tree Financial Corp. The loan document Randolph signed included a clause requiring that "all disputes, claims, or controversies" related to the loan be resolved through arbitration. The clause said nothing about how the costs and fees associated with arbitration would be allocated. Randolph later sued Green Tree, alleging violations of various federal laws aimed at protecting borrowers. Green Tree filed a motion to compel arbitration. (You can review Chapter 5 for more on these mechanics.) Randolph argued that the arbitration clause was unconscionable because the expenses associated with arbitration were so high that she might be effectively incapable of pursuing her claims against Green Tree. On appeal, the Court acknowledged the possibility that *some* arbitration clauses might create such a significant burden on prospective plaintiffs as to be unconscionable. In this case, however, a divided Court found that Randolph had not adequately demonstrated a sufficient risk that she would be encumbered with an actually unmanageable expense. It wrote, "where, as here, a party seeks to invalidate an arbitration agreement on the ground that arbitration would be prohibitively expensive, that party bears the burden of showing the likelihood of incurring such costs. Randolph did not meet that burden."

As a side note, we should mention that the analysis for unconscionability (and the other contract-based challenges we discuss) are driven primarily by state law. In Chapter 8, we will turn to the question of the FAA's impact on all of this. The short preview is that state law still governs the unconscionability analysis — provided the state unconscionability doctrines do not single out arbitration. If a class waiver is unenforceable as a matter of general state contract law, for example, a class waiver in the context of arbitration will also be unenforceable. (See Chapter 8 for more.)

§6.3.2 Who Decides Whether the Contract is Enforceable?

You may recall from the text above that courts (rather than arbitrators) are the ones who determine whether a contract exists at all. You might, therefore, reasonably imagine that a similarly simple answer exists to the question of *who* decides challenges to a contract's enforceability. But that is not the case. Instead, the answer to "who decides" challenges to enforceability depends on the *nature* of the challenge.

§6.3.2.1 Challenges to the Arbitration Clause Specifically

Two parties with an existing dispute could (and sometimes do) enter a stand-alone agreement that specifically commits them to arbitrate the dispute. For example, imagine that your classmate's laptop spontaneously combusts, causing damage to some of your property. You and your classmate surely do not have an existing contract that would cover such a contingency. So one option for you would be to file a lawsuit against your classmate (and/or possibly many other parties, thanks to liberal joinder doctrines). Alternatively, your classmate could approach you and suggest that the two of you enter an agreement to have your claim resolved by an arbitrator instead. If the two of you enter such an agreement to arbitrate, it will be just as binding as any other agreement. Now, what if you have second thoughts and want to challenge the enforceability of that agreement you entered with your classmate (for example, by saying that the agreement to arbitrate was unsupported by consideration, that it was procured by fraud, or that it was unconscionable). Who would hear your objections? The answer: *a court*. The idea is that the challenge is directed specifically at the agreement to arbitrate, and if the agreement to arbitrate was itself so flawed as to be unenforceable, the allegation should not be referred to an arbitrator to decide. A challenge to the enforceability of the contract that only contains an arbitration agreement is the domain of a court.

In most contexts, however, parties who enter an agreement to arbitrate do so in the context of a larger contract. For example, when you rent a car, you and the rental agency undertake many different commitments, only one of which relates to arbitration. If you take a job with an employment contract, it will typically spell out your duties, your wages and benefits, and any number of other things (and it might also contain an arbitration provision). These larger contracts, in which the arbitration provisions sit, are commonly referred to as "container agreements." They contain an agreement to arbitrate, in addition to other commitments.

In the context of arbitration agreements appearing inside container agreements, the same basic principle applies: A challenge focused entirely on the validity of an arbitration clause is the province of the courts. For example, if a party says that it was coerced into accepting the arbitration component of the contract, the matter will appear before a court. In short, if the challenge is to the arbitration clause itself, rather than to the container agreement, the merits of the objection will be determined by a court, rather than by an arbitrator.

§6.3.2.2 Challenges to the Container Agreement

As a practical matter, though, most of the time when a party has one or more of the contract-based arguments against the enforceability of a contract, its objections apply to the entire contract, not just to the arbitration clause. A party is likely to claim that the *entire container agreement* was fraudulently induced, rather than merely the arbitration provision falling within the container agreement. Or a party will claim that the entire agreement is unenforceable because it is unconscionable. Attacks on enforceability typically target the container agreement, not just the arbitration clause.

Who decides those challenges? The accurate, but not usually helpful, answer is "whoever the parties agreed to have hear these challenges." The parties could have, for example, specifically contemplated the prospect of such challenges. If they agreed to have all such challenges heard by a court, those challenges would fall outside of the arbitration agreement and would be heard by a court. The far more common condition, however, is one in which the parties' contract is silent on the question of who decides challenges to the container agreement, or one in which the parties generically say that "any and all disputes related to the contract" will go to arbitration. What happens then?

At the heart of answering the "who decides" question related to contract-based challenges is a concept called "separability." The principle articulation of the concept of separability comes from the Supreme Court's opinion in *Prima Paint Corp. v. Flood & Conklin Mfg.*, 388 U.S. 395 (1967). The *Prima Paint* case is significant enough that it warrants a more detailed explanation.

The case began with a contract between Prima Paint and F&C. According to their contract, F&C would provide certain services to Prima Paint in exchange for certain payments. The contract contained an agreement to arbitrate "any controversy or claim arising out of the agreement." Not long after the parties entered the contract, a dispute arose. F&C accused Prima Paint of failing to live up to certain payment obligations and sought to commence an action in arbitration. Prima Paint responded by commencing an action in federal court, alleging that because F&C had fraudulently induced Prima Paint into signing the contract in the first place, Prima Paint should not be bound by the agreement to arbitrate. (Prima Paint's specific allegation was that F&C knowingly misrepresented its financial solvency at the time of the agreement.) The merits of the case, of course, would ultimately hinge on this relatively basic contract dispute. The preliminary question, however, was *who* (the court or an arbitrator) would be assessing the merits of the challenge to the contract.

The Supreme Court answered this preliminary question by sending the dispute to an arbitrator to assess both the breach alleged by F&C and the fraud alleged by Prima Paint. The Supreme Court explained:

> [E]xcept where the parties otherwise intend, arbitration clauses . . . are "separable" from the contracts in which they are embedded, and that where no claim is made that fraud was directed to the arbitration clause itself, a broad arbitration clause will be held to encompass arbitration of the claim that the contract itself was induced by fraud.

Section 4 of the FAA requires a court to compel arbitration once it is satisfied that "the making of the arbitration agreement" is not in issue. In the case of *Prima Paint*, the Court concluded that the making of the arbitration agreement was not in issue, even if the enforceability of the entire contract *was* in issue.

As a practical matter, most of the contractual defenses we listed above are usually asserted as challenges to the container agreement, rather than to the arbitration clause in particular. Alleged fraud is likely to be fraud about the entire contractual relationship. Alleged duress applies to the entire agreement, not just the clause about arbitration. And so forth. Under the logic of *Prima Paint*, therefore, virtually all of these challenges will be heard by an arbitrator rather than by a court.

§6.4 A PREVIEW OF THE PREEMPTION DOCTRINE

As we said at the start of this chapter, arbitration is a creature of contract. And you surely remember from your first year of law school that contract law is a state law issue. There is no Federal Contracts Act. There is, however, a Federal Arbitration Act. And that fact complicates matters considerably. According to the preemption doctrine, if a valid federal law is in conflict with a state law, the federal law will trump. To what extent do the terms of the FAA conflict with (and therefore preempt) state contract laws? What can (or can't) a state do if it wants to regulate arbitration agreements? In Chapter 7, we will examine the question of the interaction between state law and federal law in resolving questions about enforcing arbitration agreements.

Examples

1. **The Burger Pit's Falling Arches.** The Burger Pit is a local drive-thru fast food restaurant. You pull up in your car and place an order at the window of the restaurant. While you are waiting for your Belly Buster Bacon Burger, the enormous silver-colored arches that normally sit on the roof of the Burger Pit come crashing down onto your car. You receive your burger and a ride to the hospital. After you recover from your injuries, you file a lawsuit against Burger Pit in the local county court. Burger Pit appears in court and files a motion to stay the litigation and compel arbitration. What would a court do with the motion?

2. **The Burger Pit's Drive-Thru Waiver.** The Burger Pit is a local drive-thru fast food restaurant. You pull up in your car to place an order at the window of the restaurant. While you are waiting for a Burger Pit employee to take your order, you notice a small sign that says, "By placing an order with us you are agreeing to arbitrate any and all disputes arising out of or relating to the purchase. For details of the arbitration agreement, visit our website." You order, pay for, and receive a Belly Buster Bacon Burger. Shortly after you eat it, you become terribly ill with food poisoning. After you recover, you file suit against Burger Pit in the local county court. Burger Pit appears in court and files a motion to stay the litigation and compel arbitration, which you oppose. What arguments is each side likely to make, and how is the court likely to rule on the motion?

3. **The Burger Pit Doesn't Deliver.** During your planning for the company picnic, you enter a catering contract with Burger Pit. Burger Pit's catering

contract contains a clause that says, "By signing this agreement, you are agreeing to arbitrate any and all disputes arising out of or relating to this catering agreement." You and Burger Pit negotiate over the price and the specifications for the catering job, and eventually you both sign the agreement. You send Burger Pit payment in advance, as is required under the contract, and you wait. The day of the company picnic arrives, but Burger Pit never does. Despite your frantic calls to the Burger Pit hotline, no food is ever delivered. You file a lawsuit in the local county court alleging breach of contract. Burger Pit files a motion to stay the litigation, citing the arbitration clause in the catering contract. What would the court do with Burger Pit's motion?

4. **Le Burger's Arbitration Menu.** Le Burger is an upscale hamburger restaurant, complete with crisp table linens and snooty servers. At the bottom of each page of the Le Burger menu is a notice that reads, "By placing an order with us, you are agreeing to arbitrate any and all disputes arising out of or relating to your purchase. For a complete copy of the arbitration agreement, see the back side of our menu." On the back of the Le Burger menu appear the details of an arbitration agreement. After waiting for weeks to secure a reservation at Le Burger, you finally get a table late one evening. You order a range of food from the menu, and the snooty server has you initial a short form indicating that you read, understood, and accepted the Le Burger arbitration policy. Shortly after your meal is over, you become terribly sick with food poisoning. You bring suit against Le Burger in the local county court, and Le Burger seeks to stay the litigation, citing the arbitration policy on its menu. What is a court likely to do with Le Burger's motion?

5. **Le Burger's Pricy Arbitration Menu.** Le Burger has the same menu as the one described in Example 4 above, except that the arbitration agreement included on the back of its menu specifies a set of arbitration procedures under which a claimant must pay an unrecoverable filing fee of $2,000 in order to commence an action. Does this clause change the enforceability of the arbitration agreement?

6. **Le Burger: Home of Chauvinist Pigs.** You and a group of your female friends go to Le Burger after work one day. The Le Burger maitre d' seats you, and you notice that the menu includes an arbitration clause that purports to cover "any and all claims arising out of or related to your visit to Le Burger." You and the waiter joke about the clause, and you agree to its terms in writing when you place your order. The waiter brings you and your friends your entrees. When it comes time for dessert, your waiter tells you and your party, "Women don't need dessert. That's particularly true for your group. You are done with

your meal." You are so offended that you storm out. You and your friends want to sue Le Burger for unlawful discrimination. Will you be able to file the claim in court, or will you be forced to bring it in arbitration?

7. **Le Burger: Home of Bigots.** You have eaten at Le Burger a number of times in the past. The positive reputation of its food far outweighs any negative impression it creates with its conspicuous arbitration policy. You and a group of friends arrive at Le Burger one evening, eager for a gourmet feast. The head waiter shouts racial epithets at you and your friends when you walk into the main dining area and refuses to seat you. You and your friends file a lawsuit alleging a violation of your civil rights, and Le Burger files a motion with the court seeking to stay the litigation, citing the restaurant's arbitration policy. How would the court rule on Le Burger's motion?

8. **Le Burger: Home of Stone Age Policies.** Tonya Tartare works as a Charbroiling Engineer in the Le Burger kitchen. When she accepted the job with Le Burger, she signed an employment contract, one part of which included an arbitration clause covering "any and all claims related to this employment or the termination thereof." After six months of working at Le Burger, Tartare discovers that all of her male colleagues make considerably more money than she does. Tartare confronts her manager, who tells her that it is "Le Burger policy to offer women one-third less than guys, because the silly dames always seem to accept lower pay without question." Tartare files a lawsuit against Le Burger, and Le Burger files a motion to stay the litigation, citing the arbitration clause in Tartare's employment contract. How would the court rule on Le Burger's motion?

9. **Le Burger: Home of No Class.** Assume the same facts as Example 8 except that the arbitration clause also specifically prohibits representative or class action suits. Tartare wants to bring an action on behalf of all female Le Burger employees. Will she be able to do so?

10. **Le Burger: Home of the Home Court Advantage.** Reuben Rubin, a busboy, was one of the longest-serving employees at Le Burger, having been there for almost a decade. One day at the beginning of his shift, his supervisor handed him a document entitled, "New Arbitration Policy." The document spelled out the terms of a new arbitration provision applicable to all Le Burger employees. According to the policy, "any and all disputes related to or arising out of" Rubin's employment were subject to arbitration. The agreement also specified that all arbitrations would take place in the forum selected by Le Burger and that the arbitrator of any such disputes would be required to have "at least 15 years' experience in restaurant ownership

or management." Rubin's supervisor told him that he had until the end of his shift to accept or decline, and indicated that he could continue his employment only if he accepted. Rubin hastily accepted, signed the policy, and began his shift. About a month later, Rubin was fired, and he brought a federal lawsuit against Le Burger alleging breach of contract and violation of state and federal antidiscrimination laws. Le Burger files a motion to stay the litigation, and Rubin contests the enforceability of the arbitration agreement. What is the likely outcome?

11. **Burger Pit: Home of Liars.** You enter into a franchise agreement with Burger Pit to operate a fast food restaurant in your hometown. During negotiations over the franchise agreement, you specifically ask the Burger Pit representative about the availability of their mouth-watering "secret sauce." The Burger Pit representative tells you, "As part of your agreement, you will have access to an unlimited amount of our secret sauce. After all, that sauce is the heart and soul of Burger Pit's business." Burger Pit requires six months' payment up front. Immediately after signing the agreement, you learn that the Food and Drug Administration had just listed Burger Pit's "secret sauce" as a banned, toxic substance. You are convinced that Burger Pit knew about the FDA ban at the time of your negotiations. You file a lawsuit alleging fraud and breach of contract against Burger Pit. Burger Pit appears in court and files a motion to stay the litigation, citing an arbitration clause in the franchise agreement that says that "any and all disputes arising out of or related to the formation, performance, breach, or nonperformance of this contract" shall be arbitrated. What would a court do with Burger Pit's motion?

12. **Le Burger: Home of Creative Signatures.** One day during the busiest season of the year, the manager of Le Burger was in desperate need of additional help in the kitchen. She hastily agreed to hire the first applicant who came to the restaurant, a man named Stephen Stylo, and put him to work immediately that evening. After only a few weeks, Stylo was fired. Shortly after that, Stylo files a lawsuit in federal court against Le Burger alleging that his termination was unlawful and discriminatory. Le Burger appears in court and moves to stay the litigation. To its motion, Le Burger attaches a copy of its employment contract, with a broad arbitration clause highlighted and with a signature appearing just above Stylo's name. Stylo argues that he has never seen this contract before, swears that he never signed any employment contract with Le Burger, and says that the signature appearing on the contract looks nothing like his own. What will the court do with Le Burger's motion to stay the litigation?

Explanations

1. **The Burger Pit's Falling Arches.** Burger Pit's motion will be denied, and your case will stay in court. Nothing in the facts suggests that you and Burger Pit ever entered a contractual relationship of any sort, beyond the purchase of your burger. No agreement to arbitrate exists. (You could have agreed to arbitrate this dispute with them after the incident but nothing in these facts suggests that you did.) Burger Pit may now want to arbitrate, but it never offered you arbitration, and you certainly never accepted it. Without an agreement to arbitrate, there is no basis for the court to compel arbitration.

2. **The Burger Pit's Drive-Thru Waiver.** The court would be unlikely to enforce the arbitration agreement in this case, though this one is less clear than the previous example.

   The arguments against arbitration in this case are strong. First, the sign was small, hard to notice, and you were probably trapped in line already by the time you saw it. Second, you were very likely not made aware of the actual terms of the arbitration agreement. If you didn't know the actual terms of the arbitration agreement (assuming you didn't go to the website and read the rules while waiting in line), there was no "meeting of the minds" about this bargain. If you didn't know the terms of the offer, you didn't accept them. And finally, there is some question about whether the notice of arbitration would constitute a "written agreement" under the FAA's terms. It is true that the FAA does not require a signature to deem an arbitration agreement to have been "written." For example, in *Caley v. Gulfstream Aero. Corp.*, 428 F.3d 1359 (11th Cir. 2005), employees were given copies of the new employee handbook containing an arbitration clause, and the employees' continued employment was deemed constructive acceptance of a written arbitration clause. Here, however, the link between your ordering and your accepting an arbitration clause that was written *somewhere* is more tenuous.

   Burger Pit's best argument is that it provided clear notice of the arbitration agreement's inclusion in any transaction. Burger Pit would point out that you saw the sign and ordered food nonetheless, implying that you accepted the terms. Surely, no matter how hungry you were, this is not a circumstance that constitutes duress.

3. **The Burger Pit Doesn't Deliver.** The court would almost certainly stay the litigation. These facts describe a perfectly enforceable contract. Nothing in the description suggests a defect in the offer, the acceptance, or the consideration. There was enough of a balance in the bargaining power (as evidenced by the fact that you got Burger Pit to change some of the terms in the contract) to dispel any scent of procedural

unconscionability. Nothing in the facts suggests that the arbitration clause was remarkable or problematic in any way. You agreed to arbitrate disputes about this catering contract, and this is a dispute about the catering contract. You are going to have to bring your claim in arbitration.

4. **Le Burger's Arbitration Menu.** The court is likely to grant Le Burger's motion to stay the litigation. A court will not proceed with litigation if it is satisfied that an agreement to arbitrate was made. In this case, no contractual defects appear in the facts. You had notice of the arbitration clause, and nothing suggests that the clause itself was somehow flawed. Your claim against Le Burger will likely be heard by an arbitrator, pursuant to the arbitration procedures printed on the back of the Le Burger menu.

5. **Le Burger's Pricy Arbitration Menu.** Probably yes. You have a much better chance of avoiding arbitration in this circumstance than in the one described immediately above. You could argue, for example, that the fee structure renders the arbitration agreement unconscionable. Normally, to demonstrate unconscionability, you would need to show both procedural and substantive unconscionability. In this case, nothing appears to be fatally wrong with the process by which this contract was formed. But there is a reasonable chance that the burden created by the arbitrator fees (particularly compared to the product prices) will be significant enough that a court would refuse to enforce the arbitration agreement.

In the case of *Brower v. Gateway 2000, Inc.*, 676 N.Y.S.2d 569 (N.Y. App. Div. 1998), a computer manufacturer included a form contract in the boxes in which it shipped computers to consumers. According to the arbitration clause appearing on that form, consumers had to pay at least $4,000 to the arbitration provider up front, and at least half of that fee was nonrecoverable. The New York appeals court considered an unconscionability argument (in light of the fact that these sums exceeded the cost of virtually all of the products the manufacturer sold) and sent the case back for the parties to substitute a less expensive alternative.

To prevail in this line of argument, however, the burden will be on you to demonstrate that the fees create an *actual*, prohibitive burden, rather than merely the risk of a burden. This was the conclusion of the Supreme Court in *Green Tree Fin. Corp.-Ala. v. Randolph*, 531 U.S. 79 (2000). In that case, the arbitration clause was silent about the allocation of arbitration fees, and the Court refused to strike the arbitration clause down on the basis of a mere "risk." Here, therefore, you would have to demonstrate that the fee in fact creates the kind of burden that would effectively bar you from an opportunity to bring a claim. The arbitration fee of $2,000, which when compared to your dinner bill makes it highly unlikely that you would ever pursue a claim, may just be sufficient to demonstrate that burden.

6. **Le Burger: Home of Chauvinist Pigs.** Your discrimination claim is probably destined to be heard before an arbitrator. As with each of the examples immediately above, nothing appears to be wrong with the process by which the arbitration agreement was formed. Nothing in these facts suggests that there is anything wrong with the substantive provisions of the arbitration agreement itself. And nothing in the language articulating the scope of the arbitration agreement could be read to exclude any categories of disputes.

This is not to say that *every* possible arbitration agreement will be consistent with statutory rights. But in order to prevail, you will need to demonstrate that some aspect of the particular arbitration agreement in question frustrates the public policy underlying the statute. And nothing in the facts suggests that Le Burger's arbitration provision is inconsistent with antidiscrimination laws. As a result, your claim is likely headed to arbitration.

7. **Le Burger: Home of Bigots.** A court would deny Le Burger's motion to stay the litigation. The nature of your claim is irrelevant. The contents of their arbitration policy are irrelevant. The simple fact is that you and your friends never entered any contractual relationship with Le Burger that evening. You intended to enter a contract with them, but the head waiter's behavior prevented it. There is no basis for sending you and your friends to arbitration.

8. **Le Burger: Home of Stone Age Policies.** Given these facts, the court would grant the motion to stay the litigation. Even if the discrimination in this case is terrible and clearly unlawful, the question of who will decide the merits of the claim is governed by the parties' agreement. And in this case, nothing suggests any defect in the formation of Tartare's employment agreement or the arbitration clause contained therein. Tartare has a great claim, and she is going to have to present it to an arbitrator.

9. **Le Burger: Home of No Class.** Unless Tartare succeeds in convincing a court that the class action waiver is unenforceable, she will be barred from initiating a representative action — in court or in arbitration. The most likely avenue for Tartare to make her argument against the enforceability of the class action waiver would be through the doctrine of unconscionability. In some contexts (for example, one in which many consumers might suffer identical but relatively small injuries), a ban on representative actions might very well constitute a substantively

unconscionable provision. But the mere existence of a class waiver does not per se render the contract unenforceable.

In this case, Tartare's argument is reasonably strong, but it is not a guaranteed winner. She would point to the adhesive process by which the contract's terms were reached. She would argue that precluding class actions will prevent her from vindicating important rights, and she would note that the ban on class actions effectively operates unilaterally against her versus Le Burger (since it is unlikely that Le Burger would initiate a class action against its employees). Weighing against her argument is the fact the claims most easily anticipated at the time of the contract formation would be sufficiently large and sufficiently individualized that the class remedy is not necessary for her to vindicate her rights. Courts have split over the impact of class waivers in the context of arbitration, so without knowing more about the jurisdiction in particular, we cannot be certain about the fate of Tartare's claim.

10. **Le Burger: Home of the Home Court Advantage.** Rubin's challenge will almost certainly be based on unconscionability, and while there are no bright-line rules or precise definitions for unconscionability, this arbitration clause appears to overreach enough to be unenforceable.

On the issue of procedural unconscionability, Rubin will point to the process by which his consent was secured. Although it is not per se procedurally unconscionable to require an employee to agree to an arbitration provision as a condition of employment, the fact that Le Burger drafted it, presented it in an adhesive manner, gave him only a brief opportunity to review it, and provided no opportunity to revoke his acceptance weighs considerably against Le Burger. On the matter of the substance of the agreement, Rubin can make at least two arguments, each of which has merit. First, he will point to the unilateral choice of forum granted to Le Burger and will argue that it presents an unbearable risk of creating excessive costs. Recall that the mere risk of costs is not necessarily dispositive of an arbitration provision's enforceability. (This was the crux of the Supreme Court's opinion in *Randolph*, described above.) But in this case, Le Burger retains the option to designate a forum in a way that makes it particularly difficult for Rubin to specify the expenses he would incur.

Second, Rubin will point to the restriction on the identity of the arbitrators and argue that by restricting the arbitrators to experienced restaurant owners, Le Burger has created a sham procedure with structural biases against claimants. On balance, the combination of these factors makes it likely that the arbitration agreement is unconscionable.

Now, who is the appropriate decision maker? In this case, the alleged unconscionability is specific to the arbitration agreement itself — not to the container agreement more broadly. Under the *Prima Paint* reasoning, attacks specific to the arbitration agreement are the province of the courts. It is a court, therefore, who will judge the merits of Rubin's challenge.

11. **Burger Pit: Home of Liars.** Your claim against Burger Pit is almost certainly headed to arbitration. The Burger Pit representative's statements about the availability appear to be fraudulent, on the basis of these facts. (It was a knowing misrepresentation of a material fact, and your reasonable reliance on that assertion caused you harm.) But the question is not whether your claim has merit. The question is which forum will hear your claim.

   The "separability" doctrine, articulated in the Supreme Court's decision in *Prima Paint*, guides the analysis in this case. According to the facts, the contract clearly contained a broad agreement to arbitrate. Nothing in the facts suggests a defect in the formation of the arbitration clause in particular. Instead, the alleged defect (the fraud) tainted not just the arbitration clause, but also the entire container agreement. Under the logic of the *Prima Paint* decision, therefore, the court must give effect to the parties' intent to have disputes (including challenges to the container agreement in which the arbitration clause sits) resolved by an arbitrator.

12. **Le Burger: Home of Creative Signatures.** In this case, Stylo is not merely attacking the enforceability of a contract with an arbitration provision. Instead, he is attacking even the *existence* of a contract with an arbitration provision. A court will not compel arbitration until it is satisfied that the parties entered an agreement with an arbitration provision. If the challenge is about the *existence* of a contract, rather than just its enforceability, the challenge must be resolved by a court.

   In this way, fraud in the inducement is treated differently from forgery of a signature on a nonexistent contract. Judge Easterbrook, in *Sphere Drake Ins. Ltd. v. All American Ins. Co.*, 256 F.3d 587 (7th Cir. 2001), explained the distinction this way:

   > A claim of fraud in the inducement — which boils down to "we wouldn't have signed this contract had we known the full truth about our trading partner" — supposes that the unhappy party did agree, but now wishes it hadn't. If a claim of "we wish we hadn't agreed" could be litigated, even when the arbitration clause is so broad, this would move a good portion of contract disputes back to court and defeat this part of the agreement at the outset, for it is easy to cry fraud. . . . But whether there was *any* agreement is a distinct question. . . . A person whose signature was forged has never agreed to anything.

163

6. Is This Agreement to Arbitrate Enforceable?

This does not mean that Stylo will necessarily have the substance of his discrimination claim heard by a court. If Stylo prevails in his assertion that the signature in question is a forgery, the court will proceed to hear the substance of Stylo's claim against Le Burger. However, if the court finds the signature to be valid, it will grant Le Burger's motion to stay the litigation, and Stylo will be forced to arbitrate his discrimination claim.

Must This Dispute Go to Arbitration? The Question of Arbitrability

§7.1 INTRODUCTION

As we mention earlier in Chapter 5, much of the litigation surrounding arbitration (and therefore much of the law you are likely to need to know about arbitration) has centered on the question of whether a disputant will be required to submit her or his case to arbitration for resolution. At the simplest level, the answer is that a party will only be sent to arbitration if she or he agreed to go to arbitration. But as you might expect, contracts (and contract law) are not always so simple.

In the previous chapter, we explored one of the two major approaches a disputant might take to try to avoid sending a dispute to arbitration: challenging the enforceability of the contractual agreement to arbitrate. To summarize Chapter 6 in a sentence: Because arbitration is a creature of contract, if there is no enforceable contract, there will be no arbitration.

In this chapter, we describe the second of the two major avenues available to disputants who seek to avoid arbitration. We consider circumstances in which the disputants contest neither the existence of a contract containing an arbitration clause nor the enforceability of the agreement to arbitrate. Instead, they contend *as a matter of contractual interpretation* that the contract does not compel them to arbitrate this case, in this circumstance.

The set of objections within this umbrella of contractual interpretations are commonly referred to as questions of *arbitrability*. We should warn you, though, that the term lacks a precise and uniformly shared definition. In fact,

165

the term "arbitrability" is sometimes even used to describe the questions from Chapter 6 — things like whether a contract was formed at all. For purposes of clarity, we intend to limit our usage of the term "arbitrability" in this chapter, but you should be aware that the term operates almost as a chimera in this area of the law.

Arbitrability presents two distinct avenues for parties seeking to avoid arbitration. The first, commonly called *substantive arbitrability*, examines the scope of the parties' agreement to arbitrate. A challenge based on substantive arbitrability asserts that even if there is a valid agreement to arbitrate, the parties never intended for that arbitration agreement to cover the particular dispute in question. The second, commonly called *procedural arbitrability*, examines the processes and conditions spelled out in the parties' agreement to arbitrate. A challenge based on procedural arbitrability asserts that the dispute should not be sent to arbitration because the party seeking to send the case to arbitration failed to satisfy some procedural prerequisite from the arbitration agreement (and therefore is not entitled to go to arbitration at all).

§7.2 SUBSTANTIVE ARBITRABILITY: "THIS DISPUTE DOES NOT FALL WITHIN THE TERMS OF OUR AGREEMENT TO ARBITRATE"

One of the many ways in which parties can customize or tailor their agreement to arbitrate is with the *scope* of the arbitration agreement. Arbitration need not be a binary matter. ("Either we arbitrate everything, or we arbitrate nothing.") Instead, parties can specify precisely the kinds of disputes they want to send to arbitration. When a dispute arises, the substantive arbitrability question simply asks whether the dispute falls within the scope specified by the parties in their arbitration agreement.

For example, imagine that two companies entering a joint venture include a provision in their contract in which they agree to arbitrate "any disputes regarding the formation of this contract or the representations made prior to the launch date of this joint venture." If a dispute arose in which one company claimed that the other misstated its assets during the negotiations, the arbitration clause would cover it. (It would be "substantively arbitrable.") If, on the other hand, a dispute arose in which one company claimed that the other side subsequently failed to make the final installment payment under the terms of the contract, the dispute would fall outside of the scope of the arbitration agreement. Neither company could force the other into arbitration on that claim because it would not be substantively arbitrable.

§7.2.1 Standards for Deciding If a Dispute Is Substantively Arbitrable

Sometimes the scope of an arbitration agreement will be so plain that no detailed analysis will be necessary to determine substantive arbitrability. For example, some arbitration clauses are narrowly and precisely crafted, spelling out in great detail which kinds of disputes are to be resolved through arbitration. ("We agree to arbitrate any and all disputes regarding whether the widgets in question conform to the contractual specifications set forth in Appendix B.") Other arbitration clauses are so broad that they encompass absolutely any dispute that could possibly arise. ("We agree to arbitrate any and all disputes related to or arising out of the formation, performance, nonperformance, breach, termination, or interpretation of this contract.") Substantive arbitrability is not a significant issue in either of these circumstances, because the scope of the agreement is clear.

But what if the contract's scope is ambiguous? You surely recall from your Contracts class that it is not easy to draft provisions in a way that prevents multiple interpretations. If an arbitration agreement has a scope that is *arguably* broad enough to encompass the particular dispute in question, what should happen?

The U.S. Supreme Court first tackled this question in an opinion from the famous *Steelworkers'* trilogy, a series of Supreme Court cases in 1960 addressing arbitration questions. In *United Steelworkers v. Warrior & Gulf Navigation Co.*, 363 U.S. 574 (1960), the union claimed that the somewhat ambiguous terms of a contract required the arbitration of a particular grievance involving work that had been contracted outside of the union, and the company argued that the grievance fell outside the scope of the arbitration clause. In its ruling favoring the union's position, the Supreme Court announced that all "doubts should be resolved in favor of coverage." This is a *strong* presumption of arbitrability. As long as the dispute arguably falls within the scope of the arbitration agreement, the dispute is sent to arbitration.

For some time, a question remained whether this presumption of arbitrability applied only in the relatively narrow context of collective bargaining. In 1985, however, the Supreme Court returned to the question of substantive arbitrability—this time outside the context of a labor-management contract. It reaffirmed the broad presumption of arbitrability in *Mitsubishi Motors Corp. v. Soler Chrysler-Plymouth, Inc.*, 473 U.S. 614 (1985), a commercial dispute between an automobile manufacturer and an automobile dealer. The Supreme Court said, with respect to substantive arbitrability, "the parties' intentions control, but those intentions are generously construed as to issues of arbitrability." In other words, the presumption that an arbitration clause is broad enough to encompass a dispute is strong, and it applies even beyond the collective bargaining context.

Why make this assumption? Why not the opposite assumption? Part of the reason lies in the Supreme Court's consistent finding since the early 1980s that there is a strong federal policy favoring arbitration. The other part is that this is a circumstance in which the parties have clearly agreed to arbitrate *some* things. As the Court reasoned, the parties knew they would be called upon to arbitrate in some contexts, and it would have been easy enough for the parties to specify if there were certain kinds of instances in which they would prefer *not* to arbitrate.

§7.2.2 Who Decides Whether a Dispute Is Substantively Arbitrable?

The scope of an arbitration clause is to be broadly construed, so that the presumption is in favor of declaring a dispute to be substantively arbitrable. But who makes this determination — a court or an arbitrator?

The question of "who decides" substantive arbitrability was the subject of a significant Supreme Court case, *First Options of Chicago, Inc. v. Kaplan*, 514 U.S. 938 (1995). In this case, First Options submitted a claim to arbitration, citing a contractual arbitration provision. Kaplan asserted in the arbitration that the claim in question was not subject to arbitration, but the arbitrators ruled that First Options properly brought the claim to arbitration, and then ruled against Kaplan on the merits of First Options' claim. Kaplan sought a court order vacating the arbitral award against him, again arguing that a court (rather than the arbitrators) should have heard Kaplan's objections to arbitrability. The Supreme Court eventually sided with Kaplan, ruling that a court should review the arbitrability of the claim.

The Supreme Court's logic in *First Options* had at least two important components. First, the Court returned to the principle that arbitration is a matter of contract between the parties. "[T]he question 'who has the primary power to decide arbitrability' turns upon what the parties agreed about *that* matter." If the parties agreed to have arbitrability determined by a court, the question should be resolved by a court. And if the parties agreed to have arbitrability resolved by an arbitrator, an arbitrator's decision should control on this question.

But what if there is ambiguity or silence on the question of "who decides arbitrability," as there is in many arbitration clauses? This is where the second part of the *First Options* opinion is important. The Court held that *a court* is the presumptive decision maker in a dispute over substantive arbitrability, unless the parties "clearly and unmistakably" contracted for it to be resolved by an arbitrator.

This creates an interesting dichotomy: The court has a presumption in favor of arbitration for resolving the *merits* of a substantive arbitrability fight, but a presumption in favor of having a judge decide *who* decides whether the case is arbitrable. The Court in *First Options* called this discrepancy "understandable." It suggested that parties who knowingly enter into an agreement to arbitrate can reasonably be expected to anticipate that they would need to be clear if they want a particular type of dispute to stay out of arbitration. By contrast, with respect to the question of who decides substantive arbitrability, the Court admitted that the question is "rather arcane." The Court reasoned that making arbitrators the presumptive decision makers about arbitrability questions "might too often force unwilling parties to arbitrate a matter they reasonably would have thought a judge, not an arbitrator, would decide."

The short answer, therefore, to who decides substantive arbitrability is "whomever the parties said should decide substantive arbitrability." But if there is any doubt about whom the parties intended to decide whether an arbitration agreement applies to a particular dispute, the determination should be made by a court. For instance, in *AT&T Technologies, Inc. v. Communications Workers of America*, 475 U.S. 643 (1986), a union challenged AT&T's decision to lay off a set of employees, claiming the layoffs violated the collective bargaining agreement. The union demanded arbitration, which was available for many kinds of disputes under the collective bargaining agreement. But AT&T asserted that the layoffs in question were because of a "lack of work," a condition it claimed fell outside the scope of the collective bargaining agreement's arbitration clause. The Supreme Court held that, in the absence of specific language providing that such an assessment should be made by an arbitrator, a district court must review the agreement to determine whether the parties intended to submit such disputes to arbitration. (Recall from *Steelworkers* and *Mitsubishi*, however, that the court's presumption in the analysis will be in favor of sending disputes to arbitration.)

§7.3 PROCEDURAL ARBITRABILITY: "THEY DIDN'T DO WHAT THE ARBITRATION AGREEMENT REQUIRES THEM TO DO"

The terms of an arbitration agreement are, in some ways, like a set of privately constructed litigation procedures. If you think back to Civil

Procedure, you'll recognize that such rules have to be filled with considerable detail in order to cover the range of circumstances that arise during the course of a dispute. Mercifully, most contracting parties do not have to craft their arbitration rules from scratch. Typically, they choose a fully written set of arbitration rules from one of a number of sources. For example, some arbitration organizations promulgate rules for their arbitrators (in part because they hope disputants will hire their organization to administer arbitrations). Some professional associations have sample arbitration procedures. Homebuilders have a set of proposed arbitration rules. So do architects. So do developers. The idea is that contracting parties might, with relatively little investment of time, easily find a set of arbitration procedures to govern future disputes.

Now, what happens if one or both of the parties fail to follow the procedures that appear in their arbitration agreement? And who decides whether the parties have, in fact, followed the agreed-upon procedures?

For minor procedural rules governing the conduct of the arbitration, the question clearly sits in the lap of an arbitrator. If, for example, the arbitration procedures indicate that parties must give each other 72 hours' notice of any witnesses they intend to call, and one of the parties (arguably) gives the other side only 60 hours' notice, the resulting dispute falls clearly within the province of the arbitrator to determine. Such intra-arbitration disputes are virtually never subject to judicial review. (For more on the possibility of judicial review of arbitrators' decisions, see Chapter 5.)

The important questions within this category arise when the dispute in question concerns a so-called gateway matter. We should warn you that the term "gateway dispute," like the term "arbitrability," is used in such a wide range of settings that it risks being unhelpful. Nevertheless, the Supreme Court continues to refer to certain matters as "gateway," and it is, therefore, important to discuss the various things that might fall under this umbrella. Some gateway disputes concern the question of whether a binding contract exists at all. (This is the subject of Chapter 6.) Other gateway disputes hinge on whether the parties have done the things they need to have done, under the terms of their arbitration agreement, in order to bring the arbitration clause into effect. It is this latter category of concerns that we are calling issues of "procedural arbitrability" in this section.

§7.3.1 Standards for Deciding if Conditions Precedent to Arbitration Have Been Satisfied

Like many of the other areas of arbitration law we have been discussing, regular contract law governs the question of how to decide if a party has followed the arbitration procedures or has met the prerequisites to arbitration. Unlike many other subtopics we have discussed, however, no arbitration-specific presumptions tip the balance one way or the other. A party alleging that some contractual condition precedent to arbitration was not met by the other party has the burden of showing that failure. Similarly, a party alleging that some arbitration procedure was not followed has the burden of demonstrating that failure. For example, ADR clauses frequently require both parties to engage in some nonbinding ADR process before filing a claim in arbitration, and they often spell out procedures for giving each other notice of claims. If one party believes that the other has failed to adhere to these requirements (and therefore believes that arbitration is not proper), the party seeking to avoid arbitration has the burden of showing that these contractual conditions were not met.

§7.3.2 Who Decides Whether a Dispute Is Procedurally Arbitrable?

As with the question of the enforceability of an arbitration contract, many of the procedural arbitrability disputes center on the question of *who* decides whether the parties have properly satisfied the contractual conditions that would send them to arbitration. The short answer is that disputes over procedural arbitrability are resolved by arbitrators, not by courts.

In *Howsam v. Dean Witter Reynolds, Inc.*, 537 U.S. 79 (2002), the Supreme Court addressed the question of allocating decision-making authority regarding procedural arbitrability issues. In that case, Howsam, on the advice of her Dean Witter advisor, bought an interest in a set of limited partnerships. The partnerships did not fare as well as Howsam hoped, and she believed that Dean Witter had misrepresented certain aspects of the purchase. The terms of Howsam's investment contract with Dean Witter included an arbitration provision, which specified that the arbitration rules of the National Association of Securities Dealers (NASD) would apply. Howsam sought to bring her claim against Dean Witter to arbitration. Dean Witter responded by pointing to a clause in the NASD rules that held that no dispute would be eligible for arbitration "where six (6) years have elapsed from the occurrence or event giving rise to the dispute." The question before the Supreme Court was not whether that amount of time had passed, but rather *who decides* whether Howsam's claim was timely. The Supreme Court held that this was a matter "where parties would likely expect that an arbitrator would decide the gateway matter. Thus, 'procedural' questions which grow out of the dispute and bear on its final disposition are presumptively *not* for the judge, but for an arbitrator, to decide."

7. Must This Dispute Go to Arbitration? The Question of Arbitrability

With some hesitation about oversimplifying what is an evolving and complex area of the law, therefore, we offer the following summary of the past two chapters:

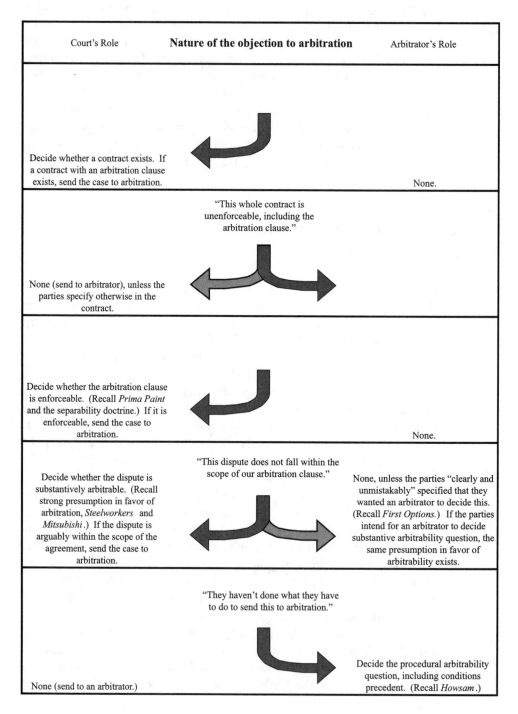

Court's Role	Nature of the objection to arbitration	Arbitrator's Role
Decide whether a contract exists. If a contract with an arbitration clause exists, send the case to arbitration.		None.
None (send to arbitrator), unless the parties specify otherwise in the contract.	"This whole contract is unenforceable, including the arbitration clause."	
Decide whether the arbitration clause is enforceable. (Recall *Prima Paint* and the separability doctrine.) If it is enforceable, send the case to arbitration.		None.
Decide whether the dispute is substantively arbitrable. (Recall strong presumption in favor of arbitration, *Steelworkers* and *Mitsubishi*.) If the dispute is arguably within the scope of the agreement, send the case to arbitration.	"This dispute does not fall within the scope of our arbitration clause."	None, unless the parties "clearly and unmistakably" specified that they wanted an arbitrator to decide this. (Recall *First Options*.) If the parties intend for an arbitrator to decide substantive arbitrability question, the same presumption in favor of arbitrability exists.
None (send to an arbitrator.)	"They haven't done what they have to do to send this to arbitration."	Decide the procedural arbitrability question, including conditions precedent. (Recall *Howsam*.)

Examples

Working for the Grape

Grapalicious Grapes is a small vineyard and winemaking operation. All of its employees agree, in their employment contract, to abide by the Grapalicious Employee Handbook. Among other things, the Handbook includes a dispute resolution provision. It reads, in part:

> Employer and Employee agree to endeavor to resolve any and all differences, grievances, and disputes through the most efficient, least formal mechanism possible. To that end, Employer and Employee agree that any complaint or grievance will be presented to the other side, in writing, within four months of the circumstances giving rise to the complaint or grievance.
>
> Further, neither the Employer nor the Employee will initiate any formal action against the other without having first engaged in a good faith effort to resolve the matter consensually.
>
> In the event Employer and Employee are unable to resolve their differences through informal negotiations, Employer and Employee agree to submit to binding arbitration the following disputes:
>
> 1. Any and all disputes concerning wages and benefits, and
> 2. Any and all disputes concerning the termination of this employment relationship.
>
> Except as provided herein, the arbitration will be conducted according to the Commercial Arbitration Rules of the American Association of Grapegrowers.

1. **Sour Grapes.** Ernest was a Grapalicious employee for more than a year. Three months ago, he was fired from his job. Having now examined his final paycheck more carefully, Ernest believes that Grapalicious incorrectly calculated his overtime pay for the weeks before he was fired. Ernest called Grapalicious and tried to work things out, but he got nowhere. If Ernest were to bring a claim against Grapalicious, would Grapalicious be able to force him to bring it before an arbitrator, rather than in court?

2. **Sour Grapes, Version 2.** Assume the same set of facts as in Example 1, except that Ernest brought his claim concerning the overtime calculations directly to an arbitrator, immediately upon discovering the error in his paycheck. Would Grapalicious have any grounds for opposing the submission of the case to arbitration? Who decides this?

3. **Overripe Grapes.** Emilia was a Grapalicious employee for almost a decade. For the entire period of her employment, she worked a somewhat irregular schedule. She and her supervisor would simply

set a schedule at the start of each month, customizing it to her needs and to the needs of the company. Some weeks, she would work as many as 50 hours, and some weeks, she would work as few as 10. On average, by the end of the year, it always worked out that she was working about two-thirds time with Grapalicious. About a year ago, Emilia got a new supervisor. About 10 months ago, her supervisor stopped giving her large assignments. In the past 8 months, she has never worked more than 15 hours a week. Emilia is convinced that her new boss has made these adverse employment decisions for discriminatory reasons, and she files a lawsuit against Grapalicious. Would Grapalicious succeed in an effort to compel Emilia to bring her claim before an arbitrator instead? Who decides this?

4. **Grape Gripe.** Emmanuel is a salesman for Grapalicious. For years, he has been assigned to the Rocky Mountain region. When he is not on the road, Emmanuel works from the basement of his home (which is located in the region). Grapalicious paid for all of the costs of maintaining the home office — something it has done for no other members of its sales force. Three months ago, Emmanuel's boss told him that he would soon be responsible for the Southeast region and advised him to put his house on the market right away. Emmanuel filed a letter of complaint with his boss, citing, among other things, the extraordinary burden it would cause on his family. Grapalicious refused to change the assignment, and it now is also refusing to pay to set up a similar home office in Emmanuel's new home in the Southeast. After trying unsuccessfully to resolve this matter with Grapalicious, Emmanuel filed his complaint — about the transfer and about the refusal to pay for a new home office — with an arbitrator. If Grapalicious filed a motion in court seeking to stay the arbitration, what arguments would it make, and would Grapalicious be successful?

5. **Discriminating Palate?** Eleanor was an executive at Grapalicious for several years. Almost immediately after a new CEO came on board, Eleanor was fired. She is convinced that her discharge was the product of unlawful discrimination. Three months later, she filed a lawsuit against Grapalicious in federal court. Grapalicious attempted to contact Eleanor to discuss the matter, which she refused to do. Would Grapalicious succeed if it sought to compel Eleanor to pursue her claim in arbitration?

Doing Business with the Grape

6. **Missing Bottles.** Grapalicious has a contract with BottleCo to supply bottles for wine and other products made at the Grapalicious vineyard. One shipment of bottles never arrived at Grapalicious, causing

Grapalicious to fail to meet the deadline for entering and selling wine at the biggest wine show of the season. Grapalicious files a claim in arbitration against BottleCo, citing the arbitration clause in the contract between Grapalicious and BottleCo. BottleCo responds by filing a motion to stay the arbitration, pointing out that the contract's arbitration clause provides that it only applies in cases of "intentional breaches of contract." As part of its motion, BottleCo maintains that the missing shipment was an innocent mistake, rather than an intentional breach. Who rules on the motion and how will the court or arbitrator rule on the motion to stay arbitration?

7. **Complaining on the Clock.** Grapalicious gets another shipment of bottles from BottleCo. This time, several of the bottles are cracked, and others are misshapen. Grapalicious promptly calls BottleCo to complain. BottleCo responds by saying, "Let's meet in person to work all of this out." Because of scheduling difficulties, the parties are not able to meet until a few months later. At the meeting, BottleCo tells Grapalicious that it cannot discuss the problem because Grapalicious failed to bring the defective bottles to the meeting. Their meeting adjourns. Grapalicious later sends photos of the broken bottles to BottleCo. After some further delay, about a year after the disputed shipment in question took place, BottleCo responds by saying, "We're going to need you to put all of this in writing." Grapalicious, finally fed up with dealing with BottleCo, files an arbitration claim against BottleCo. BottleCo then files a motion in court to stay the arbitration, citing the contractual provision requiring the complaining party to bring any arbitration action under the contract within one year of the event giving rise to the claim. How will the court (or arbitrator if applicable) rule on the motion to stay arbitration?

8. **Impasse over Impasse.** In handling its vineyard labor needs, Grapalicious has a contract with unionized grape pickers, represented by the Harvesters Union of Grape Employees (HUGE). The collectively bargained contract contains an arbitration clause that provides, "In the event any dispute arises regarding hours, wages, or benefits, Grapalicious and HUGE will bargain in good faith. In the event that the good faith bargaining results in an impasse, the dispute shall be resolved by binding arbitration according to the procedures set forth in section 45 of this agreement." During harvest season, several HUGE members believe that Grapalicious failed to pay them according to the overtime schedule set forth in the collective bargaining agreement. A HUGE representative storms into the office of the Grapalicious CEO, demanding an adjustment to the employees' salaries. "What the hell are you talking about?" replies the Grapalicious CEO. The HUGE representative storms out of the office, and HUGE immediately files an arbitration claim against Grapalicious.

Grapalicious heads to court and files a motion to stay the arbitration on the grounds that HUGE did not follow arbitration procedures. Specifically, Grapalicious alleges that HUGE failed to satisfy its obligation to bargain in good faith and that, in any event, no impasse had yet occurred. How will a court (or arbitrator if applicable) treat this motion to stay the arbitration action?

9. **The Grape's Rules.** Grapalicious has a supply contract with SuperScrewper, to manufacture screw tops to seal all of Grapalicious's wine bottles. According to the contract with SuperScrewper, "any and all disputes regarding the quality of the bottle screw tops described in this contract shall be resolved through arbitration." A dispute arises from the most recent SuperScrewper shipment. Grapalicious files a lawsuit in court against SuperScrewper, alleging that (1) the entire shipment of screw tops was late, (2) too few screw tops were sent, and (3) some of the screw tops were bent and unusable. Will SuperScrewper be able to compel Grapalicious to bring these claims in arbitration instead of court?

10. **The Grape's Rules, Part 2.** Assume the same set of facts as in Example 9. The arbitration agreement between Grapalicious and SuperScrewper also specifies that "any such arbitration shall be conducted according to the Commercial Arbitration Rules of the American Association of Grapegrowers." What impact would this clause have if, according to those rules, questions of substantive arbitrability are to be resolved by the arbitrator?

Explanations

Working for the Grape

1. **Sour Grapes.** Yes. Based on the facts before us, the Grapalicious employment contract — including the arbitration clause contained in the contract — appears to have no defects. For example, nothing in the contract suggests that the employee handbook was imposed inappropriately on the employees, and nothing suggests that the handbook's provisions unconscionably favor Grapalicious over the employees. We might want to know more about the American Association of Grapegrowers' arbitration rules to assess their fairness, but on these facts, nothing suggests that the contract itself is anything but binding.

As to the question of substantive arbitrability, the arbitration clause within this contract specifies a relatively narrow scope of disputes that are subject to arbitration. Rather than saying "any and all disputes about anything," it names two categories of disputes that must be arbitrated. Such terms are to be read expansively, however, under the logic of the federal policy favoring arbitration, as articulated in the Supreme Court's *Steelworkers'* trilogy. Here, the dispute concerns both wages and benefits, and the termination of Ernest's employment. The dispute is, therefore, substantively arbitrable, and Grapalicious will be able to compel Ernest to arbitrate this dispute.

2. **Sour Grapes, Version 2.** Yes. Although it may appear counterintuitive, Grapalicious might be able to resist having this heard in arbitration by arguing that Ernest failed to satisfy the conditions precedent to arbitration specified in the employee handbook. According to the handbook, Ernest was supposed to present his complaint to Grapalicious in writing, and he was supposed to exhaust good faith bargaining efforts. Nothing in the facts suggests that he did so. Therefore, Ernest may be blocked from imposing the arbitration provision against Grapalicious, if Grapalicious wishes to avoid having an arbitrator resolve the dispute.

   Notice, however, that all of these objections that Grapalicious might raise fall into the category of "procedural arbitrability" questions — so-called "gateway issues" the parties would reasonably expect the arbitrators to decide. As a result, an arbitrator (rather than a court) would resolve disputes about Ernest's compliance with these provisions. A court would only wind up resolving the substance of this dispute if an arbitrator determined that Ernest's failure to adhere to the procedural requirements of the contract bars him from compelling arbitration.

3. **Overripe Grapes.** Probably not. This question hinges on the substantive arbitrability of Emilia's claim. The contract specifies the two types of claims subject to arbitration. Unless the dispute falls within the categories the parties consented to present to an arbitrator, Grapalicious would have no grounds to compel arbitration. Emilia's claim does not, on its face, appear to be a dispute over wages and benefits, though one could argue that the customized work schedule was a benefit of some sort. Nor does the dispute technically concern the termination of her employment (as evidenced by the fact that she remains employed at Grapalicious). As a result, therefore, unless the arbitration clause is read extraordinarily expansively, Grapalicious is unlikely to succeed in compelling arbitration.

   Now, who makes this determination — a court or an arbitrator? In most cases, a court would resolve this question of substantive arbitrability. Some states appear to resolve this question differently, sending the matter to arbitration. But as a general matter, under the logic of *First Options*, the question of substantive arbitrability would be sent to an arbitrator only if the parties' agreement evidenced a "clear and unmistakable" intention to do so. Here, no such indication exists, so a court would resolve the question.

   Notice that how the parties frame the litigation can make a big difference. Is this a simple matter of work assignments — a matter not identified as subject to arbitration? If so, a court would refuse to compel arbitration. Or is this a case of a wage and hour dispute, and because both were significantly decreased, a case of constructive termination? If so, the matter appears to fall within the scope of the arbitration clause, particularly given the broad presumption in favor of substantive arbitrability.

4. **Grape Gripe.** Grapalicious's best argument would be that Emmanuel's claims are not substantively arbitrable. Grapalicious would argue that nothing in these facts relates to the termination of Emmanuel's employment, and that the transfer itself does not involve wages and benefits. Quite plainly, Emmanuel was not fired, so that aspect of the arbitration clause's scope does not affect the analysis.

The question is whether any of this involves a dispute over "wages and benefits." The transfer itself does not appear to fall within the arbitration clause's scope. But the company's refusal to reimburse expenses for setting up a new home office *might* constitute a dispute over benefits. Given the strong federal policy favoring arbitration and the corresponding presumption of arbitrability, it is certainly conceivable that one might consider this to be at least partially a dispute over benefits — and therefore, at least partially substantively arbitrable.

If the dispute over benefits (the home office expenses) is deemed substantively arbitrable, Grapalicious would fail in its motion to stay the arbitration — at least as to that issue. To the extent the parties contracted to arbitrate disputes like this one, a court would hold off on deciding the merits of the remaining legal claims until the arbitration had run its course. (Recall the preclusion doctrine reasons requiring this sequence. If the court were to go first, it might make a ruling that precluded an arbitrator from deciding that which the parties agreed to have an arbitrator decide.)

In all events, at least based on the facts before us, Emmanuel appears to have a tough road ahead with his various claims. Unless Grapalicious's employment contract has a provision guaranteeing company-funded home offices, Emmanuel is unlikely to be able to insist upon being compensated for those costs. And unless Grapalicious's employment contract has a provision permitting employees to dispute assigned transfers, Emmanuel is unlikely to succeed in avoiding the transfer altogether. But notice that the fight in question in this chapter is not about whether a claimant wins. Instead, it is about the forum in which an aggrieved party must bring a claim. And in this case, conceivably, Emmanuel might have to bring his claims in two separate fora.

5. **Discriminating Palate?** Yes. Eleanor might object to being compelled to arbitrate a claim involving a statutory right (in this case, antidiscrimination laws). However, as we discussed in Chapter 6, a public policy

objection such as this is extraordinarily unlikely to succeed absent some statutory language making it clear that the type of discrimination claim in question is not subject to arbitration agreements. The agreement, therefore, is enforceable. Grapalicious appears to have complied with any of the conditions precedent to arbitration, so the matter is likely to be deemed procedurally arbitrable. The only other possible objection would be if this claim were not substantively arbitrable. However, Eleanor's claim appears to be plainly within the scope of the arbitration agreement, which provides for arbitration of "any and all disputes concerning the termination of this employment relationship." As a result, Grapalicious can compel Eleanor to bring her claim in arbitration.

Doing Business with the Grape

6. **Missing Bottles.** The enforceability of the contract between BottleCo and Grapalicious is not in question, so this raises a substantive arbitrability question, at the outset. Responsibility for determining whether Grapalicious's claim falls within the scope of the arbitration clause rests initially with the court.

   In deciding the motion to stay litigation (which hinges on a determination of substantive arbitrability), the court will be guided by the *Steelworkers'* presumption of arbitrability. The clause specifically limits arbitration to incidents of "intentional breaches of contract," and it might be difficult for Grapalicious to demonstrate that BottleCo's breach was intentional. Nevertheless, given the broad presumption of arbitrability, the court may decide that the matter is at least arguably within the scope of the clause.

   The Supreme Court addressed a somewhat similar question in *PacifiCare Health v. Book*, 538 U.S. 401 (2002). In that case, the arbitration clause in question prohibited the arbitrator from awarding any "punitive" damages. The plaintiffs brought a claim alleging a RICO violation, and sought the treble damages that statute makes available to successful claimants. When the defendants sought to compel arbitration, the plaintiffs objected on the grounds that they might be unable to receive the relief they deserved in arbitration. The litigants argued over whether treble damages were an example of "punitive" damages (which the arbitrator was not empowered to award) or "remedial" or "compensatory" damages (which would fall within the arbitrator's authority). The Supreme Court found that argument premature and compelled arbitration, largely on the grounds that arbitrators should resolve questions concerning ambiguous contractual terms.

   In the dispute involving Grapalicious's claim, it is therefore likely that a court would deny BottleCo's motion to stay the arbitration.

7. **Complaining on the Clock.** This raises a procedural arbitrability issue. Neither party contends that the contract is unenforceable, and neither party contends that the dispute does not fall within the scope of the disputes they agreed to arbitrate. Instead, BottleCo is asserting that Grapalicious failed to adhere to the procedural requirements of the arbitration agreement and, therefore, should be barred from proceeding in arbitration against BottleCo.

   This procedural arbitrability issue falls within the scope of "gateway matters" the parties would, as the Supreme Court in *Howsam* wrote, "likely expect that an arbitrator would decide." The arbitrator might decide that Grapalicious gave BottleCo constructive notice or that BottleCo engaged in misbehavior that prevents it from asserting this defense to arbitration. In that case, the arbitrator would then proceed to determine the merits of the claim. Alternatively, the arbitrator might decide that the contract's procedural requirements were clear and that Grapalicious failed to meet them. If that happens, the dispute would be dismissed from arbitration, and Grapalicious would have to pursue its claim in court. (And a court may very well interpret the time clause as creating a waiver of any right to pursue an action in court, even if the otherwise relevant statute of limitations would not yet bar the action.)

   In either event, BottleCo's procedural arbitrability defense would be sent to an arbitrator to decide, and as such, BottleCo's motion to stay arbitration would be denied.

8. **Impasse over Impasse.** Grapalicious's motion raises a procedural arbitrability question. Although the motion is before a court, procedural arbitrability issues like this are generally matters for the arbitrator to resolve (absent some contractual language to the contrary). The court will, therefore, likely deny the motion to stay the arbitration, and Grapalicious will need to raise its procedural arbitrability issue before the arbitrator. On these facts, it is entirely possible that the arbitrator will determine that no impasse was yet reached on the dispute, and that arbitration is therefore not (yet) appropriate. This initial matter of whether on the facts an impasse occurred is not for the court to resolve, however.

9. **The Grape's Rules.** Any effort by SuperScrewper to compel arbitration will hinge on the substantive arbitrability question of whether Grapalicious's claims fall within the category of "disputes regarding the quality of the bottle screw tops." Remember, the language of the contract itself is the first element to examine. Such matters are properly for a court to resolve, so the trial court would make this determination. Operating under the presumption of arbitrability articulated in the *Steelworkers'* trilogy, the court would almost certainly find that the third of Grapalicious's allegations (that some tops were bent and

unusable) falls within the scope of the arbitration clause. The question of the timing and quantity of the shipment are less obviously disputes "regarding the quality of the screw tops." Even with the "generous" construction dictated by the Supreme Court in *Mitsubishi*, a court would likely find only the last of these disputes arbitrable. It would, therefore, grant an order compelling arbitration of the third (but not the first two) of Grapalicious's claims.

10. **The Grape's Rules, Part 2.** The usual presumption is that questions of substantive arbitrability are the province of courts, rather than arbitrators. In the *First Options* case, the Supreme Court held that a court "should not assume that the parties agreed to arbitrate arbitrability unless there is 'clear and unmistakable' evidence that they did so." The contract clearly incorporates the arbitration rules of the American Association of Grapegrowers. (Incidentally, many of today's major arbitration providers' standard rules contain this provision.) The question is whether this incorporation by reference constitutes the parties' "clear and unmistakable" intention to arbitrate arbitrability. The majority of federal courts that have looked at this question have held that incorporation by reference is sufficient to meet the demands of *First Options*, particularly where, as in the case here, the contract drafters are both sophisticated parties. However, some federal courts have held, in similar circumstances, that the incorporation by reference is not enough, suggesting that the parties were unlikely to have truly considered the matter when just referencing boilerplate arbitration provisions. If the incorporated arbitration rules declare an intention to arbitrate arbitrability, the court will send the matter to an arbitrator to determine whether the claims fall within the scope of the arbitration agreement.

Federal Preemption and the Law(s) of Arbitration

§8.1 INTRODUCTION

The law of arbitration is, in many ways, more complex than the laws related to other dispute resolution processes (other than litigation). In part, the complexity stems from the comparatively greater formality one finds in arbitration than in other ADR processes. Another factor in the complexity of arbitration law is the juxtaposition of both state and federal laws. In this final arbitration chapter, we examine the relationship between these state and federal laws and their effects on arbitration.

At least two fundamental principles inform this area of the law. Each, independently, is relatively straightforward. The first principle is that not everyone loves arbitration. You probably realized this while reading earlier chapters in this book. Just as individual preferences vary, so do those of several states. And you would probably not have a hard time imagining why variation among states exists. States' legislative processes are influenced by a variety of factors. For example, a state with a history of strong consumer protection laws likely has a different set of laws than a state with a history of laws supporting unfettered commerce. Again, on its own, this principle — that states' laws vary in their treatment of this area — is neither surprising nor particularly complex.

The second of the important principles in this area is that federal law strongly promotes the enforcement of arbitration agreements. At the heart of the state vs. federal relationship pertaining to arbitration is §2 of the Federal Arbitration Act. FAA §2 provides that an arbitration provision "shall be valid, irrevocable, and enforceable, save upon such grounds as exist at law or in equity for the revocation of any contract." Again, this is not surprising, given what you have already learned about the FAA.

So we have two simple principles — not everyone loves arbitration, and federal law promotes arbitration. The combination of these two principles, however, creates a complex patchwork of laws governing arbitration. What happens when these two principles collide? What if a state law is less favorable to arbitration than is suggested by the FAA? Does it matter if the dispute appears in state court, as opposed to federal court? To what extent should the answer to these questions be influenced by the parties' arbitration agreement? These difficult, but critically important, questions form the basis of this chapter.

§8.2 SOME BACKGROUND ON THE PREEMPTION DOCTRINE

Because we have a federal system of government, we frequently encounter circumstances in which federal and state laws might diverge. Before examining the peculiar intersection of state and federal arbitration laws, we offer the following brief overview of the general laws of preemption.

Put most basically, the preemption doctrine provides that federal laws generally trump state laws. Drawn from the Supremacy Clause of the Constitution, the preemption doctrine is the vehicle for assuring that federal law is the "supreme law of the land." In *Jones v. Rath Packing Co.*, 430 U.S. 519 (1977), for example, the U.S. Supreme Court considered competing federal and state standards regarding bacon packaging. According to both federal and state laws, bacon labels must accurately state the weight of the packaged food. However, the federal law provided for "reasonable variations caused by loss or gain of moisture during the course of good distribution practices," while the state law had no provision allowing for variation. A bacon producer who was fined for violating the state standard asserted that its bacon packages met the looser federal law and that the federal law preempted the stricter state standard. The Supreme Court agreed, finding that the federal law required preemption of the state standard.

In some cases, Congress clearly intends for a particular law to preempt specific state laws to the contrary. For example, when Congress passed the federal CAN-SPAM Act, it specifically stated that the Act supersedes any state statute, regulation, or rule that expressly regulates the use of electronic mail to send commercial messages. In circumstances like these, preemption is not complicated.

Preemption can also occur when the federal law is silent about preempting state laws, but when the federal laws dominate the area. For example, some federal schemes of laws are so complete that they really leave no room in the field for state law. In *Campbell v. Hussey*, 368 U.S. 297 (1961), for example, the Supreme Court held that a state law pertaining to the labeling of tobacco was preempted by federal regulation of the tobacco industry because Congress intended to create "uniform standards" for tobacco labeling. Preemption, therefore, sometimes occurs even when a state law does not directly contradict any federal law, and Congress has not expressly denied states the power to create laws in the area. In still other cases, a state law would be preempted if it creates obstacles (or actually made it impossible) to comply with federal law. For example, in *McDermott v. Wisconsin*, 228 U.S. 115 (1915), the Court held that the state could not enact legislation regarding the labeling of syrup that interfered with federal regulation of the same activity. Still, these articulations of the boundaries of the preemption doctrine leave considerable room for ambiguity.

You probably encountered the Supremacy Clause for the first time during your Civil Procedure course, in the context of the *Erie* doctrine. The *Erie* doctrine addresses questions about which law (state or federal) should govern the various questions that arise in litigation. In brief, federal courts have a set of rules of civil procedure. And federal courts sometimes hear cases involving federal subject matter such as patent cases, antitrust cases, or federal discrimination cases. In those cases, a federal court would clearly apply federal laws and federal procedures in overseeing the adjudication. But federal courts also hear "diversity of citizenship" cases — ones in which the underlying basis of the claim is state law (a tort claim, a property dispute, or a contract claim, for example). What laws should a federal court apply in those cases? A gross generalization is that federal courts sitting in diversity apply federal procedures and state substantive law. (This is, of course, dangerously overbroad for purposes of answering a Civil Procedure exam, but it will do for our purposes here.) Finally, state courts often hear claims that are based at least in part on federal law. State courts wind up using state procedures, while enforcing the federal substantive law. This collection of broad principles is often referred to as the *Erie* doctrine, though in reality the relevant legal issues are broader than the *Erie* case alone. At the heart of it all is the Supremacy Clause and its effects on the enforceability of state laws.

§8.3 FEDERAL ARBITRATION LAW AS SUBSTANTIVE LAW

The Federal Arbitration Act forms the basis of the federal law of arbitration. Almost all of the FAA's provisions refer to the duties and obligations of "United States courts" or of "any United States district court." FAA §2, however, does not make specific reference to federal courts. Instead, it merely provides that arbitration agreements "shall be valid, irrevocable, and enforceable, save upon such grounds as exist at law or in equity for the revocation of any contract." A fundamental question, therefore, is whether Congress intended for the parameters of FAA §2 to be binding on state courts as well as federal courts. Should FAA §2 be enforced as substantive federal law? The text and the legislative history of the FAA do not necessarily point to an obvious answer to these questions. Nevertheless, the Supreme Court answered these questions in the affirmative in *Southland Corp. v. Keating*, 465 U.S. 1 (1984). As a result, the FAA is treated as substantive federal law, preempting state law to the contrary.

In *Southland*, a group of franchisees who operated 7-Eleven stores brought suit against Southland, the owner of the 7-Eleven franchise. Citing the franchise agreement's arbitration clause, Southland filed motions to compel arbitration. The California Supreme Court refused to compel arbitration, because the California Franchise Investment Law required that franchisees' claims be brought to court, rather than to arbitration. Southland appealed, and the U.S. Supreme Court reversed. The Court cited the federal policy favoring arbitration, and held that FAA §2 rests on the constitutional authority of the Commerce Clause. It wrote that the FAA "creates a body of federal substantive law . . . applicable in state and federal courts."

Despite this far-reaching language, the *Southland* opinion has not been viewed as a declaration that the FAA preempts the entire field of arbitration. Room still exists for some state laws in the area of arbitration. The question becomes which state laws avoid preemption.

§8.4 FIVE CATEGORIES OF STATE LAWS RELATED TO ARBITRATION

For purposes of simplicity, we suggest five categories of state laws potentially relevant to arbitration. As you might expect, the boundaries between these laws may, in some cases, be blurry. And to be clear, this categorization is our own, rather than a framework memorialized in a particular judicial opinion. However, we think that it captures the current legal landscape.

At the far left of the preemption chart below are two categories of state laws that are clearly enforceable and *not* preempted by the FAA.

1. State laws affecting *all* contracts
2. State laws enforcing arbitration clauses

At the far right is one category of state law that is clearly preempted by the FAA, under the logic of the *Southland* case.

> 3. State laws disfavoring *only* arbitration clauses

In between these two sides rest the battlegrounds and remaining grey area of federal preemption law in the context of arbitration.

> 4. State laws disfavoring arbitration clauses *and* some other subset of contracts
> 5. State laws enforcing arbitration clauses, but only with some modifications or restrictions

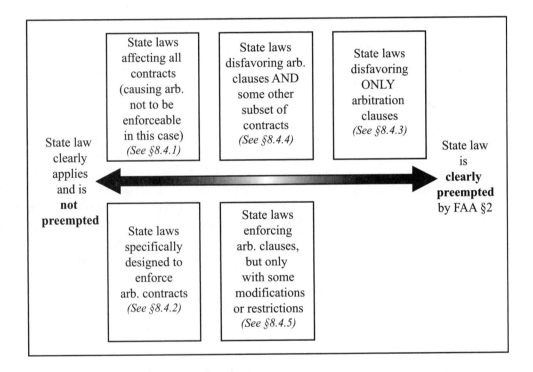

§8.4.1 State Laws Affecting *All* Contracts

A very considerable portion of the law of contracts is a matter of state law. State law governs what constitutes adequate consideration. State law sets the parameters of the doctrines of fraud and duress. State law establishes tests for determining whether a contract is unconscionable. And so forth.

Each of these state laws is potentially relevant to arbitration because arbitration is a creature of contract. An arbitration clause is enforceable, therefore, only if it satisfies the laws governing contract formation and performance.

At a basic level, nothing in the FAA disrupts states' predominance in this area. FAA §2 provides that an arbitration clause is enforceable "save upon such grounds as exist at law or in equity for the revocation of *any* contract" (emphasis added). State laws related to consideration, unconscionability, and the like, are applicable to *any* contract. Even if they are applied in a way that causes an arbitration clause to be unenforceable, they do not run afoul of the FAA. The preemption doctrine will not disrupt them.

§8.4.2 State Laws Enforcing Arbitration Clauses

As we described in Chapter 5, the FAA provides a statutory basis for giving effect to arbitration agreements. Under the FAA, a party to an arbitration agreement can file a motion to compel arbitration or to stay litigation. Similarly, the FAA provides the basis for entering an arbitrator's award as a judgment of the court, making it enforceable through the familiar machinery of the judiciary.

But what about state courts? The FAA's provisions routinely refer to "courts of the United States." What happens to parties whose case presents no basis for appearing in federal court? The answer is that state law routinely provides for enforcement of arbitration in ways similar to (and in some cases, identical to) the federal provisions. Many states, for example, have adopted either the Uniform Arbitration Act (UAA) or the Revised Uniform Arbitration Act (RUAA). Both the RUAA and the UAA have provisions that permit parties to compel or stay arbitration, to enter an arbitral award, or to challenge the award on some narrow basis.

State arbitration laws such as these provide a simple illustration of the principle that state law is not entirely preempted by the FAA, particularly when they promote arbitration. As an initial matter, preemption occurs only when the state law and the federal law are in conflict. Where the state law accomplishes the same thing as the federal law, a preemption analysis is unnecessary.

§8.4.3 State Laws Disfavoring *Only* Arbitration Clauses

Some states are sufficiently skeptical of arbitration in certain contexts that they have passed laws designed to prevent the enforcement of arbitration clauses in those contexts. Typically, a state's concerns focus on commercial and employment settings — ones characterized by a large disparity in the power or sophistication of the parties.

For example, California's Franchise Investment Law — the one at issue in the *Southland* case — aimed to protect franchisees from abusive contractual terms imposed by franchisors. Among the terms deemed invalid under the

California law were arbitration clauses. As you know from the *Southland* case, the Supreme Court struck down these laws that single out arbitration and render them unenforceable. FAA §2 permits state law to invalidate arbitration contracts, but only "upon such grounds as exist at law or in equity for the revocation of any contract."

Laws targeting arbitration specifically are, by definition, *not* grounds as exist for the revocation of any contract. The Supreme Court arrived at this conclusion in the case of *Doctor's Assocs., Inc. v. Casarotto*, 517 U.S. 681 (1996). In *Casarotto*, a Montana state law provided that arbitration clauses would be enforceable only if the first page of the contract in question contained a notice of an arbitration clause printed in underlined, capital letters. A dispute arose involving a contract containing an arbitration agreement, but the first page included no notice of arbitration, much less one in underlined, capital letters. The Supreme Court held that the Montana state law could not be applied consistent with the FAA. Noting that the state law singles out arbitration for separate treatment, the Supreme Court deemed the state law to be preempted, and it enforced the arbitration agreement.

§8.4.4 State Laws Disfavoring Arbitration Clauses *and* Some Other Subset of Contracts

Up until this point, we have dealt with the relatively "easy" cases at the far ends of the continuum we described above. On one end, we have discussed laws that are clearly not preempted (state laws applied to all contracts, and state laws enforcing arbitration agreements). On the other end, we have discussed state laws that are clearly preempted (state laws that single out arbitration for nonenforcement). We now turn to the murkier, grey area.

Some state laws do not single out arbitration specifically, but nonetheless have the effect of treating arbitration clauses (and some other kinds of contracts) differently from contracts generally. Although not as clearly contrary to the FAA as those state laws that specifically target arbitration, these state laws are nonetheless likely to be preempted by the FAA.

For example, the case of *OPE International v. Chet Morrison Contractors*, 258 F.3d 443 (5th Cir. 2001), revolved around a Louisiana statute regulating construction contracts and subcontracts. Under the terms of the Louisiana statute, a construction contract is "null and void and unenforceable as against public policy" if it "requires a suit or arbitration proceeding to be brought in a forum or jurisdiction outside of this state." A dispute arose between a Texas corporation and a Louisiana subcontractor. According to their contract, any disputes were to be resolved by arbitration in Texas. In contesting a motion to compel arbitration, the subcontractor argued that the arbitration contract was invalid because its choice of forum provision violated the Louisiana statute. Notice here that the Louisiana statute does not single out arbitration as the only type of contract to be unenforceable. Instead, it invalidates all contracts — including arbitration contracts — that would require a forum outside of the state. The court in OPE International held that the FAA preempts the state statute in this case and compelled arbitration. It treated the Louisiana statute largely as if it were directed specifically at arbitration clauses, and even cited Southland in explaining its preemption decision. Under the OPE International court's logic, because the state statute had the effect of invalidating an arbitration clause, the FAA would not permit the state statute to operate.

Similarly, the Delaware Supreme Court upheld arbitration in the case of Graham v. State Farm, 565 A.2d 908 (Del. 1989), despite the presence of a state law right to a jury that was arguably implicated by the agreement. In Graham, an insurance company sought to enforce an arbitration agreement found in the plaintiff's insurance policy. The plaintiff argued that the insurance policy was a contract of adhesion, that the arbitration clause was not even part of the agreement at the time the plaintiff signed up for the insurance, and that enforcement of the arbitration clause would constitute a waiver of the plaintiff's state-law-protected right to a jury. Citing the strong policy in favor of arbitration, the Delaware Supreme Court held that the arbitration clause should be enforced against the plaintiff.

Not all courts, however, arrive at the same conclusion. For example, Keystone v. Triad Systems, 971 P.2d 1240 (Mont. 1998), presented a case very similar to OPE International. The parties in Keystone entered a contract in Montana that included an arbitration clause that specified that arbitration would take place in California. Relying on a Montana state law that invalidates clauses specifying an out-of-state forum, one of the disputants sought to compel arbitration in Montana, rather than in California. The Montana Supreme Court rejected the assertion that the Montana statute was preempted by the FAA. Instead, the Montana Supreme Court reasoned that the Montana law is "consistent with the FAA because [it does not] nullif[y] either party's obligation to arbitrate their dispute. Rather [the law] preserve[s] the obligation to arbitrate and constitute[s] no more of an intrusion than on any other general contract entered into in this State." This, the court said, distinguishes the case from those in which the state law specifically targets arbitration.

The Montana Supreme Court also rejected a preemption-based argument when it refused to compel arbitration in Kloss v. Edward D. Jones & Co., 54 P.3d 1 (Mont. 2002). In Kloss, an elderly woman signed a contract with an investment firm without being aware that her contract included an arbitration clause. When a dispute arose and she sought to avoid arbitration, the Montana Supreme Court held that she had not knowingly or intelligently agreed to arbitrate. Instead, it held that "the arbitration provision by which Kloss waived her right of access to this State's courts, her right to a jury trial, her right to reasonable discovery, her right to findings of fact based on the evidence, and her right to enforce the law applicable to her case by way of appeal were clearly not within Kloss' reasonable expectations." And as a result, after pointing to the Montana state constitution's strong protection of the right to a jury trial, the court held that the arbitration clause in question was unconscionable and invalid under Montana contract law. The majority in *Kloss* explained that the FAA did not preempt the state law's strict protection of jury rights because the state law did not single out arbitration. Instead, Montana's protection of jury trial rights affected a wide array of different clauses that would have the effect of eliminating jury trials.

Most courts are likely to treat state laws that invalidate a subset of contracts (including arbitration contracts) as being preempted by the FAA. In examining the specifics of the state law in question, however, a court is likely to ask whether the state law is more like a law targeting arbitration, or a state law generally applicable to all contracts. The more it appears to be a general law affecting all contracts, the more likely the court is to uphold it against an assertion of federal preemption. It may not be surprising, however, to note that it was a state court in *Keystone* that held state law enforceable, while it was a federal court in *OPE International* that deemed state law preempted. Nor should it be surprising that different states (here, for example, Montana and Delaware) view arbitration differently.

§8.4.5 State Laws Enforcing Arbitration Clauses, but Only with Some Modifications or Restrictions

Some state laws target arbitration specifically, but cannot properly be characterized as singling out arbitration for wholesale hostile treatment like the laws described above in §8.4.3. Instead, these state laws provide for the enforcement of arbitration contracts — with some caveats or conditions. In general, the more onerous the conditions, the more likely a court is to view the state law as unlawfully in conflict with the federal law governing arbitration.

For example, the California Judicial Council promulgated a set of state ethics standards regarding arbitrators' disclosures. The standards required more disclosure than would be required under FAA §10 (the provision that spells out the bases upon which a court can vacate an arbitral award). In a high-profile dispute between Hollywood figures Michael Ovitz and Catherine Schulman, an arbitrator issued an award in favor of Ovitz. Schulman then sought to have the award vacated, after discovering that the arbitrator had not disclosed that he was engaged in arbitrating another dispute involving Ovitz's law firm. Schulman argued that disclosure of this relationship was required under the California arbitrator ethics rules, and Ovitz argued that the

FAA preempted the application of those rules. A California court of appeals sided with Schulman, finding that the state ethics rules do not

> reflect hostility to arbitration or an attempt to limit the ability to enter arbitration agreements. The California scheme seeks to enhance both the appearance and reality of fairness in arbitration proceedings, thereby instilling public confidence. With increased public confidence, arbitration is more attractive as a means of resolving private disputes. Hence, far from posing an obstacle to implementing the purpose of the FAA, [the disclosure requirement] actually *serves* that purpose.

Ovitz v. Schulman, 133 Cal. App. 4th 830, 35 Cal. Rptr. 3d 117 (App. 2 Dist. 2005).

As you might expect, however, this area of the law is evolving and filled with grey areas. Those seeking to enforce state laws affecting arbitration frame the laws as if they are mere "modifications" or "enhancements," arguing that they are consistent with the letter and the spirit of the FAA. Those seeking to avoid state laws affecting arbitration frame the laws as "hostile" to the FAA and to arbitration generally. The more tinkering a state attempts to do with the enforceability of arbitration contracts or arbitral awards, the more likely it is to be preempted under the FAA.

§8.5 WHAT IF THE PARTIES SPECIFICALLY *CHOOSE* TO HAVE STATE LAW GOVERN THE QUESTION?

A final potential complication in the law of arbitration preemption arises when the parties' contract specifies that a particular state's law should govern the resolution of the dispute. Choice of law clauses (for example, "this contract shall be governed by the law of Oklahoma") are common in modern contracts, and you probably encountered them in your Civil Procedure course. The idea behind a choice of law provision is to add clarity and predictability to the contract. Absent a choice of law provision, there is some risk that the parties will wind up fighting not only about what happened, but also about what body of law should govern the question of what should happen. And so these clauses are common, particularly in commercial contracts.

The arbitration wrinkle is quite easily illustrated this way: Assume the parties' contract specifies that the laws of State X will govern all disputes related to the contract. And now assume that certain laws in State X would disallow an arbitration clause that would otherwise be permitted under federal law. Which law controls?

Recall the two competing, important policies at play in this circumstance. On the one hand, the whole idea of arbitration is to permit parties, through the contracting process, to agree mutually to shape their own dispute resolution procedure. This logic would suggest that the state's law should be applied, because doing so permits the parties to "have their own way." On the other hand, the whole idea of the FAA is to prevent states from overriding parties' agreements to arbitrate. This logic would suggest that the state's law should be preempted, because doing so results in the case being resolved through arbitration.

The question turns on the choice of law provision. Choice of law provisions come in three basic flavors, two of which produce clear answers to the preemption question. In the third case, unfortunately, we are stuck with "it depends" — or its even-less-satisfying cousin, "it's hard to say."

§8.5.1 An Easy Case: The Parties Specify State Law Only as to Substance

Imagine that the parties' choice of law provision says simply, "If either party alleges that the other committed fraud in connection with this contract, we want our conduct to be judged against the standards set forth in State X's articulation of the law of fraud." In that case, if a dispute arose in which one party alleged that the other committed fraud, it is clear that the contract specifies State X law for determining whether the conduct in question constitutes fraud.

What if State X also had a set of arbitration laws that would cause some aspect of the parties' arbitration agreement to be nullified? It would not matter. This is a simple case of parties intending to arbitrate a dispute and state law trying to prevent them from doing so. Because the parties have not expressed an intention to be bound by state arbitration law, there is no conflict between the pro-arbitration federal law and the parties' autonomy. Federal law would preempt any such state law as easily as it did in the *Southland* case.

§8.5.2 Another Easy Case: The Parties Specify State Law as to Arbitration

Imagine that the parties' choice of law provision says simply, "If any dispute arises about the enforcement of any aspect of the arbitration clause in this contract, the laws of State X will govern the dispute, even if the effect of such law is to modify or nullify some aspects of this arbitration provision." In that case, if a dispute arose regarding the enforceability of the arbitration agreement, the laws of State X would govern. Even if the FAA would normally preempt the laws of State X, if the parties agreed specifically to have those state laws govern, no preemption problem arises. The parties' autonomy can be respected without offending the FAA's basic purpose of putting arbitration contracts on equal footing with all other contractual terms.

For example, imagine that two parties entering a contract include an arbitration clause and a choice of law provision specifying that the law of Kansas will govern "any and all disputes, including any disputes about the scope, meaning, or enforceability of the arbitration clause in this contract." Now imagine that under Kansas state law, arbitration agreements are unenforceable with respect to tort claims. If the parties had no choice of law provision, the Kansas law would clearly be preempted. (Think about *Southland* or *Casarotto*.) But with the choice of law provision, no preemption problem arises. The parties are, of course, free to negotiate the scope of their arbitration agreement, and they clearly would have had the authority to agree to exclude tort claims from the scope of the agreement. Given the choice of law clause, the Kansas state law would be treated as if the parties had spelled out, in their agreement, that the arbitration clause would not apply to tort claims. Therefore, no preemption problem arises.

§8.5.3 A More Complicated Case: The Parties' Choice of Law Provision Is Ambiguous About the Scope of Its Coverage

Imagine that the parties' choice of law provision is less precise and says simply, "All disputes regarding this contract shall be resolved pursuant to the laws of State X." What happens if a dispute arises, and one party challenges the enforceability of some aspect of the arbitration clause in the contract, pointing to State X laws? Should State X laws be applied (even though they are not entirely hospitable to arbitration)? Or should federal law preempt State X law (even though doing so ignores the parties' choice of law provision)?

This circumstance demands a tradeoff between the two competing policies underlying this area of the law. And what courts are most likely to do is to try to guess whether the parties' choice of law is more like the first easy category — choice of law as to substance — or the second easy category — choice of law as to arbitration. That is, a court will ask itself, "Did the parties intend to name State X law to govern just the substantive legal questions related to this dispute, or did they intend to incorporate State X arbitration law as well?"

In some circumstances, the state law in question will be such that the most reasonable assumption about the parties' intention is that the parties intended to incorporate the state laws' provisions into their arbitration agreement. For example, in *Volt Info. Sciences, Inc. v. Bd. of Trustees of Leland Stanford*

Junior Univ., 489 U.S. 468 (1989), the parties outlined broadly that California law would govern any disputes. A multiparty dispute arose, one piece of which involved parties who had not signed the arbitration agreement. As a result, some pieces of the dispute would be heard in arbitration, and some pieces would be heard before a court. The question became which pieces of the dispute would go first (with some of the parties obviously concerned about the prospect of preclusion, depending on the outcome of whichever went first). California state law authorized the court to stay the arbitration between some parties, pending the result of the litigation involving the other parties. Under the FAA, however, the court would not be entitled to stay the litigation. The Supreme Court upheld the trial court's decision to stay the arbitration, explaining that the parties' choice of law provision "incorporated California rules of arbitration into their arbitration agreement." In essence, the Court said this was more like easy category #2 above — that the parties intended for California's arbitration stay provisions to be available in the resolution of their disputes. The Court saw no FAA preemption problem here because "parties are generally free to structure their arbitration agreements as they see fit. Just as they may limit by contract the issues which they will arbitrate, so too may they specify by contract the rules under which that arbitration will be conducted."

In other circumstances, however, courts will view broad choice of law provisions as not intending to include state law *limitations* on arbitrators. For example, in *Mastrobuono v. Shearson Lehman Hutton, Inc.*, 514 U.S. 52 (1995), the parties designated New York law in their choice of law provision. A dispute arose, proceeded to arbitration, and the arbitrator awarded punitive damages against the defendant. The defendant sought to have the award vacated on the grounds that New York state law does not permit arbitrators to award punitive damages. The Supreme Court upheld the arbitrator's award, explaining that the parties' choice of law provision intended to include only "New York's substantive rights and obligations, and not the State's allocation of power between alternative tribunals." In other words, the Supreme Court believed that these parties intended for New York law to govern only substantive disputes (for example, what legal standards should be applied to determine whether a fraud occurred), not arbitration-related disputes (for example, what powers an arbitrator has).

Examples

1. **The Sweat Factory's Youthful Look.** The Sweat Factory is a fast-growing set of fitness center franchises, targeted at a young, urban clientele.

   Ben, a baby-faced 16-year old health fanatic, applied for a position as a fitness coach at the first Sweat Factory to open its doors in his home state. Nowhere on the employment application did the Sweat Factory ask about Ben's age, and he never mentioned it. In the course of filling out his application for employment, Ben did initial a box labeled "acknowledgment of receipt and acceptance of arbitration provisions." The arbitration provision contained in the contract mandates arbitration of "any and all disputes related to the applicant's employment or termination thereof."

Two weeks into his employment, Ben's boss fired him for "unprofessional and unacceptable personal hygiene." Ben sued the Sweat Factory for wrongful termination. The Sweat Factory filed a motion to compel arbitration, citing the employment agreement. Ben responded by revealing his age and claiming that the arbitration clause appearing in the contract is not binding on him as a matter of state law. The state in which Ben lives and worked provides that the age of majority for contract formation is 18. The Sweat Factory contends that the arbitration clause is binding on Ben because the FAA preempts the application of this state law in this case.

Will a court or an arbitrator hear the merits of Ben's claims against the Sweat Factory?

2. **That Isn't Just Sweat I Smell.** In a fit of post-holiday guilt, Jen decides to sign up for a membership at the Sweat Factory. After an unusually quick tour of the facilities, the manager of the Sweat Factory presents her with their standard membership form. He invites her to take it home and read it, but she insists on signing up immediately. Included in the membership agreement is an arbitration clause that reads, "The Member agrees to resolve any and all claims against the Sweat Factory through binding arbitration." Jen separately initialed the arbitration clause, signed the agreement, and paid the membership fees.

One week later, as she was working out, Jen noticed a curious musty odor and later contracted a severe cough. Her health deteriorated enough that she sought medical attention, and her doctors speculated that she had been exposed to extensive harmful mold. After a full recovery, she returned to the Sweat Factory and noticed that almost all of the walls and many of the machines had a thin (but disgusting) layer of mold on them. Jen also noticed that the Sweat Factory's posted health license had expired six months before her membership began.

Jen filed a lawsuit against the Sweat Factory, alleging improper maintenance and violations of the state health code. The Sweat Factory filed a motion to compel arbitration, citing Jen's membership agreement. Jen responded by arguing that the arbitration clause is unenforceable as a matter of state law because the Sweat Factory was unlicensed when she signed her membership agreement. Under the relevant state law, a consumer contract is per se unenforceable if it is issued by an unlicensed business. The Sweat Factory argues that the FAA preempts the application of state law in this case.

Who will hear the substance of Jen's claim against the Sweat Factory, an arbitrator or a court?

3. **Buy a Bottle, Get Arbitration for Free.** Veronica was passing by a Sweat Factory center one hot day when she noticed a stack of giant plastic "Sweat Factory Thirstquencher" water bottles in the window. She went inside and asked to purchase one of the enormous water bottles. Upon learning that Veronica was not a member of the Sweat Factory, the Sweat Factory cashier asked Veronica to sign a "Sweat Factory Non-Member Consumer Agreement" before selling her the bottle. The agreement consisted of nothing more than an arbitration clause providing that "any and all" disputes related to any consumer purchases at the Sweat Factory would be resolved through arbitration. Veronica signed the agreement, purchased the $10 water bottle, filled it with cold water, and went on her way.

   Later that day, Veronica became terribly sick, and she believes that her illness was caused by toxic chemicals leaching from the Sweat Factory water bottle. She filed a lawsuit against the Sweat Factory, and the Sweat Factory moved to compel arbitration, citing the consumer agreement.

   In preparing to oppose the motion to compel arbitration, Veronica's attorney discovered a state law that provides, in part, "As a matter of state law, no clause requiring the arbitration of a dispute will be enforceable if it is contained in a contract for purchase or sale of a consumer good costing less than $1,000."

   What effect is this state law likely to have on the enforceability of the arbitration agreement?

4. **Arbitration Clauses in the Small (Electronic) Print.** Archie, a perennial couch potato, saw a Sweat Factory advertisement on television late one night. Inspired, he immediately went online to sign up for a Sweat Factory membership. The membership agreement on the Sweat Factory website included an all-encompassing arbitration clause. Archie skimmed the agreement quickly and clicked "I accept."

   One month later, Archie was shocked to receive his first bill from the Sweat Factory. The bill included a $500 startup fee and a monthly fee of $150. Archie claims that the website included no mention of a startup fee, and that it listed the monthly fee as $15, rather than $150.

   Archie filed a lawsuit in state court against the Sweat Factory seeking treble damages under the state's consumer protection statute. The Sweat Factory moved to compel arbitration, citing the clause in the contract Archie "accepted" online. Archie opposes the motion to compel arbitration on the grounds that the state's consumer protection laws specifically require that any arbitration clause be separately signed (if it is in hard copy) or be separately accepted (for example, by clicking a separate "I accept" button in a popup window, if the contract was entered online). Here, Archie argues, he neither signed nor separately accepted the arbitration clause.

Will the state consumer protection law help Archie to avoid having his claim heard in arbitration?

5. **Fraud and the Franchisee.** Betty, an aspiring entrepreneur with a passion for fitness, decided to open a Sweat Factory franchise. The franchise agreement between Betty and General Urban Training Corporation (GutCo), the owner and franchisor of the Sweat Factory fitness centers, included a broad arbitration clause.

Betty's operation of her first Sweat Factory franchise did not have nearly the success she expected. She stopped paying the franchise fees set forth in her agreement with GutCo. GutCo then filed a claim against her in arbitration, consistent with the terms of the franchise agreement.

Betty intends to file a counterclaim against GutCo, alleging fraud in the financial projections GutCo provided to her as a prospective franchisee. She would prefer, however, for the entire dispute to be litigated, rather than arbitrated.

Betty files a motion to stay the arbitration, citing a state law that expressly prohibits franchise agreements from containing binding arbitration clauses. Will Betty's motion to stay the arbitration succeed, in light of the state law on point?

6. **How to Waive a Jury.** Ricardo signed a membership agreement with the Sweat Factory. Buried deep in the membership agreement was an arbitration clause requiring "any and all disputes" related to Ricardo's membership to be resolved through binding arbitration.

After Ricardo failed to pay his monthly fee, the Sweat Factory imposed a fine of $1,000 on Ricardo, along with a notice that the fine would increase exponentially if it went unpaid. Ricardo claims that the fine is a violation of the membership agreement, and he thinks it may violate state usury laws as well. He files a complaint in state court against the Sweat Factory, and the Sweat Factory moves to compel arbitration.

In opposing the motion to compel arbitration, Ricardo cites a State Supreme Court decision in which the court struck down a jury waiver provision in a consumer contract. In that case, the State Supreme Court wrote:

> Our state's constitution tolerates the enforcement of a contractual waiver of the right to a jury only when such waiver is entered voluntarily, knowingly, and intelligently. Further, such waiver must clearly, unequivocally, and unambiguously express a waiver of this right.

What, if any, effect is the State Supreme Court's decision on jury waivers likely to have on the motion to compel arbitration in Ricardo's case?

Explanations

1. **The Sweat Factory's Youthful Look.** The question here hinges entirely on whether the FAA preempts the state contract law defining the age of majority for contract formation. The arbitration clause in the contract clearly covers this dispute, and no other potential contract defects appear in the facts to make us question whether the claim should head to arbitration. If state law declares Ben, a minor, to be incapable of entering this contract, he will be able to have his claim heard in court. If, however, the FAA were to preempt the application of the state majority law, Ben will be bound by the terms of the contract and an arbitrator would hear the merits of his claim.

   Here, the state law in question does nothing to target or single out arbitration. Instead, this state law declares the age of majority for any contract formation. The law applies to all contracts in all contexts — including arbitration agreements. As such, it is entirely consistent with the FAA because its application strikes down arbitration contracts only on a ground that "exist[s] at law or in equity for the revocation of any contract." (Recall that this language is drawn directly from FAA §2.) Because preemption kicks in only when a conflict arises between federal law and state law, the FAA does nothing to disrupt the application of this state law.

2. **That Isn't Just Sweat I Smell.** If, as Jen asserts, the relevant state law is applicable to all consumer contracts involving unlicensed businesses, the FAA will not preempt the state law. Under the FAA's terms, an arbitration contract must be enforced "save upon such grounds as exist at law or in equity for the revocation of *any* contract." The state law rendering these contracts unenforceable renders *any* contract unenforceable — not just arbitration contracts. As a result, Jen should prevail in her efforts to have the merits decided by a court rather than an arbitrator.

3. **Buy a Bottle, Get Arbitration for Free.** The state law is unlikely to have any effect, because it is almost certainly preempted by the FAA. The state law singles out arbitration for nonenforcement, and, therefore, does not treat arbitration clauses on par with other contractual provisions. This is precisely the kind of state law the Supreme Court has determined to offend the FAA. The state law treats arbitration provisions less favorably than it treats all contract provisions. As a result, it conflicts with FAA §2 and its application will be preempted in this case.

   If Veronica wants to avoid arbitration, therefore, she will need to find a basis other than this state consumer protection statute. Recall from Chapter 6 that a party to a contract containing an arbitration clause can challenge the enforcement of that clause on any of the bases one can use to challenge *any* contract. So, for example, Veronica might make an argument that the arbitration clause is unenforceable because it is unconscionable. She might argue that arbitration would be so expensive, when compared with the small amount in controversy, that it risks depriving all consumers of any potential remedy. As we discussed in Chapter 6, some courts have been willing to void arbitration clauses that necessarily involve inordinately high expenses.

4. **Arbitration Clauses in the Small (Electronic) Print.** The state law will not prevent the enforcement of the arbitration clause in Archie's case. The state law here is inconsistent with the Supreme Court's interpretation of the FAA because it forces arbitration clauses to adhere to higher standards than all other contract provisions. As such, it will be preempted.

5. **Fraud and the Franchisee.** Betty will be bound by the arbitration clause appearing in her franchise agreement with GutCo.

    It is easy to understand why the state may have an interest in protecting franchisees, given their relative lack of sophistication in most circumstances. And it may be easy to understand why a state would view arbitration clauses drafted by franchisors skeptically. As a policy matter, the state law may make sense. The problem for Betty is that *Southland* clearly held such anti-arbitration laws to be inconsistent with the FAA.

6. **How to Waive a Jury.** It probably depends on the jurisdiction. Some courts treat arbitration clauses as a form of jury waiver, and subject them to the same strictures as other jury waivers. Others view arbitration clauses as enforceable even in contexts in which other kinds of agreements that have the effect of eliminating the jury would not be upheld. If Ricardo is in a jurisdiction that treats arbitration clauses as a form of jury waiver, he may argue that his agreement did not satisfy the state law requirements for jury waivers.

    Therefore, if Ricardo's state strongly protects against jury waivers, he may succeed in arguing that the arbitration clause in question is unenforceable as a matter of state law. He would then argue that the state law is generally applicable to all contracts (including arbitration contracts) and would seek its enforcement. Whether he would succeed in this argument depends on where he lives.

CHAPTER 9

Dispute Resolution Within the Court System

§9.1 INTRODUCTION

Even though your law school probably teaches dispute resolution as a separate course from those courses focused on litigation, dispute resolution and litigation are in many ways inextricably linked in modern practice. It is inaccurate to assume that ADR is what happens outside of a courthouse and litigation is what happens inside a courthouse. The judiciary is involved in both formal and informal ADR conduct. Sometimes, judges engage in mediation-like behaviors in an effort to resolve disputes. Other times, judges or other court personnel suggest that litigants consider using the services of one or another ADR provider to search for possible settlements. And of course, private negotiations and settlement efforts take place "in the shadow" of what each party expects a court might do with the case.

In this chapter, we focus on the most intertwined version of this relationship between the judiciary and various forms of dispute resolution: court-ordered ADR. First, we examine the sources of courts' authority to compel parties to engage in ADR. Second, we consider the boundaries of courts' authority, looking at what courts can and cannot order. Third, we focus on the requirements of participation and what "good-faith" participation entails. And finally, we look at what happens when parties disobey a court's order to participate in ADR.

§9.2 WHY A COURT HAS THE AUTHORITY TO ORDER ADR

At some point, virtually every parent has asserted the authority to impose some unwanted restriction, deadline, or responsibility on an offspring, citing the authority, "Because I said so, and because I am your mother/father." Judicial authority, at least theoretically, is more limited than this vision of parental authority. If the court is compelling litigants to participate in ADR, some rule, statute, or common law principle must give the court the authority to do so.

In re *Atlantic Pipe Co.*, 304 F.3d 135 (1st Cir. 2002), provides a useful survey of the possible basis of judicial authority to order ADR. In that case, the First Circuit Court of Appeals listed four potential sources of authority for a court to order mediation: (1) the Federal Rules of Civil Procedure; (2) applicable federal statutes; (3) a court's local rules; and (4) the court's inherent powers. Below, we examine each of these four sources. We also note that a fifth source, state rules, provide the foundation for the vast array of ADR processes made available in state judicial systems.

§9.2.1 Federal Rules of Civil Procedure

Rule 16 has been on the books ever since the adoption of the Federal Rules of Civil Procedure in 1938. In its original form, Rule 16 provided for relatively straightforward judicial conferences in which judges and litigants set expectations about the nature, schedule, and boundaries of the forthcoming litigation. For example, Rule 16 conferences routinely produce a limit on certain discovery practices and a timetable for dispositive motions. In 1983, however, Rule 16(a) was amended to include the explicit suggestion that these Rule 16 conferences also be used for the purpose of "facilitating the settlement of the case." On the basis of Rule 16(a), judges have seen fit to engage in a variety of activities to promote the settlement of claims.

Rule 16(c) also explicitly anticipates the creation of local rules concerning ADR, stating that "courts may take appropriate action, with respect to . . . (9) settlement and the use of special procedures to assist in resolving the dispute when authorized by statute or local rule." Courts have interpreted "appropriate action" to include not only encouraging, but also requiring that litigants engage in ADR. Once these local rules (which we discuss below) exist, Rule 16 authorizes the court to order the parties to use ADR procedures.

§9.2.2 Federal Statutes and Local Rules

A second potential source of a court's authority to compel participation in ADR comes from federal statutes such as the Civil Justice Reform Act of 1990 and the subsequent Alternative Dispute Resolution (ADR) Act of 1998. The Civil Justice Reform Act of 1990 created pilot programs in which federal courts required ADR programs. The ADR Act of 1998 extended the pilot programs to all federal jurisdictions. In fact, the ADR Act, 28 U.S.C. §652, requires that each federal district establish some type of dispute resolution system for the cases within its jurisdiction and that the district court "require that litigants in all civil cases consider the use of an alternative dispute resolution process at an appropriate stage in the litigation."

Based on this requirement, each federal district has established an ADR system. In some cases, the system includes a brief protocol for a single ADR process. For example, in the court-annexed mediation program for the Eastern District of Pennsylvania, the local rules include guidelines about the selection and training of mediators, the assignment of cases, and the mediation process. The mediation may be ordered by the judge or requested by the parties. In other jurisdictions, like the local rules for the courts in the Ninth Circuit, the model rules for district courts include descriptions of a wide range of ADR processes, case management rules, pre-process requirements, and far more detail about the options available to litigants. In these and many other jurisdictions, local rules explicitly authorize judges to order the parties to some type of ADR process. Some local rules go further and spell out the requirements of that participation as well as sanctions for violating the court order to participate in ADR.

§9.2.3 The Court's Inherent Powers

The most sweeping source of judicial authority to order the parties to pursue settlement opportunities may well lie in the inherent power of the court. For example, in In re Atlantic Pipe Co., described above, the parties were involved in a complex web of claims and counterclaims originating from the failure of a massive public works construction project. Hoping to simplify matters, the district judge ordered the parties to participate in mediation and to share the costs of mediation equally. One of the parties objected and claimed the district court did not have the authority to order participation on these terms, even though the mediation itself would be nonbinding. The Court of Appeals noted that the district court had the power to enact local rules pursuant to either a statutory provision or under the ADR Act of 1998. Further, the court stated that even in the absence of these forms of authority, the district court could order mediation through its inherent judicial powers. The Court of Appeals qualified this grant of discretionary power by asserting that when the district court uses this inherent power to mandate mediation, the mediation must include certain safeguards. The opinion in *In re Atlantic Pipe Co.* suggested that a court's inherent powers are constrained by

> at least four limiting principles. First, inherent powers must be used in a way reasonably suited to the enhancement of the court's processes, including the orderly and expeditious disposition of pending cases. Second, inherent powers cannot be exercised in a manner that contradicts an applicable statute or rule. Third, the use of inherent powers must comport with procedural fairness. And, finally, inherent powers "must be exercised with restraint and discretion."

The Court of Appeals held that the mediation in this case must have a time limit and that the mediator's fees must be capped at a reasonable amount. This case illustrates that courts are given substantial discretion in mandating mediation as long as they order a reasonable process.

§9.2.4 State ADR Systems

Many states have adopted one or more ADR systems in association with their courts. Some states mandate forms of nonbinding ADR for entire categories of cases. In California, for example, the civil procedure code requires mediation for all civil cases valued at less than $50,000. Texas allows judges discretion to order mediation in any civil cases. In Minnesota, all parties in civil cases are required to discuss ADR options, and the court has the authority to require an ADR process at its discretion. So some states have been far ahead of the federal courts in their development of ADR systems, and others have relatively less robust ADR systems in place. Most important, you should keep in mind that court-ordered ADR is not a uniquely federal phenomenon.

---

§9.3 WHAT A COURT CANNOT COMPEL THE PARTIES TO DO

As outlined in the section above, courts frequently do have the authority to order litigants to participate in certain nonbinding forms of ADR. To help to give shape to the scope of that authority, we begin by exploring that which a court cannot do.

§9.3.1 A Court Can't Make Me Settle!

It may sound obvious, but we start with the basic proposition that a court cannot (under *any* of the sources of authority listed above) compel litigants to settle. A court cannot, therefore, order litigants to mediation and threaten to hold them in contempt if they fail to settle their case. Similarly, in the context of a judicial settlement conference, a judge can try to persuade parties to settle, but cannot force them to do so under threat of penalty. For example, in *Kothe v. Smith*, 771 F.2d 667 (2d Cir. 1985), the trial court judge, in a pretrial conference, suggested that the $2 million claim should be settled for between $20,000 and $30,000. The plaintiff indicated to the judge that she would accept an offer in that range, but the judge never communicated this willingness to the defendant. The defendant did not settle the claim in the pretrial conference, but did later make a $5,000 offer (which the plaintiff refused). After one day of the trial, the defendant offered to settle the case for $20,000, and the claim settled. The trial court judge then imposed sanctions on the defendant, citing the defendant's unwillingness to settle earlier during the pretrial conference. On appeal, the Second Circuit described the settlement process as complex and ruled that sanctions for a failure to settle were inappropriate, especially since the plaintiff's indication that it would be willing to settle in that range was never expressed to the defendant. The court stated that Rule 16 "was not designed as a means for clubbing the parties — or one of them — into an involuntary compromise." The courts can order the parties to the bargaining table and require the parties have the authority to settle, but the court cannot require a settlement.

§9.3.2 A Court Can't Make Me Make an Offer!

The court also cannot require the parties to make an offer. In *Avril v. Civilmar*, 605 So. 2d 988 (Fla. Dist. Ct. App. 1992), the defendant offered $1,000 in mediation to settle the plaintiff's claims against him, stemming from an automobile accident. The defendant's explanation for the relatively low offer (the plaintiff had demanded $2 million) was that the plaintiff had suffered only soft tissue injuries, and the defendant and his insurer had not yet conducted an investigation in the two months since the accident. Upon motion from the plaintiff's attorney, the Florida trial court imposed sanctions on the defendant for not acting in good faith during the mediation and for delaying the investigation. An appellate court overturned that ruling, stating that the "plaintiff's only basis for sanctions is merely that defendants were unwilling to make an offer of settlement satisfactory to him. . . . There is no requirement that a party even make an offer at mediation, let alone offer what the opposition wants to settle." Thus, a court can order parties to mediation, but it cannot punish parties who fail to make an offer or fail to make an offer that is attractive to the other party.

§9.3.3 A Court Can't Force the Terms of an Offer (But Can Punish Me If I Turn Down a Good Offer)!

Although it is true that a court cannot order parties to make offers or to accept particular terms of an agreement, many judges and many policies strongly "encourage" parties to settle. And in some cases, that "encouragement" may be so strong that parties wind up feeling real pressure to resolve their claims. An example of permissible "encouragement" appears in offer-of-judgment provisions such as the one found in Federal Rule of Civil Procedure 68. Under Rule 68, if

1. a defendant makes an offer of settlement in writing,
2. the plaintiff rejects that offer,
3. the dispute goes forward in litigation, and
4. the plaintiff's eventual recovery is less than the defendant's prior offer of settlement,

the plaintiff has to pay the court costs and fees the defendant incurred after the date of the offer of judgment. Many states also have offer-of-judgment statutes in their rules of civil procedure, and they tend to operate in similar ways. For example, assume that the defendant offers to settle the dispute with the plaintiff for $50,000 on October 15. The plaintiff refuses and takes the dispute through litigation. On December 15, at the conclusion of trial, the plaintiff is only awarded $20,000. The plaintiff is now responsible for paying the defendant's costs incurred from October 15 to December 15, excluding attorneys' fees.

The theory behind an offer-of-judgment rule is twofold. First, the rule is supposed to discourage plaintiffs from rejecting reasonable offers. On the theory that some cases persist needlessly in court because plaintiffs have fantasies about jackpot juries, offer-of-judgment statutes can provide extra incentive for a plaintiff not to roll the dice. If plaintiffs are punished for continuing through litigation when they should have accepted the offer, they will be more likely to accept the offer. Second, this rule is also designed to encourage defendants to make a reasonable offer and to make it sooner rather than later. (A defendant's incentive is to offer early, of course, so as to maximize the costs and fees potentially recovered if the plaintiff inappropriately turns down the offer.)

The parties must meet both express and implicit requirements in order to trigger Rule 68 protection. First, the offer must be made in writing. Second, the offer of settlement must have been presented to the plaintiff in a timely manner, as determined by each jurisdiction (under the federal rule, at least ten days before trial begins). Third, the terms of the offer must be clear. Finally, if the plaintiff is planning to accept the offer, this acceptance must be unconditional and in writing. Note that once trial commences, the offer is automatically withdrawn and inadmissible as evidence. Prior to trial, however, the defendant can make additional offers, with each offer being subject to the same conditions.

Offer-of-judgment statutes, therefore, represent an example of "encouraging" settlement (which is permitted), without imposing particular terms of settlement (which is not permitted).

§9.4 WHAT A COURT CAN COMPEL THE PARTIES TO DO

§9.4.1 A Court Can Compel a Particular (Nonbinding) Form of ADR

Up until now, we have largely been speaking of the court's authority to order litigants to go through *some* form of ADR. In certain jurisdictions, this is all that courts do. The court presents litigants with a menu of different ADR options and says, in effect, "Choose one, and don't come back until you've given it a try." In other jurisdictions, courts order litigants to participate in a particular form of ADR — either one mandated for all litigants or one specially selected by the judge for the particular case in question.

In all cases, the courts' authority to compel participation in ADR mechanisms is limited to nonbinding forms of ADR. A court order compelling parties to engage in binding ADR would amount to a deprivation of the litigants' opportunity to present their claims in court. In some cases, this would violate the litigants' right to a jury trial (a right that is available in only certain circumstances of civil litigation, contrary to popular belief). In all events, such an order would violate the litigants' due process rights. As a result, courts may only compel nonbinding forms of ADR.

§9.4.1.1 Mediation

One of the most recognizable forms of court-ordered ADR is mediation. As we discuss in Chapter 3 in this book, mediation can take many different forms, and the court-ordered versions are no different. Litigants sent to court-ordered mediation must still navigate strategic and practical issues about mediator selection and type of mediation. Further, the court systems ordering mediation must carefully consider the mechanisms for providing adequate judicial supervision of the mediation system. Many of the issues raised elsewhere in this book about quality control in mediation and about confidentiality become even more salient when a court is overseeing the process. Some jurisdictions have created rosters of mediators and established certain qualifications (training, education, experience, etc.), trying to ensure that parties have a quality mediation experience. Courts are also concerned with the type of participation that parties have in a court-ordered process, and we will examine this issue of good-faith participation later in this section.

§9.4.1.2 Nonbinding Arbitration

A second major form of ADR to which litigants are frequently ordered to attend is nonbinding arbitration. As you learned earlier, an arbitration (even a nonbinding one) looks much like a trial. It involves a decision maker, similar to a judge, who hears the arguments of each side and then renders a decision. Nonbinding arbitrations rarely have all of the formality of court and are commonly designed to move quickly and efficiently. For example, because parties often believe that arbitrators have sufficient expertise to assess evidence appropriately, without formal exclusionary rules, arbitrations often proceed with more relaxed (and speedier) evidentiary rules.

Unlike court-ordered mediation, which largely reflects the broad diversity of private mediation processes, court-ordered arbitration is less diverse than its private counterpart. The most significant distinction is that court-ordered arbitration is always nonbinding. As you read earlier in this book, many forms of private arbitration are binding. Although binding arbitration serves as a substitute for litigation, nonbinding arbitration merely supplements it.

Why would litigants want to go through arbitration if the arbitrator's decision is not binding? First, there is some chance that the arbitration process will satisfy the range of different interests the litigants may have in bringing their claims. It may provide them with an opportunity to tell their stories, to confront their counterparts, and to hear the opinion of an impartial third party. That alone could make the process worthwhile to some litigants. Second, the opinion of the arbitrator provides useful information to both parties about how their cases are perceived, and this might push the parties to settle.

Third, nonbinding arbitration can have an effect on litigants because the order to participate in it frequently includes a cost-shifting mechanism similar to the one we described with respect to offer-of-judgment rules like Rule 68. For example, in *Richardson v. Sport Shinko*, 880 P.2d 169 (Haw. 1994), a nonbinding arbitrator issued a $60,000 award in favor of the plaintiffs to compensate for an injury suffered at the defendant's hotel. Dissatisfied with the amount, the plaintiffs demanded a trial *de novo*, but at trial, the jury found entirely in favor of the hotel. Immediately after the trial, the defendant filed a motion for sanctions under a Hawaii statute that provides for recovery in the event the party demanding a trial *de novo* fails to improve upon the arbitrator's award by a certain percentage. The Hawaii Supreme Court upheld the sanctions against the plaintiffs in this case. And as a result, in lieu of receiving the $60,000 the arbitrator ruled they should receive, the plaintiffs wound up *owing* the defendants more than $5,000.

§9.4.1.3 Early Neutral Evaluation

Early neutral evaluation (ENE) is another form of nonbinding arbitration that can be ordered by the court. The ADR Act of 1998 specifically mentions the possibility of courts adopting rules regarding ENE, and many have done so. ENE is typically even more casual than nonbinding arbitration, although it operates similarly in some regards. For example, ENE parties prepare memos, outline the dispute and their respective legal positions, and give short explanations of their desired outcomes to an evaluator. The evaluator (who is typically selected on the basis of significant prior experience with similar cases) can ask questions before rendering a written case evaluation. The evaluation, in most cases, takes the form of a prediction—either a specific figure the evaluator believes represents the likely recovery at trial, or the range the evaluator determines is the most reasonable, under the circumstances. In this regard, this process resembles evaluative mediation (discussed in Chapter 3 on mediation). The ENE highlights both the legal merits of each party's position and the likely outcome of litigation. The parties can then use the evaluation as the settlement or use this information to pursue a different agreement.

§9.4.1.4 Summary Jury Trials

A summary jury trial differs from a regular trial in two important ways. First, as the name suggests, it is a shorter version of trial. Typically, each side is permitted a short amount of time in which to present its best case, and then a jury deliberates and renders a decision. The second important distinction is that the jury's verdict is nonbinding. The jury often knows that its verdict is nonbinding, although in some cases the jury deliberates believing it is a "regular" jury, rather than a jury for a summary trial.

Like nonbinding arbitration and ENE, the principal intention of a summary jury trial is to promote settlement. However, unlike nonbinding arbitration, summary jury trials virtually never include a cost-shifting mechanism. Instead, they typically seek to promote settlement by requiring the principals or key decision makers from each side to attend the summary jury trial. The theory is that the lawyers' clients may be more inclined to settle once they have seen the other side's best arguments presented to a jury and heard the jury's interpretation of those best arguments.

§9.4.2 A Court Can (But Doesn't Always) Compel Good-Faith Participation

When two disputants appear in a binding dispute resolution process, like litigation or arbitration, there is good reason to imagine that each disputant will take the matter seriously. After all, if they do not, the decision maker is more likely to find against them, given the adversarial nature of those proceedings. Further, the decision maker in each of those binding processes typically has the ability to penalize bad behavior that goes beyond simple inattention or lack of seriousness.

When two parties voluntarily agree to engage in an ADR process, there is also at least some reason to believe that they will engage in the process seriously. After all, they are there because they choose to be there. Each party can walk away whenever it wants to do so. What would be the point of behaving badly? Unfortunately, even in voluntary ADR processes, there is some risk that one or both of the parties will seek to use the process for a purpose other than settlement. At worst, a party might use an ADR process as a "fishing expedition," to try to assess the other side's case before trial. Or a party might use an ADR process as a means of delaying trial, or to harass the other side, or to drive up expenses.

But when courts *order* parties into nonbinding ADR processes, there is even more reason to worry about potential abuse and bad behavior. We are *not* suggesting that ADR only works if both parties behave well and like each other. Few disputants like each other much by the time a dispute reaches the point of litigation. And many parties, driven by all that unhappiness and by strategic or competitive considerations, act in less than helpful ways during the course of an ADR process. If the success of ADR processes hinged on the parties behaving perfectly, ADR processes would virtually never be all that useful. But there is some boundary beyond which parties' behavior is certain to scuttle the effectiveness of any ADR process. What would it mean to say that a court can order parties to ADR, but the parties are then free to engage in behavior that thwarts any chance the ordered ADR process has of producing a settlement?

Thus, in the context of court-ordered ADR in particular, we see a clash of policy interests. On the one side, you have the interest in preserving the integrity of the court's order and in promoting settlement through nonbinding ADR mechanisms. On the other side, you have the interest in preserving the parties' autonomy and control over the fate of their own dispute.

The policy response to these considerations, in many jurisdictions, has been to permit courts to order nonbinding ADR processes in which the parties are compelled to participate "in good faith." At least two dozen states currently have a good faith statutory requirement, and a similar number of federal district courts have adopted local rules with a "good faith" requirement.

§9.4.2.1 What Constitutes Good-Faith Participation?

There are plenty of reasons why parties might not settle a lawsuit. They might believe that the case is important to take to trial in order to establish some principle. They might paint themselves into a corner publicly in a way that makes settlement too costly. They might hate each other so much that they cannot bring themselves to agree to anything. They might have terrible attorneys giving them bad advice. They might lack sufficient information, or resources, or time, or authority to reach a deal. They might not be sufficiently creative to see their way through the problem.

As we noted above, courts cannot compel parties to settle. What courts *can* do, through the mechanism of a good-faith requirement, is remove at least some of the potential barriers to settlement. For example, we might reasonably imagine that a case is less likely to settle if one of the parties is absent, if one of the parties is unprepared, or if one of the parties lacks the authority to reach an agreement. Courts have, therefore, focused on the elements of attendance, preparation, and authority in shaping the legal boundaries of what constitutes good-faith participation.

Attendance at the mediation is the easiest item to measure in terms of good faith, and courts have consistently found that failing to show up to an ordered mediation constitutes bad faith. For example, in *Graham v. Baker*, 447 N.W.2d 397 (Iowa 1989), a seller was commencing forfeiture proceedings against a buyer who had defaulted on installment payments for the land. Pursuant to a statute requiring parties to such disputes to "participate" in mediation, they began mediation. Once at the mediation, the seller's attorney, Flagg, insisted that the entire matter was "non-negotiable." A court reviewing the debtors' objection to Flagg's behavior wrote:

> Flagg's behavior, which ranged between acrimony and truculency, precluded any beneficial result to the parties from the mediation process. It has cost his clients considerable time and expense. Nevertheless, his inappropriate behavior is not determinative. We find that Flagg's presence at the mediation meeting satisfied the minimal participation required by the statute.

Clearly, a court would not deem *every* absence to constitute a sanctionable lack of good-faith participation. But having a good excuse after the fact is far less likely to be forgiven than having a good excuse beforehand and seeking the court's approval for your absence. For example, in *Hernando County School Bd. v. Nazar*, 920 So. 2d 794 (Fla. Dist. Ct. App. 2006), a party and his attorney both failed to appear at a court-ordered mediation. When the party who did appear filed a motion for sanctions, the absent party explained that he was out of town assisting relatives victimized by a hurricane, and his attorney informed the court that he had experienced medical problems requiring a doctor's appointment. The court nevertheless imposed sanctions for failure to attend, indicating that the parties should have cleared their absences in advance of the mediation, rather than after the fact. Another court took the same basic approach in *Raad v. Wal-Mart Stores, Inc.*, 1998 WL 272879, 1998 U.S. Dist. LEXIS 11881, a case in which some of the parties unexpectedly telephoned into a mediation session, rather than appearing in person. The court held that mere telephone presence was not in compliance with the requirement to attend mediation, but left open the possibility that if telephone presence had been discussed prior to the mediation, it may have been allowed.

A second component of good faith participation hinges on the **preparation** each party has engaged in prior to the ADR process. For example, two disputants (or even worse, two attorneys for two disputants) who show up to a mediation without really understanding the nature of the case or the relevant interests have little chance of engaging in the process in a meaningful way. Preparation, however, is not always easy to measure. For the most part, therefore, courts reviewing complaints based on inadequate preparation look at externally verifiable forms of preparation. For example, if a mediator has requested a premediation memorandum, experts' reports, or other preparation in advance, failure to comply will be treated as an example of bad faith participation.

A third component of good faith participation in the context of ADR relates to assuring that those who attend the mediation have sufficient **settlement authority** to make resolution possible. A mediation in which the CEOs of each company are present is far more likely to settle than one in which one side sends only the summer intern from the accounting department. In *G. Heileman Brewing Co. v. Joseph Oat Co.*, 871 F.2d 648 (7th Cir. 1989), the court specifically ordered corporate representatives with settlement authority to appear at a pretrial settlement conference. Upholding this order, the Seventh Circuit declared the power to compel participation to be within the court's "inherent authority." This holding has been extended to other court-ordered ADR processes as well. Although the court cannot force the parties to settle, this requirement seeks to assure that mediation at least has a possibility of reaching a settlement.

Measuring good faith is more difficult when the conduct in question is more subjective. Is it bad faith to have a nasty attitude? Is it bad faith to seem disengaged? Is it bad faith not to listen carefully? And so on. Trying to punish behavior like this poses at least two significant challenges. First, it raises considerable questions of proof. Demonstrating that I was not at the mediation is one thing. Demonstrating that I was not paying careful attention is quite another. Second, complicating all of this is the question of confidentiality. In almost all jurisdictions, mediators are barred (because of confidentiality considerations) from testifying about mediation parties' behavior.

Foxgate Homeowners' Ass'n v. Bramalea, 25 P.3d 1117 (Cal. 2001), provides a useful example of the tension between enforcing good-faith requirements and maintaining confidentiality. The plaintiff homeowners' association brought a claim for a construction defect against the developer Bramalea. After working with the parties for several months, the mediator scheduled a five-day mediation session to which both sides were ordered to bring experts and claims representatives. The parties were also supposed to serve experts' reports on each other before the mediation. On the first morning, the plaintiff showed up with its attorney and nine experts. In contrast, the defendant's attorney showed up 30 minutes late and with no experts. When the defendant would not promise to show up with experts at any time, the subsequent mediation sessions were cancelled. The mediator filed a report with the court supporting plaintiff's motion for sanctions, detailing the attorney's "obstructive bad-faith tactics," and then resigned from the case. The California Supreme Court held that, under the relevant California confidentiality statute, a mediator is not allowed to report sanctionable bad faith behavior. Here, the court had no problem with the concept of sanctioning what was clearly a series of nonappearances and failure to comply with even the most basic premediation discovery orders. Yet the issue of who reports this bad faith was problematic, and the court held that the rules concerning confidentiality trumped the interest of good faith participation.

A second challenge in seeking to punish bad behavior in mediations is the risk that doing so will create unmanageable and unwise restrictions on parties' autonomy. Some parties will choose to adopt a problem-solving stance in bargaining. Some will be passive. Some will be aggressive. And some will engage in "hard bargaining." Parties are (and must be) permitted to choose their approach to negotiating with their counterparts. Hard bargaining, or even obnoxious behavior, might not be pleasant, and we do not even think it is very effective in most circumstances. (See Chapter 1 on negotiation.) But that does not mean that the behavior is (or should be) subject to sanction.

Even an explicit good faith requirement does not mean that a party has to give up on its positions or cave in to the other party. It is certainly not bad faith for someone to bargain hard to get a favorable settlement. For example, in Hunt v. Woods, 1996 WL 8037, 1996 U.S. App. LEXIS 1420 (6th Cir. 1996), the plaintiff, Hunt, was injured in a car accident, and sued Woods, the driver of the other car, for damages. Hunt and Woods were sent to pretrial mediation to try to work out a settlement. Woods's attorney attended the mediation with authorization to settle for some amount less than the limit of Woods' $25,000 policy. Hunt, however, entered mediation with a firm anchor of not less than $25,000. The mediator told Woods that that it would be a waste of time to make an offer below that anchor point. Agreeing, Woods did not respond to Hunt's $25,000 proposal. The case went to trial, where Woods stipulated to liability and Hunt was awarded $37,000. Hunt then tried to get pretrial interest, arguing that because Woods knew he didn't have a defense against his liability, and because he didn't make a settlement offer, he was not mediating in good faith.

On appeal, the court rejected the idea that Woods was bargaining in bad faith. The court noted that he entered mediation prepared to make an offer, but was convinced by the mediator that anything below $25,000 would be rejected out of hand. Woods adopted a strategy that, ultimately, may have been unwise. But it was not evidence of bad faith.

Hard bargaining with a nominal offer of settlement can also be perfectly defensible. In *Gray v. Eggert*, 635 N.W.2d 667 (Wis. Ct. App. 2001), a school bus driven by Gray and a county transit bus driven by Eggert collided. Gray sued for damages, but Eggert denied all liability, arguing that the school bus had run into him while he was stopped, and any injuries she sustained were due to her own negligence. The trial court ordered the two parties to mediation, where Eggert stuck to his assertion that he was not liable. Gray offered to settle for $5,000, and Eggert responded by offering $100. The trial court then imposed sanctions on Eggert for failing to make a good faith effort to settle. The appeals court, however, overturned this decision, holding that although the trial court could order mediation, it could not require that the parties settle, nor could the trial court judge (who was not present at the mediation) use the nominal settlement offer as evidence that Eggert was acting in bad faith.

§9.4.2.2 What Happens to Those Who Cross the Line?

If a judge finds that a party has acted in bad faith, the judge has considerable discretion in crafting an appropriate sanction. Typically, the judge chooses a sanction designed to make the aggrieved party whole. For example, in *Raad v. Wal-Mart Stores, Inc.*, discussed previously, Wal-Mart failed to follow the judge's order to mediate when it did not send a representative with settlement authority to the mediation. The trial court judge issued penalties that included the plaintiff's attorneys' fees, the expense of bringing the motion for sanctions, the money the defendant saved by not sending someone to the mediation, and the costs to other litigants from the court taking time to resolve this motion and not other cases. The trial judge in this case was mainly concerned with returning all of the adversely affected parties to their financial situations prior to the failed mediation.

On occasion, the penalties can be far more severe for failure to participate in good faith. At the far end of the spectrum of sanctions, some incidents of bad faith result in dismissal or default. For example, in *Triad Mack Sales & Serv. v. Clement Bros. Co.*, 438 S.E.2d 485 (N.C. Ct. App. 1994), the court ordered each party to send someone with settlement authority to a mediation session. The defendant failed to do so. In a hearing on sanctions, the attorney for the defendant offered only an unsworn statement that the president of the defendant corporation was ill and that "all other officers, directors, and employees were out of state." The court issued an order striking the defendant's answer and placing the defendant company in default. The appellate court reviewing an appeal of the order acknowledged that the trial court judge could have crafted a lesser sanction, but upheld the default as falling within the discretion of the trial court judge.

Examples

Snow White has been the talented and trusted bookkeeper for the Seven Dwarfs for many years. Keeping track of the Dwarfs' spending habits, while managing the accounting of their diamond mining business, is not easy. Snow White was under the impression that every year she would receive a salary increase for her dedicated efforts, and she received a raise every year until two years ago. But for the past two years, she has been receiving the same measly $9.50 an hour. After she heroically handled an accounting disaster when Dopey failed to report a purchase for an entirely new mine (he forgot where the old one was located and decided to buy another), she decided to sue for back wages. The Dwarfs claim that her past raises were purely discretionary and she is not entitled to any past wages.

1. **Hi Ho Hi Ho, It's Off to Mediation We Go.** During an initial judicial conference with the judge assigned to the case of *Snow White v. Seven Dwarfs*, the judge issued the following order: "The parties shall, within 30 days of this order, select a mediator from the approved court roster. Within 30 days of the selection of the mediator, the parties shall meet at least once to try to work out a settlement." Before even engaging in the mediator selection process, the Dwarfs indicated to Snow White that they had no intention of going to mediation. If the Dwarfs believe the court lacks the authority to order mediation, could they simply ignore the order? If they ignore the order, what options would Snow White have?

2. **The Wicked Mediator.** The judge orders Snow White and the Dwarfs to mediation and the judge's order specifies that the mediator in the case will be Wicked Witch. Wicked Witch is not listed on the court's approved mediator roster, does not appear to have conducted any mediations prior to this one, and has not taken any mediation courses. However, Wicked Witch is a close personal friend of the judge in this case. What options does Snow White have if she would prefer not to participate in a mediation with Wicked Witch?

3. **Hi Ho, It's Off to Summary Jury Trial We Go?** In lieu of sending the parties to mediation, the judge orders Snow White and the Dwarfs to conduct a summary jury trial. As part of the order, the judge specifies that the principal clients must attend in person. Snow White and her attorney are worried about the summary jury trial because their best witness, Sleeping Beauty, is a secret. At a minimum, Snow White and her attorney would prefer not to have Sleeping Beauty testify about the diamond industry until the trial. What options does Snow White have?

4. **Don't Be a Dope in Mediation.** Snow White and the Dwarfs are ordered into mediation, and the relevant local rules specify that the parties must participate in good faith. Snow White arrives at the mediation ready to discuss the merits of the case. She expected the Dwarfs to send Doc, the Dwarf who possesses full settlement authority in this matter. Instead, the only Dwarf to show up was Dopey. Dopey arrived at the mediation 20 minutes late, eating a cupcake from a party he had just attended. When confronted about his failure to submit a premediation memo and documents, he simply attempted to appease Snow White with a bite of his cupcake. Outraged that the Dwarfs did not appear to be taking the mediation seriously, Snow White stormed out. She files a motion for sanctions, accusing the Dwarfs of participating in bad faith in the mediation. How is the court likely to rule on Snow White's motion?

5. **While You Were Sleeping.** After making no progress in the first mediation session, which Dopey attended, the Dwarfs decide to send Sleepy to the next session. Once Sleepy arrives, the mediator convinces both participants to sit down together and begins to ask each side to discuss their underlying interests. Snow White goes into depth about her feelings, shedding some tears about not being appreciated at the Dwarf house. After Snow White is done wiping her eyes, she looks up and finds that Sleepy has been asleep the whole time! Snow White is outraged that she just poured her heart out to a dwarf who did not hear a word — he might as well have stayed home! She files another motion for sanctions with the court, again asserting that the Dwarfs have not engaged in the mediation in good faith. How is the court likely to rule on Snow White's motion?

6. **Grumpy Behavior in a Mediation.** In their third mediation session, the Dwarfs realize that they need to take this situation seriously. Their lucrative diamond mining industry will not be able to survive the negative press that would follow if this case were litigated. Seeking to protect their business, they send Grumpy to the next round of negotiations. Grumpy is easily the shrewdest negotiator among the Dwarfs, having personally negotiated many big money deals for the Dwarfs' business. However, Grumpy is primarily known for his angry and uncompromising personality. He has a long track record of strained relationships with Snow White (and with many of the Dwarfs). Because he feels that Snow White was an ungrateful and demanding employee, Grumpy approaches these negotiations with an even bigger chip on his shoulder than normal. Grumpy starts out with an unreasonably low settlement offer, and he then refuses to engage in any meaningful discussion about a compromise. As the session continues, it becomes clear that he does not take Snow White's claim seriously and has no desire to offer her a larger settlement. Annoyed and offended with Grumpy's lack of respect for her

claim, Snow White files a motion for sanctions with the judge who ordered the mediation. How is the court likely to rule on Snow White's motion?

7. **Too Shy to Show Up.** In a closed door meeting, the Dwarfs evaluate their negotiation strategy and conclude they have made some big mistakes in choosing their representatives. They decide that they will have more success if they send someone with a calm and welcoming personality to foster a productive mediation session. They choose to send Bashful as their representative to day four's mediation session. However, on the morning of the mediation, Bashful becomes, unsurprisingly, bashful at the thought of having to speak candidly in front of Snow White and her attorney. On the verge of an anxiety attack, Bashful decides that the only effective way he can represent the Dwarfs' interests at the mediation is to appear by telephone. He calls into the session and begins talking in calm and friendly tones. Snow White, however, is outraged that the Dwarfs did not send a representative in person. She storms out and files a motion for sanctions with the judge who ordered the mediation. How is the court likely to rule on Snow White's motion? Would the outcome have been any different if it had been a nonbinding arbitration to which the Dwarfs failed to show, rather than a mediation?

8. **Too Short on Cash.** Outside of the context of mediation, the Dwarfs send Snow White a written settlement offer. Under its terms, Snow White's salary going forward would be $11 an hour, and she would receive backpay stemming from that raise dating back two years. The Dwarfs also offer to pay all of Snow White's costs and attorneys' fees, bringing the total offer to $10,000. Fed up with the Dwarfs and uncertain that she has any interest in returning to work for them, Snow White refuses the settlement offer. The case goes to trial, and a jury sides with Snow White, but awards only $5,000 in damages. Following the entry of judgment, the Dwarfs file a motion to recover the litigation costs and attorneys' fees they incurred since the date of their offer to Snow White. How is the court likely to rule on the Dwarfs' motion?

Explanations

1. **Hi Ho Hi Ho, It's Off to Mediation We Go.** The Dwarfs are at risk of being found in contempt of court if they refuse to follow the court's order. Even if the Dwarfs are correct in their assertion that the court lacks the authority to order the parties into mediation, it is a terrible idea simply to ignore a court's order. In terms of procedure, if the Dwarfs never objected to being sent to mediation in the first place, they could try filing a motion with the judge seeking to be excused from the mediation. If they raised an objection at the time of the order, the Dwarfs could file a

motion to reconsider the court's order. And if all else fails, they might be able to seek interlocutory appellate review of the trial court judge's order.

However, the Dwarfs are unlikely to succeed in challenging the court's order that the case go through mediation. Recall that in *In re Atlantic Pipe Co.*, the court named inherent powers as one of four possible sources for a court's authority to order parties into mediation. Nothing in the facts of the case as presented suggests that the order is improper or beyond the scope of the court's inherent powers. Nothing suggests that the order conflicts with local rules or statutes, that the ordered mediation is somehow unfair, or that the court's order was otherwise improper. Even if the Dwarfs appeal the court's order compelling mediation, therefore, the court's order will almost certainly stand.

The question here also asks about Snow White's options. Assuming Snow White does not want to find herself at risk of being held in contempt along with the Dwarfs, she will need to take independent steps to carry out at least as much of the court's order as she can. For example, she should send letters to the Dwarfs, urging their participation in the mediator selection process. She should indicate her willingness to participate in mediation. And so on. Snow White cannot yet file a motion with the court seeking to enforce the court's order that the Dwarfs participate in mediation. Technically, because the 30 days specified in the judge's order have not yet passed, the Dwarfs are not yet in violation of the court's order. Presumably, they may yet change their minds and engage in mediation—a prospect made even more likely if Snow White takes steps to give effect to the judge's order.

2. **The Wicked Mediator.** Under the logic of *In re Atlantic Pipe Co.*, a court's authority to compel parties into mediation is bounded by certain constraints. For example, it suggests that a court's use of its inherent powers "must comport with procedural fairness." In this case, we know nothing of the actual mediation process Wicked Witch would conduct, so we cannot say for certain that Snow White would succeed in characterizing the process as unfair. But Snow White would probably argue that parties' autonomy and self-determination in mediation must include at least some say in the selection of the mediator—particularly here, because the parties have not independently chosen to go to mediation.

Snow White might further argue that the judge's reliance on the court's inherent powers here was not done with "restraint and discretion." If Wicked Witch were merely unqualified, Snow White might not be able to overcome the deference that would normally be afforded to the trial court's discretionary order. If Wicked Witch were merely a friend of the judge, the appearance of impropriety might not be sufficient to overcome an order specifying a particular mediator for this case. But the combination of these two factors weighing against propriety makes it very likely that a court reviewing the trial judge's order would side with Snow White and order mediation with a different mediator.

We do not have enough information about the facts here to know whether the judge would face the prospect of independent sanctions for improper behavior. Clearly, government officials cannot self-deal — they cannot expend public resources or use their public offices in ways to enrich themselves. In many circumstances, this ban extends to relatives and even friends. But without knowing more of the details, it is unclear whether, for example, Snow White could bring a complaint against the trial judge for this order. In all events, though, if Snow White objects to the appointment of Wicked Witch, she should raise the matter with the trial court in order to preserve the objection.

3. Hi Ho, It's Off to Summary Jury Trial We Go? As an initial matter, Snow White could seek to have the order compelling participation in summary jury trial reversed. She could file a motion with the court asking it to reconsider its order, or she could file an appeal seeking the same. The prospect of success with either of these efforts is likely to hinge on the degree to which the court has the authority to order parties to summary jury trial. Some jurisdictions plainly view summary jury trials as within the scope of ADR mechanisms to which courts have the inherent power to order parties. (For example, in *Cincinnati Gas & Elec. v. General Electric*, 854 F.2d 900 (6th Cir. 1988) (discussed in Chapter 4), the Sixth Circuit upheld orders to attend a summary jury trial.) In *Strandell v. Jackson County*, 838 F.2d 884 (7th Cir. 1987), however, the Seventh Circuit found that neither the court's inherent powers nor the relevant rules permitted a judge to order this particular form of ADR. Snow White might, therefore, have an avenue for escaping the judge's order altogether, depending on her jurisdiction.

If Snow White is not released from the order compelling summary jury trial (SJT), Snow White and her attorney would need to weigh carefully the possibility of conducting the SJT *without* calling Sleeping Beauty to the stand. Nothing in an order compelling SJT could compel a disputant to take a particular approach to prosecuting or defending its case. That would infringe far too much on party autonomy. And there is no precedent suggesting that a party would be limited in a full trial to that which he or she presented in an initial, summary jury trial. If she otherwise put on her case in earnest, she runs little risk of being held to have participated in violation of the court's order.

Depending on the terms of the summary jury trial process, however, Snow White may have a strong incentive to perform as well as possible in the process — including by calling her secret, star witness. If the SJT included a cost-shifting mechanism akin to that found in Rule 68's offer-of-judgment statute, Snow White would find herself functionally compelled to do her best, even if no technical legal rule requires it. However, as we describe above, such a cost-shifting mechanism virtually never accompanies a SJT process. To impose such a feature on the parties would truly illustrate the tension between a party's autonomy with respect to the course of its lawsuit and the court's inherent powers to manage cases.

Further, Snow White probably exaggerates the potential benefit of keeping Sleeping Beauty's testimony (and even her identity) out of the summary jury trial process. Television often suggests that trials are filled with surprise witnesses that turn a case in dramatic fashion. The reality of modern litigation, with procedures ranging from liberal discovery to pretrial practice, make trial by ambush exceedingly rare.

4. **Don't Be a Dope in Mediation.** The court is likely to find that the Dwarfs' participation failed to meet the "good faith" standard required under the terms of the court order. Good faith is not a self-defining concept, of course, but we can draw guidance from the various jurisdictions that have considered the boundaries of good faith in other contexts. For example, courts appear to have reached relative consensus on the idea that good faith includes, at a minimum, having a representative at the mediation who has appropriate settlement authority. To the extent that Dopey lacked settlement authority, the participation may be found to be in bad faith. Further, if mediators require an initial submission (for example, a mediation memo), and a party fails to provide it, courts have held that party to have breached a duty to participate in good faith. These externally measurable criteria (attendance, authority, submissions) all point to an absence of good faith, and probably make this a relatively easy case for a court.

By contrast, behaviors within the mediation session (for example, Dopey's bizarre introduction of a partially eaten cupcake into the conversation), are much more difficult for a court to consider in assessing the extent to which parties have engaged in good faith. Confidentiality and the subjectivity involved in assessing mediation behaviors make these internal-to-mediation activities less prone to judicial review under good-faith standards. Here, however, the case is relatively easy because Dopey's lack of settlement authority is sufficient to support Snow White's complaint.

The punishment for failure to participate in good faith rests in the discretion of the court. Typically, a court would fine the Dwarfs for the costs of that day's mediation, including the costs of the mediator, the mediator's travel costs, the costs Snow White incurred by taking the time away from her bookkeeping, and Snow White's attorneys' costs for the day. For example, in G. Heileman Brewing Co. v. Joseph Oat Corp., 871 F.2d

648 (7th Cir. 1989), Heileman, a brewery, and Joseph Oat Company, a waste water treatment facility builder, were engaged in a bitter dispute. A federal magistrate ordered each party to send a corporate representative with the authority to settle to a pretrial conference for the purpose of discussing the positions of the parties and discussing possible settlements. Oat sent an attorney authorized to speak for the company, but with no authority to settle. The court imposed sanctions on Oat for not sending a representative with full authority to settle. On appeal, the court upheld the sanctions imposed on Oat for violating the court order. The court imposed sanctions of nearly $6,000 for Heileman's costs and attorneys' fees.

5. **While You Were Sleeping.** If Snow White is able to demonstrate to the court that, in fact, Sleepy was sleeping throughout the mediation, she has a chance of prevailing. Although a court would not normally inquire deeply into the nature of a disputant's participation in the course of a mediation, Snow White may successfully argue that a participant who is asleep is the functional equivalent of a participant who is absent. And then using the line of cases holding that presence is a minimal component of good faith participation, Snow White would make the case for sanctions.

In his defense, Sleepy would probably (1) dispute the allegation that he was asleep the whole time, and (2) point out the difficult line-drawing exercise this case presents even if he did doze off at some point. As to the first, Snow White may face a difficult proof issue stemming from the confidentiality that typically attaches to mediation sessions. (For more on the confidentiality that attaches to mediation sessions, see Chapter 4.) As to the second, Sleepy would probably suggest a slippery slope to the court. Is it bad faith to be tired? To be distracted? To fail to pay careful attention? Again, if the proof were easy to access, a court would probably rule in favor of Snow White's motion for sanctions, but the proof would probably be elusive.

If the court does find bad faith, it is likely to order the Dwarfs to pay all costs associated with the mediation for that day, including attorneys' fees, making Snow White technically whole again (even though she is likely to be emotionally drained at this point). Because this is the Dwarfs' second attempt at mediation and their second good-faith violation, a judge may find it necessary to give them a harsher punishment. Local court rules can permit a court to impose fairly harsh penalties on parties that fail to mediate in good faith. Penalties may range, depending on the jurisdiction, from a simple fine all the way to dismissal, and in most cases, the decision rests in the discretion of the trial court judge.

6. **Grumpy Behavior in a Mediation.** Grumpy's behavior might not meet the conventional, popular definition of "good faith" participation. But it

is very unlikely that a court would fine him for any of the behaviors described here. Grumpy was present. Grumpy had settlement authority. Grumpy had prepared his case. Grumpy even made a settlement offer (albeit a very low one). As the court in *Gray v. Eggert*, described above, concluded, a low settlement offer is not, alone, evidence of bad faith participation. Courts typically examine the full range of circumstances surrounding an allegation of bad faith before making a determination. For example, in *Francis v. Women's Obstetrics & Gynecology Group*, 144 F.R.D. 646 (W.D.N.Y. 1992), the defendant was physically present at the mediation. However, the defendant arrived at the mediation without having submitted the required preparation materials in a timely fashion. Once the mediation commenced, the defendant informed the plaintiff that the defendant had not yet secured authorization from its insurance carrier for coverage, making the exercise largely moot. In granting the plaintiff's motion for sanctions, the court decried the defendant's "cavalier attitude" toward the process. Here, however, Grumpy was "merely" a hard bargainer. His strategy might not be successful. It might not even comport with the vast majority of existing "best practices" among negotiators. A court would not, however, find that his participation here breached the requirement to participate in good faith.

7. **Too Shy to Show Up.** The court would be well within its discretion to sanction the Dwarfs for failing to participate in good faith. Bashful's reluctance to appear in person may be understandable. Indeed, there are surely circumstances in which the best, most efficient arrangement would be to have some or all of the participants in a mediation appear by phone. But a disputant should not assume that he or she can unilaterally opt for this nonconventional mode of participation at the last minute. In this case, Bashful made no mention of the possibility that he would appear by phone. Instead, he simply called in rather than appearing in person. Just as in the *Raad v. Wal-Mart Stores, Inc.* case, described above, Bashful did not secure permission ahead of time for this mode of appearance. In this case, it is not clear that Snow White's reaction (storming out immediately) was entirely justified. However, without prior or contemporaneous consent to the appearance by phone, the court could deem Bashful's absence a failure to participate in good faith. As with previous examples, the court will have broad discretion in crafting an appropriate punishment for failure to adhere to the court's order. The most likely sanction would be fee shifting aimed at making Snow White whole for the failed mediation session.

If the proceeding had been a mandatory, nonbinding arbitration hearing, rather than a mediation, the Dwarfs might be in even more trouble. Under some arbitration rules, if one party fails to appear, the absent party is considered in default. Even if no rules providing for default exist, if only one party is present to offer evidence to the arbitrator, the arbitrator will almost certainly find in favor of the party who is present. In a binding arbitration, that would be the end of the story. But what about a nonbinding arbitration? In theory, as the name suggests, the arbitrator's finding is nonbinding and the losing party can demand a trial *de novo*. But at least some courts have concluded that a party who fails to appear at a mandatory, nonbinding arbitration has waived any right to demand a trial *de novo*, essentially rendering the nonbinding arbitrator's decision final. See, e.g., *New England Merchants National Bank v. Hughes*, 556 F. Supp. 712 (E.D. Pa. 1983) (refusing to grant trial *de novo* following defendant's failure to appear in a nonbinding arbitration).

8. **Too Short on Cash.** The Dwarfs' motion would be filed under Federal Rule of Civil Procedure 68 (or the state equivalent, if this case is in state court and the state has a similar provision in its rules). The facts do not specify otherwise, so we should assume that the Dwarfs' written offer was sufficiently unambiguous and unconditional to fall within the scope of the rules. Under Rule 68, because "the judgment finally obtained by the offeree [Snow White] is not more favorable than the offer, the offeree must pay the costs incurred after the making of the offer." The Dwarfs' *costs*, therefore, will be recoverable. However, Rule 68 limits the opportunity for recovery to costs (which include small-ticket items like filing fees, stenographers' fees, etc.). The largest portion of the Dwarfs' expenses most likely came in the form of attorneys' fees. Unlike some of its state equivalents, the Federal Rules do not provide for the recovery of attorneys' fees under the offer of judgment provisions. The Dwarfs, therefore, would recover only some of the money they seek from Snow White.

Attorneys, Clients, and Dispute Resolution

§10.1 INTRODUCTION

Lawyers have a set of ethical duties with respect to their clients, their counterparts, and the court. Because each state has a separate Bar, each state sets the specific parameters of these duties. We are saved from a 50-state survey, however, because virtually all states model their legal ethics on one of two documents — the ABA Model Rules of Professional Conduct (the Model Rules) or the ABA Model Code of Professional Responsibility (the Model Code). Because the Model Rules are, by far, the more commonly employed set of standards, this chapter focuses on the Model Rules. We will, however, indicate if the Model Code has provisions substantially different from those in the Model Rules.

We will first examine the lawyer's duty to advise a client of available ADR options prior to litigation. Second, we consider the lawyer's duty to communicate offers of settlement to a client and the consequences when a lawyer fails to do so. Finally, we focus on the lawyer's duty to maintain client confidences during mediation, arbitration, or other settlement negotiations.

§10.2 THE DUTY TO ADVISE A CLIENT OF ADR OPTIONS

A lawyer's core task is to counsel and represent clients effectively. In some contexts, effective counseling and representation will involve litigation. In

Model Rules of Professional Conduct

Rule 1.2   (a) Subject to paragraphs (c) and (d), a lawyer shall abide by a client's decisions concerning the objectives of representation and, as required by Rule 1.4, shall consult with the client as to the means by which they are to be pursued. A lawyer may take such action on behalf of the client as is impliedly authorized to carry out the representation. A lawyer shall abide by a client's decision whether to settle a matter. . . .

(c) A lawyer may limit the scope of the representation if the limitation is reasonable under the circumstances and the client gives informed consent.

(d) A lawyer shall not counsel a client to engage, or assist a client, in conduct that the lawyer knows is criminal or fraudulent, but a lawyer may discuss the legal consequences of any proposed course of conduct with a client and may counsel or assist a client to make a good faith effort to determine the validity, scope, meaning or application of the law.

Rule 1.4   (a) A lawyer shall:

(1) promptly inform the client of any decision or circumstance with respect to which the client's informed consent . . . is required by these Rules;

(2) reasonably consult with the client about the means by which the client's objectives are to be accomplished;

(3) keep the client reasonably informed about the status of the matter;

(b) A lawyer shall explain a matter to the extent reasonably necessary to permit the client to make informed decisions regarding the representation.

Rule 2.1   In representing a client, a lawyer shall exercise independent professional judgment and render candid advice. In rendering advice, a lawyer may refer not only to law but to other considerations, such as moral, economic, social and political factors, that may be relevant to the client's situation.

Comment 5 (excerpt)

Similarly, when a matter is likely to involve litigation, it may be necessary under Rule 1.4 to inform the client of forms of dispute resolution that might constitute reasonable alternatives to litigation.

Rule 3.2   A lawyer shall make reasonable efforts to expedite litigation consistent with the interests of the client.

others, clients' interests may be best served by some other legal or informal process. As a result, in most circumstances, a lawyer can only meet her or his responsibility to help clients make informed decisions by providing information about the risks and opportunities presented by a range of different approaches to addressing her or his clients' problems.

Four provisions of the Model Rules, shown below, inform a lawyer of the obligations to help clients understand various dispute resolution alternatives. Put roughly, Model Rule 1.2(a) requires a lawyer to defer to clients' decisions about the clients' objectives and to consult with clients about the means they will pursue. ("What are you trying to accomplish, and how should we try to do that?") Model Rule 1.4 requires a lawyer to provide enough information to clients so that the client can make an informed decision about the case. ("Here's what you need to know about the risks and opportunities of this situation. . . .") Similar to Model Rule 1.4, Model Code EC 7-8 states that "[a] lawyer should advise his client of the possible effect of each legal alternative." Model Rule 3.2 requires a lawyer to expedite litigation, consistent with clients' interests. ("I'll make this as painless as possible.") And finally, Model Rule 2.1 permits a lawyer to refer not only to the law, but also to social, economic, and moral factors relevant to the case. ("As I see it, this case raises the following legal and nonlegal issues. . . .") Within even this baseline framework of obligations, it is not difficult to imagine why lawyers' responsibilities often involve counseling about ADR.

Although many states have modeled their legal ethics rules on the Model Rules or the Model Code, each state is free to (and often does) add variations, creating additional or different definitions of lawyers' duties. Broadly speaking, a lawyer's state-created obligation to advise about ADR falls somewhere along a continuum, ranging from no obligation to an explicit obligation to advise clients about dispute resolution alternatives.

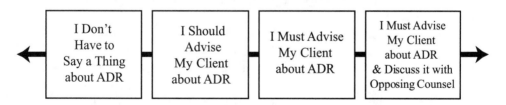

Above, we divide the universe of possible state approaches to these ethical rules into four categories. The reality, of course, is that every state can adopt whatever system of ethical codes it wishes. The line between these categories is not always bright, and we offer them simply to provide a conceptual framework for understanding the broad differences between jurisdictions. We discuss each broad category in further detail below.

§10.2.1 I Don't Have to Say a Thing

The far left end of the continuum represents an absence of any explicit duty whatsoever regarding ADR. Reflecting the reality of modern legal practice, though, few states' laws are utterly silent about ADR.

A somewhat greater (though still not very significant) obligation arises when a state suggests that discussing ADR with a client *may* sometimes be appropriate. For example, Florida Supreme Court Rule of Professional Conduct 4-2.1 provides, ". . . when a matter is likely to involve litigation, it *may be* necessary . . . to inform the client of forms of dispute resolution that might constitute reasonable alternatives to litigation. . . ." (emphasis added). Similarly, §A(3) of the Lawyer's Creed of Professionalism of the State Bar of Arizona provides, "[i]*n appropriate cases*, I will counsel my client with respect to mediation, arbitration and other alternative methods of resolving disputes" (emphasis added). Such provisions hint that the idea of ADR counseling might be helpful, without going so far as to declare it a good idea.

§10.2.2 I Should Advise My Client About ADR

Many state legal ethics provisions include clauses that explicitly suggest lawyers ought to discuss ADR with clients, as a matter of best practice. Some states accomplish this through statute. For example, Arkansas's Code states, "[a]ll attorneys licensed in this state when practicing in this state are encouraged to advise their clients about the dispute resolution process options available to them. . . ." Ark. Code Ann. §16-7-204 (2008). Other states achieve the same end through court rules. For example, Hawaii's Supreme Court Rules of Professional Conduct state, "In a matter involving or expected to involve litigation, a lawyer should advise a client of alternative forms of dispute resolution which might reasonably be pursued to attempt to resolve the legal dispute or to reach the legal objective sought." Haw. Sup. Ct. R.P.C. 2.1.

The significant thing to observe about these state provisions is that they go further than suggesting to lawyers that discussing ADR with clients may be appropriate — they *encourage* lawyers to advise clients about ADR. They do not, however, require lawyers to do so. And as you might expect, in these states, a lawyer who fails to advise a client about ADR may not face the same level of trouble as a lawyer in a state where advising about ADR is explicitly required.

§10.2.3 I Must Advise My Client About ADR

An increasing number of states are enacting a mandatory duty for lawyers to advise clients of available ADR options. These mandatory statutes vary in their scope, but all rules in this category use terms like "must," "required," or "shall." These requirements can be found in many different places: state codes, court rules, creeds, district rules, and local rules. For example, Missouri Supreme Court Rule 17.02 states, "[counsel] shall advise parties of the availability and purposes of alternative dispute resolution programs." Therefore, a lawyer in Missouri who fails to discuss ADR with a client has breached a specific obligation. Virginia places the obligation within the context of the duty to keep a client informed. Virginia Supreme Court Rule 1.4, Comment 5 states:

> The client should have sufficient information to participate intelligently in decisions concerning the objectives of the representation and the means by which they are to be pursued, to the extent the client is willing and able to do so. . . . This continuing duty to keep the client informed includes a duty to advise the client about the availability of dispute resolution processes that might be more appropriate to the client's goals than the initial process chosen. For example, information obtained during a lawyer-to-lawyer negotiation may give rise to consideration of a process, such as mediation, where the parties themselves could be more directly involved in resolving the dispute.

Similar to a number of states, Texas has a creed in its code of professional behavior, which, in order to gain membership to the Bar, requires the candidate lawyer to promise that he or she will uphold an obligation to advise clients. The Texas Lawyer's Creed, R. II.11 states, "I will advise my client regarding the availability of mediation, arbitration, and other alternative methods of resolving and settling disputes."

Finally, some states have codified the duty to advise in a way that removes all ambiguity regarding the scope and timing of this consultation. For example, Massachusetts Supreme Court Rule 1:18 states, "[a]ttorneys shall: provide their clients with this information about court-connected dispute resolution services; discuss with their clients the advantages and disadvantages of the various methods of dispute resolution, and certify their compliance with this requirement on the civil cover sheet or its equivalent." Massachusetts is serious enough about this rule that compliance requires lawyers to fill out and check a box on a form that indicates they consulted with their clients about ADR prior to filing a lawsuit. Even when a state might not have an across-the-board requirement to advise, specific practice areas may have such a requirement. For example, the United States Bankruptcy Court for the Southern District of California has a rule stating, "[p]rior to the pre-trial status conference, counsel shall confer with the client and discuss the mediation program, and shall ask the client for authorization to participate in the mediation program." U.S. Bankr. Ct. R. S.D. Cal., LBR 7016-4.

§10.2.4 I Must Advise My Client *and* Discuss with Opposing Party or Counsel

At the far end of the spectrum are states whose rules not only require lawyers to advise clients about ADR, but also to engage opposing counsel or opposing parties in discussions of ADR or settlement efforts. For example, one Ohio rule requires that "[b]efore the initial pre-trial conference in a case, counsel shall discuss the appropriateness of ADR in the litigation with their clients and with opposing counsel." Stark County, Ohio Gen. R. 16.03. Similarly, the Middle District of Louisiana Rule 16.3.1M, Rule C-1(a) states, "[b]efore the initial conference in all civil cases, counsel shall discuss the appropriateness of ADR in the litigation with their clients and with opposing counsel." Even if a state merely had an obligation for counsel to confer with opposing counsel about ADR possibilities, each lawyer would necessarily have an obligation to discuss the matter with her or his client. Requirements like these, therefore, are the strongest currently in force.

§10.2.5 Sanctions

A lawyer who fails to adhere to the standards established by the Bar is subject to a range of different possible forms of discipline. In cases of modest transgressions, a lawyer may merely be reprimanded, censured, or fined. In more serious cases, a lawyer may be stripped of her or his license to practice law for some fixed amount of time or even permanently.

Since the ethical rules concerning advising clients about ADR vary from state to state and the sanctions for violating ethical rules are so fact-specific, we cannot offer a uniform description of what happens to those lawyers who do not adequately advise their clients about ADR. In cases in which a lawyer has been in trouble for failing to advise a client about ADR, the lawyer has almost always also been guilty of a number of other misdeeds, making it hard to assess the severity the Bar would attach to an independent failure to advise a client about ADR. For example, consider the case of In re *Potter*, 952 P.2d 936 (Kan. 1998). Denise Carson, a car accident victim, hired Marcus Potter to handle her case. She did not hear from him again until 16 months later, after she had filed a disciplinary complaint against him. During that time, Potter had failed to advise his client even about the fact that the other driver's insurance company was trying to engage in settlement conversations. The court reviewing the complaint against Potter concluded that the attorney violated Model Rule 1.4 when "he did not consult with [Carson] . . . about her claim or explain the settlement negotiations to her despite numerous phone calls from [Carson]." When determining Potter's sanction, the court split on either an indefinite suspension from the practice of law or a public censure. Despite Potter's history of client complaints due to lack of communication, the court decided that the correct sanction was a public censure because Carson did not suffer any demonstrable monetary harm stemming from the lack of communication with Potter.

Beyond the prospect of Bar sanctions for ethical violations, lawyers also practice under the shadow of possible malpractice suits. Some kinds of lawyer malpractice are easy to spot and easy to quantify. For example, a lawyer who fails to submit a pleading within the prescribed time limit and thereby loses the case will have a difficult time arguing that submitting an untimely pleading is an acceptable practice. But even in this straightforward situation, an injured client must prove that the lawyer's misconduct *caused* *injury* to the client. In essence, the lawyer's defense may be, "Sure, I lost your case at the pleadings stage, but you never would have survived summary judgment anyway, so what's the harm?" The highly speculative inquiry this demands presents a real challenge to pursuing a legal malpractice claim successfully. Now imagine how much harder it would be to prove that an injury stemmed from a lawyer's failure to tell a client about mediation. Who's to say the client would have agreed to mediation, even if the lawyer had provided the advice? Who's to say the client would have settled in mediation, even if the lawyer had advised mediation? As a result of these realities in the dynamics of legal malpractice claims, malpractice claims against lawyers solely on the grounds of failure to advise a client about ADR possibilities must be rare indeed.

§10.3 DUTY TO COMMUNICATE SETTLEMENT OFFERS

One important distinction in the Model Rules is between those matters on which a lawyer must *defer* to the client's wishes, and those on which the lawyer merely is required to *consult* with the client. In general terms, a lawyer must defer to the client's wishes regarding the goals of the representation. ("What I want to do here is maximize the total dollars I recover from the insurance company" versus "What I want here is to get as much as I can quickly, because I really need the money now" versus "What I want here is to show the world what a lousy company this is.") By contrast, a lawyer is obligated ethically only to consult with clients about the means the lawyer will pursue. ("I believe you will fare best in this litigation if we join your neighbor as a codefendant, but I want to talk with you about the implications of doing that.") Similarly, Model Code EC 7-7 states that "[i]n certain areas of legal representation not affecting the merits of the cause or substantially prejudicing the rights of a client, a lawyer is entitled to make decisions on his own. But otherwise the authority to make decisions is exclusively that of the client."

As a result of this distinction, courts and Bar grievance committees give considerable deference to lawyers' judgment calls about many decisions along the way during litigation. Clients typically do not have the authority to micromanage their lawyers throughout the litigation. Nevertheless, at the end of the day, the case remains the client's, and the client retains the ultimate decision-making authority about its disposition. In short, because the client gets to decide whether to accept an offer of settlement, the lawyer is obligated to communicate such offers.

§10.3.1 Do I Have to Tell My Client About Every Offer?

In short, yes. Model Rule 1.2(a) provides that "a lawyer shall abide by a client's decisions concerning the objectives of representation and . . . shall consult with the client as to the means by which they are to be pursued. . . . A lawyer shall abide by a client's decision whether to settle a matter." Under this rule, the decision to settle and under what terms is clearly the client's choice. Following from this, Model Rule 1.4(b)'s duty to inform the client sufficiently to make an informed decision about the representation necessarily requires a lawyer to inform the client about any offers of settlement from the opposing party.

As with almost all forms of lawyer misconduct, the sanction for failing to communicate a settlement offer depends on the circumstances involved. At the most extreme, it can lead to disbarment. For example, in In re Brown, 453 P.2d 958 (Ariz. 1969), Francis Brown represented the plaintiff in a dog-bite case. On the eve of trial, the defendant offered to settle the case for $600, but Brown did not communicate the settlement offer to his client. The case went to trial, and Brown's client lost and had to pay costs and jury fees. As a result of this conduct (and a host of other unimpressive practices listed in a Bar complaint against him), Brown was disbarred.

Perhaps it is obvious, but these rules require an attorney to communicate settlement offers *accurately*. In the case of In re Ragland, 697 N.E.2d 44 (Ind. 1998), attorney Michael Ragland represented a client who brought action against a nursing home. The nursing home made an $18,000 settlement offer, which Ragland communicated to the client. Ragland also told the client that additional funds would be available through her insurance company, and the client authorized acceptance. The terms of the settlement, however, were contrary to what Ragland told his client. In fact, his client could not recover any additional money from the insurance company or from anyone else, under the terms of the agreement to which Ragland agreed on behalf of his client. As a result of a complaint alleging this and other misconduct, Ragland was suspended from practicing law for six months. The court also reduced the fee Ragland collected from this representation. The court declared that Ragland had, in essence, accepted the $18,000 settlement without his client's consent, because the client had not made a fully informed decision.

Some jurisdictions have taken the duty to convey settlement offers even further, by requiring attorneys to convey even offers of settlement *discussions*. For example, State Bar of Michigan Standing Committee on Professional and Judicial Ethics, Opinion RI-255 (1996), has interpreted Rule 1.4 to mean that "[i]f counsel for the opposing party offers to resolve the pending dispute through alternative dispute resolution forums, a lawyer is required to convey that offer to the client." Nothing in the rule requires the attorney or the client to accept the invitation to try to settle the case, but the attorney has an obligation to pass the opportunity on to the client.

§10.3.2 Does It Matter if the Other Side's Offer Is Terrible?

Nothing in the Model Rules prevents you, as a lawyer, from advising your client against accepting a terrible offer. Indeed, a lawyer who fails to provide this advice may be violating his or her ethical obligations. Clients often rely on lawyers to assess the relative merits of different possible courses of action — frequently including a comparison of litigation and settlement. The mere fact that the other side has made an offer does not affect this obligation. What the lawyer cannot do, however, is to substitute her own judgment about the settlement offer for her client's. The lawyer can say, "They made a terrible offer, and I advise you against accepting it." But if, at the end of the conversation, the client says, "Accept it anyway," the lawyer must defer to the client's decision.

§10.3.3 Does This Mean That the Client Can't Give Me Discretion?

No. Under the Model Rules, a client could certainly give you the authority to *accept* a settlement offer that falls within certain parameters. For example, a client might tell her lawyer, "Do as well as you can, and I authorize you to accept anything better than $100,000." If, during settlement negotiations, the other side presents an offer that is better than $100,000, the lawyer need not convey the offer to her client. She could, based on the authority given by her client, simply accept the offer. What the Model Rules prohibit is two scenarios: (1) a lawyer *rejecting* an offer of settlement without at least presenting that offer to his or her client for consideration, and (2) a lawyer *accepting* an offer on behalf of a client who has not authorized such an acceptance.

For example, in In re Eichholz, 2007 WL 1223613, 2007 U.S. App. LEXIS 11201, a former client and a former employee testified against attorney Benjamin Eichholz, accusing him of having settled cases without the proper authority for several clients, of having failed to discuss settlement offers with other clients, and of having committed several other Model Rule violations. The court suspended Eichholz from practice for two years.

Clearly, clients sometimes give their lawyers final authority to settle cases and give them broad discretion about the terms of the settlement. But the authority for specific settlement, separate from any other authority, must be clear. For example, in In re Lewis, 463 S.E.2d 862 (Ga. 1995), Peggy Uselton hired attorney James Lewis to represent her in a personal injury action. Uselton signed Lewis's standard retainer agreement, which provided that Lewis "shall have full power and authority to settle, compromise, or take such action as he might deem proper for the best interest of the client. . . ." Lewis subsequently accepted a settlement offer in the case without consulting Uselton, who thought the settlement terms were inadequate. Uselton filed a complaint with the Georgia State Bar against Lewis. The court rejected Lewis's argument that his contract with Uselton gave him unqualified authority to settle on her behalf, pointing in particular to Georgia's prohibition against an attorney obtaining a proprietary interest in a client's cause of action. The court suspended Lewis for 18 months. General, blanket authority imposed as a term of initial representation, therefore, does not provide an adequate basis for a lawyer to enter a final settlement without consulting the client.

§10.3.4 Do I Have to Convey My Client's Settlement Offer if I Think It Is Unwise?

With some decisions, the Bar clearly requires attorneys to defer to their clients' wishes. (For example, attorneys must defer to clients on whether to accept a settlement offer.) With other decisions, the Bar clearly does not require attorneys to defer to their clients' wishes, though attorneys certainly *can* defer. (For example, attorneys need not defer to clients on intra-litigation decisions like when to file a particular motion.) A challenge arises when the decision is sufficiently important that a client is likely to *want* deference from the lawyer, but is not explicitly described in the Model Rules as one of the matters on which a lawyer must defer to the client. That is the challenge with respect to clients' desires to *offer* settlement.

In brief, the answer to the question posed in this section is, "Probably yes — a lawyer must communicate a client's settlement offer to the other side if the client insists on making the offer." But this does not mean that the lawyer cannot try to persuade the client that making the offer is unwise (for example, because the lawyer thinks the client has misjudged the risks associated with the case, or because the lawyer thinks the offer would be more strategic if made in another form or at another time). At the end of the day, however, if the client wishes to dispose of the case in a particular way, a lawyer who does not communicate that offer may also violate Model Rule 1.2.

One case illustrating this dynamic is *In re Panel File Number 99-5,* 607 N.W.2d 429 (Minn. 2000). A client informed its lawyer that it wished to extend a settlement offer at an upcoming conference at which opposing counsel and a magistrate judge would be present. The lawyer, who was operating under a contingent fee contract, did not communicate the client's offer at that meeting. Some time later, the case settled, but the lawyer billed the client for more than $40,000, an amount *not* based on the original contingent fee contract. The attorney asserted that "because the settlement was against his advice, he was no longer bound by the contingent fee." The Minnesota Supreme Court, interpreting an earlier version of Minnesota's Rule 1.2, which did not explicitly require consultation before making an offer, nevertheless held that the lawyer had an obligation in this case to communicate the client's offer and rejected the lawyer's assertion about the fee arrangement.

The current Model Rule 1.2 (reprinted earlier in the chapter) adds a key provision making it clearly a client's decision whether to make or accept a settlement offer. In a jurisdiction that has adopted the most recent version of the Model Rules, this case from Minnesota would have been even easier to decide against the lawyer.

§10.4 CLIENT CONFIDENCES

In addition to the duty to discuss ADR and the duty to communicate settlement offers, a third lawyer duty is relevant to dispute resolution — the duty to maintain client confidences. As a matter of legal ethics and as a matter of lawyer-client privilege, confidentiality raises at least two significant questions: Under what circumstances must a lawyer keep information confidential if the client wants to keep it secret? Under what circumstances may a lawyer reveal a client's information against the client's wishes?

These two confidentiality questions produce a complex patchwork of rules and standards, arising in a broad range of contexts. Many of these will be covered in your course on Professional Responsibility, and it is not our purpose to review that course in its entirety here. Some of these obligations arise in the context of other courses as well. For example, you will likely encounter the Sarbanes-Oxley Act (which establishes the conditions under which a lawyer must whistleblow and withdraw from representing clients who commit corporate fraud related to securities) in a course on Business Entities. Again, it is beyond the scope of this volume to summarize the entirety of the law on maintaining client confidences.

For our purposes, confidentiality raises a more limited number of issues that are truly particular to confidential client information and ADR. Below, we explore three such issues.

§10.4.1 Can a Lawyer Sit Quietly in Settlement Talks While a Client Commits Fraud?

No. As you know from the detailed treatment in Chapter 2, fraud is the knowing misrepresentation of a material fact, causing detrimental, reasonable reliance. Model Rule 1.2(d) explicitly prohibits a lawyer from counseling or assisting a client in "conduct that the lawyer knows is criminal or fraudulent." In a comment to this Rule, the Model Rules acknowledge that "[w]hen the client's course of action has already begun and is continuing, the lawyer's responsibility is especially delicate." Consider the intersection of Comment [3] to Model Rule 4.1(b) and Model Rule 1.6.

Model Rule of Professional Conduct 4.1(b) Comment [3]

Ordinarily, a lawyer can avoid assisting a client's crime or fraud by withdrawing from the representation. Sometimes it may be necessary for the lawyer to give notice of the fact of withdrawal and to disaffirm an opinion, document, affirmation or the like. In extreme cases, substantive law may require a lawyer to disclose information relating to the representation to avoid being deemed to have assisted the client's crime or fraud. If the lawyer can avoid assisting a client's crime or fraud only by disclosing this information, then under paragraph (b) the lawyer is required to do so, unless the disclosure is prohibited by Rule 1.6.

Because the recently revised version of Rule 1.6 now permits lawyers to disclose information to prevent a client from committing fraud, Rule 4.1's requirements make it clear that an attorney must disclose otherwise confidential information, if doing so is necessary to prevent a client's fraud.

Model Rule of Professional Conduct 1.6

(a) A lawyer shall not reveal information relating to the representation of a client unless the client gives informed consent, the disclosure is impliedly authorized in order to carry out the representation or the disclosure is permitted by paragraph (b).

(b) A lawyer may reveal information relating to the representation of a client to the extent the lawyer reasonably believes necessary:

(1) to prevent reasonably certain death or substantial bodily harm;

(2) to prevent the client from committing a crime or fraud that is reasonably certain to result in substantial injury to the financial interests or property of another and in furtherance of which the client has used or is using the lawyer's services;

(3) to prevent, mitigate or rectify substantial injury to the financial interests or property of another that is reasonably certain to result or has resulted from the client's commission of a crime or fraud in furtherance of which the client has used the lawyer's services; . . .

(6) to comply with other law or a court order.

---

§10.4.2 Can a Lawyer Help a Client Deceive an Arbitrator or Mediator?

Model Rule 3.3 clearly requires a lawyer to be candid with a tribunal. These provisions specifically apply to contexts in which the lawyer is representing a client in court. Model Rule 1.0(m) also extends the definition of "tribunal" to include arbitrators. So a lawyer cannot assist a client in deceiving an arbitrator any more than the lawyer could do so in front of a judge.

But mediation is probably a different story — at least with respect to Model Rule 3.3. Mediators do not act as adjudicative bodies. Even when mediators provide evaluative assessments of a case's merits, the mediator is not rendering a binding decision. As a result, the Model Rules' requirement of candor to tribunals does not extend to mediators. Nevertheless, lawyers' other obligations continue to apply. For example, Model Rule 4.1's prohibition against assisting a client in committing fraud does not differentiate among the targets of fraud.

In short, Model Rule 3.3 requires "candor," which is something more demanding than "don't commit fraud." The fact that Model Rule 3.3 does not apply to mediators does not mean that lawyers have ethical license to say whatever they want to mediators. The rules still do not permit them to

---

Model Rule of Professional Conduct 3.3
Candor Toward the Tribunal

(a) A lawyer shall not knowingly:

(1) make a false statement of fact or law to a tribunal or fail to correct a false statement of material fact or law previously made to the tribunal by the lawyer;

(2) fail to disclose to the tribunal legal authority in the controlling jurisdiction known to the lawyer to be directly adverse to the position of the client and not disclosed by opposing counsel; or

(3) offer evidence that the lawyer knows to be false. If a lawyer, the lawyer's client, or a witness called by the lawyer, has offered material evidence and the lawyer comes to know of its falsity, the lawyer shall take reasonable remedial measures, including, if necessary, disclosure to the tribunal. A lawyer may refuse to offer evidence, other than the testimony of a defendant in a criminal matter, that the lawyer reasonably believes is false.

(b) A lawyer who represents a client in an adjudicative proceeding and who knows that a person intends to engage, is engaging or has engaged in criminal or fraudulent conduct related to the proceeding shall take reasonable remedial measures, including, if necessary, disclosure to the tribunal.

(c) The duties stated in paragraphs (a) and (b) continue to the conclusion of the proceeding, and apply even if compliance requires disclosure of information otherwise protected by Rule 1.6.

(d) In an ex parte proceeding, a lawyer shall inform the tribunal of all material facts known to the lawyer that will enable the tribunal to make an informed decision, whether or not the facts are adverse.

---

commit fraud. What the rules do appear to permit are those comments that are less than candid but fall short of constituting fraud.

§10.4.3 Can a Lawyer Disclose Confidential Information in a Mediation, Since Mediation Is a Confidential Process?

No. The fact that conversations are taking place within a mediation, as opposed to some other forum, does not give a lawyer license to disclose that which she is otherwise not permitted to disclose. Nothing in the Model Rules provides for a special exception for mediation communications. If the client does not want the information revealed, and the information is not on the narrow list of exceptions in Model Rule 1.6, the lawyer must not reveal the information — even in mediation.

That would be the answer even if the Model Rules were irrelevant, for at least two reasons. First, although mediation communications are often treated as confidential, they are certainly not absolutely confidential. See Chapter 4 for more on the boundaries of mediation confidentiality. Second, even if mediation were reliably confidential, that should not matter for purposes of deciding whether to reveal a client's secret. (That would be akin to saying, "It's OK for me to tell your secret to my friend, because my friend said she wouldn't tell anybody.")

The Model Rules contain no exception permitting disclosure in a confidential process like mediation. The following three bright-line rules, therefore, provide the best guidance:

1. A lawyer can divulge a client's confidential information if the client consents.
2. A lawyer can divulge a client's confidential information in the relatively narrow set of circumstances listed in Model Rule 1.6.
3. A lawyer must divulge a client's confidential information under Model Rule 4.1(b) if doing so is necessary to avoid assisting the client to commit a crime or fraud.

Examples

To Advise, or Not to Advise

Hamlet, upon learning of his father's death, made arrangements to move back home to be nearer to his mother and to the family business, Ophelia's Fresh Fruit (OFF). When he returned, Hamlet was shocked to discover that things were rotten. His mother had remarried Hamlet's Uncle Claudius and Claudius had taken over the position of CEO of OFF, even though Hamlet believed he was the rightful heir to the company. Hamlet marched into a local lawyer's office and declared, "I want to sue Claudius." The lawyer asked a few questions about the situation, and said, "Leave everything to me." Two years of protracted litigation later, with no resolution in sight, Hamlet is bemoaning his fate to a friend, when the friend says, "Have you tried to mediate or settle?" Hamlet confesses that he's never heard of mediation, and his friend suggests that Hamlet's lawyer may be part of the problem.

1. **Model Rules State.** Assume that Hamlet's state has enacted a version of the Model Rules of Professional Conduct. Has Hamlet's lawyer violated any professional obligations? If so, what sanctions might the lawyer face?

2. **State Encourages ADR Advising.** Assume that Hamlet's state has enacted a version of the Model Rules of Professional Conduct and has added a provision declaring that "in most circumstances, a lawyer should advise a client of alternative forms of dispute resolution which might reasonably be pursued to attempt to resolve the legal dispute or to reach the legal objective sought." Has Hamlet's lawyer violated any professional obligations? If so, what sanctions might the lawyer face?

3. **State Requires ADR Advice and Consultation with Opposing Counsel.** Assume that Hamlet's state has enacted a version of the Model Rules of Professional Conduct. Assume that it also has a statute that says, "A lawyer has a duty to inform the client of forms of dispute resolution which might constitute reasonable alternatives to litigation." Has Hamlet's lawyer violated any professional obligations? If so, what sanctions might the lawyer face? Does Hamlet have a case for malpractice?

Kosmo's Pool

Kosmo hired a swimming pool manufacturer to install a room-sized pool in his tenth-floor apartment. After the pool was installed, Kosmo fell asleep while sitting in the pool one afternoon. Unfortunately, Kosmo's hand became lodged in the pool's drainage system, causing serious injury. Kosmo hires a lawyer, Jack Childs, to file suit against the swimming pool manufacturer.

4. **Chlorine for Life.** Jack Childs and opposing counsel met to discuss the case. Jack Childs outlined Kosmo's product liability claim. The defendant explained that Kosmo was at fault by falling asleep in the pool. The two postured for a while, and then the pool manufacturer offered a lifetime supply of chlorine and other pool-cleaning chemicals to settle the case. Jack Childs laughed at the offer, and rejected it without ever informing Kosmo of its terms. Has Jack Childs violated his professional obligations to Kosmo?

5. **Jack Childs's Judgment.** Prior to a follow-up meeting with the lawyer for the defendant, Jack Childs meets with Kosmo and discusses the merits of the case. He explains the possible risks and the opportunities associated with the litigation, and at the end of the conversation, Kosmo tells Jack Childs, "Do the best you can for me. I trust your judgment. If they make a good offer, take it. Otherwise, let's take this to trial." At a subsequent meeting, the pool company renews its offer of lifetime chlorine. Jack Childs again laughs and says, "No. Unacceptable. I don't even need to consult with my client on this one." The pool company says their offer is final, and Jack Childs rejects it. Has Jack Childs violated his professional responsibilities to Kosmo?

6. **Kosmo's Idea of Justice.** Kosmo tells Jack Childs that he believes that the best outcome in this case would be for the pool company to pay for a pool boy to come by the apartment every day to maintain the pool. Jack Childs explains that such a result would be impossible even in the best-case scenario presented by litigation. Kosmo persists and argues that Jack should demand this for him. Jack Childs explains that making such a demand would probably infuriate the pool company, making them less likely to settle. Kosmo insists. Their meeting ends, and Jack Childs decides never to communicate the crazy demand. Has Jack Childs violated his professional responsibility to Kosmo?

7. **Kosmo's Limit.** On the eve of trial, Kosmo and Jack Childs have a final conversation about the possibility of settling the case. Kosmo rescinds his blanket grant of authority to Jack Childs and instead specifically tells Jack that he will agree to "anything above $50,000." On the courthouse steps, the pool company offers to settle the case for "$60,000, but not a penny more." Jack Childs ponders the situation for a minute. His contingency fee arrangement with Kosmo entitles Jack to one-third of any recovery. The defendant's offer would leave Kosmo with only $40,000, so Jack Childs rejects the offer without consulting his client. Has Jack Childs violated his professional responsibility to Kosmo?

8. **Jack Childs's Judgment, Part 2.** During a break in the trial, the defense lawyer approaches Jack Childs and offers a creative settlement according to which Kosmo would receive $30,000, a certificate for a new pool in ten years, and free cleaning supplies. Jack Childs accepts the offer without consulting Kosmo. Has Jack Childs violated his professional responsibility to Kosmo?

Release the Hounds, but Not the Information

Leeza was soliciting donations door-to-door as part of a project for the Young Do-Gooders Club. When she rang the doorbell at the mansion of Monty Barns, no one answered, but she heard from within, "Release the hounds!" Moments later, a pack of snarling dogs attacked Leeza, causing severe injuries. Lionel Klutz agrees to represent Barns in the ensuing personal injury action.

9. **Monty's Initial Plan.** Early in the litigation, the two sides agreed to attempt mediation. Klutz advised Barns about the process, and Barns agreed that it might be useful. "After all," Barns said, "I'm sure they'll ask me if this has ever happened before at some point. Better that it should be asked in a setting in which I'm not under oath, so that I can say this is the first time." Klutz then asked him how many times such a thing *had* occurred in the past, and Barns laughed and said, "Oh, dear

me, I've lost count. So many solicitors, so few dogs." What might Klutz do in this situation, consistent with the Model Rules of Professional Responsibility?

10. **Monty Barns, Man of His Word.** In their final preparations for mediation, Barns and Klutz agree on a strategy: Barns will show deep remorse for the injuries, will confess that this is not the first time the dogs have "gotten out," and will offer $500,000 to settle the case. In her opening statement, Leeza's lawyer describes the horrific injuries Leeza suffered, including not only physical injuries but also a complete loss of memory about the events. Barns interrupts, "Loss of memory, eh? Then she doesn't remember taunting my poor puppies? Throwing rocks at them? Hitting them with a stick? That's what she did, you know. I'm sorry she got hurt, but it's no wonder they finally bit her. She's the one to blame here!" Leeza and her lawyer look shocked. Barns looks over at Klutz and, imperceptibly to the other parties at the mediation, winks. What might Klutz do in this situation, consistent with the Model Rules of Professional Responsibility?

11. **Not a Penny More!** After a protracted pretrial process, including several failed efforts at mediation, Leeza's case is set for trial. In his last-minute preparations, Klutz asks Barns if he would consider settling the matter. Barns tells Klutz, "I'm willing to pay her $200,000, but not a penny more." On the eve of trial, the judge orders the parties to try mediation one more time. In an initial private caucus involving only the mediator, Barns, and Klutz, the mediator asks Barns, "What is the most you would be willing to pay?" Without hesitating, Barns replies, "$100,000, but not a penny more." What might Klutz do in this situation, consistent with the Model Rules of Professional Responsibility?

Explanations

To Advise, or Not to Advise

1. **Model Rules State.** The fact that Hamlet is unhappy with the way his litigation is unfolding is not necessarily evidence that his lawyer has breached any duties. The Model Rule perhaps most directly relevant to this circumstance is Rule 1.4, which requires a lawyer to "reasonably consult" with clients about the means the lawyer will undertake in pursuing the client's aims. If Rule 1.4 refers solely to the means within litigation, Hamlet's lawyer is entirely safe. Another reading of Rule 1.4, however, suggests that the Model Rule contemplates that the lawyer will consult about a range of different possibilities, including those beyond litigation.

Hamlet might make a similar argument with reference to Model Rule 3.2, which requires lawyers to "expedite litigation consistent with the interests of the client." As above, one might read Rule 3.2 as requiring merely that a lawyer expedite *litigation* (for example, by limiting discovery). Hamlet might argue, however, that his lawyer failed to expedite the litigation by failing to advise him of the possibility of a nonlitigation alternative (like mediation) that could have resolved the issue more quickly.

Finally, Hamlet might argue that the lawyer failed to discharge his duties with adequate care, thus committing legal malpractice. He might succeed in suggesting that any lawyer would at least counsel a client contemplating litigation about the possibility of ADR. But it would be difficult for Hamlet to prove any damages of significance stemming from this failure, if everything else the lawyer has done in litigation has been proper.

At the end of the day, Hamlet's lawyer is unlikely to face serious sanctions in this case.

2. **State Encourages ADR Advising.** The addition of a state provision that merely says, "in most circumstances, a lawyer should . . ." does not change the analysis from Example 1 significantly with respect to the legal ethics claim against Hamlet's lawyer. In his defense, Hamlet's lawyer would correctly point out that the language "should" means that the Bar does not require advice of this sort. And he would also probably argue that, even if advice about ADR is normally called for, this was one of the circumstances the drafters clearly acknowledged as different.

The state provision suggesting advice-giving could be useful to Hamlet if he were pursuing a malpractice claim against his lawyer. If the lawyer's defense is that advice on ADR is not normally given, the existence of this rule (and presumably local practices that accompany it) would make it easier for Hamlet to establish a breach of the normal duty of care. However, Hamlet would still face all of the challenges described in the explanation to Example 1 in establishing a causal link between the lawyer's conduct and any injury Hamlet believes he has suffered.

3. **State Requires ADR Advice and Consultation with Opposing Counsel.** In this case, Hamlet's lawyer had a duty to advise Hamlet about "forms of dispute resolution which might constitute reasonable alternatives to litigation." Given the nature of this dispute (an intrafamily clash, involving ongoing relationships and ongoing business affairs), it would be almost impossible for Hamlet's lawyer to argue that no reasonable alternatives to litigation exist. Mediation, in particular, suggests itself as at least worthy of discussion.

Hamlet could file a complaint against his lawyer with the local Bar, and under these facts, the lawyer's conduct almost certainly constitutes a breach of the relevant rules. What sanction the Bar will impose depends on the Bar's assessment of the seriousness of the misconduct.

As for a malpractice claim, Hamlet would probably only be able to pursue this successfully in a state with the requirement to advise clients about ADR. And even then, Hamlet would have to show that (a) he would have pursued the mediation had his lawyer suggested it, (b) he would have settled the claim in mediation, and (c) the settlement would have been better than the result of litigation. Demonstrating that the attorney's conduct fell below the standard expected of lawyers should not be difficult. But causation and damages will require considerable speculation.

Kosmo's Pool

4. **Chlorine for Life.** Under the facts here, it looks like Jack Childs has breached his legal obligations to his client by failing to communicate the terms of a settlement offer, as required under Model Rules 1.2 and 1.4. It may be that the offer is facially unacceptable. It may be that the attorney is confident that the client will reject the offer. But the decision to accept or reject the settlement is the client's, not the lawyer's. As a result, Jack Childs had an obligation to communicate the offer to Kosmo prior to rejecting it.

5. **Jack Childs's Judgment.** No. Model Rule 1.2 and Model Rule 1.4 require a lawyer to keep the client sufficiently informed so as to make an informed decision about the case. Jack Childs has done so here. And Kosmo granted Jack Childs discretion to assess the merits of any possible offers. Of course, if the offer had been in any way different from the first offer — in particular if it had been a better offer — and Jack Childs had any doubts about what Kosmo would think about an offer, Jack Childs should take it back. But here, Kosmo has given Jack Childs this authority, and Jack Childs can exercise that authority without concern that he might be violating his ethical obligations. This case is unlike the In re Lewis case because here the client's authority was clearly communicated and was informed (as opposed to being only the product of boilerplate language in a retainer agreement). Of course, it may have been better practice for Childs to return to his client, since Kosmo's preferences and thinking may have evolved over time. But under the circumstances, Childs's behavior satisfies his ethical duties to Kosmo.

6. **Kosmo's Idea of Justice.** Probably yes. Big picture decisions, like whether to bring a claim or settle a case, are clearly the province of the client, and a lawyer must defer as to those decisions. Minor, tactical decisions along the way, like the sequence of depositions or the framing

of a legal claim, are clearly the province of the lawyer. The decision to make a particular offer appears to fall somewhere between these two extremes. Model Rule 1.2(a), however, provides, "A lawyer shall abide by a client's decision whether to settle a matter." Assuming the state in question has adopted the Model Rules, Jack Childs appears to have violated them.

7. **Kosmo's Limit.** Maybe. Jack Childs certainly did not handle the situation as well as he probably should have. On these facts alone, however, it is unlikely that the Bar would decide that he breached a Model Rule. Still, in order to give effect to his client's desires about the settlement of the case, Jack Childs should have clarified the scope of Kosmo's parameters. In particular, he should have clarified whether Kosmo meant $50,000 *net*. If Jack Childs had any doubts, Model Rules 1.4 and 1.2 strongly suggest that he should have consulted with Kosmo.

8. **Jack Childs's Judgment, Part 2.** Yes. The circumstances surrounding the case have likely changed since their last meeting, and Model Rule 1.4(a)(1) requires the lawyer to keep clients informed about such changes. The offer does not fall neatly within Kosmo's stated parameters of cash only, suggesting strongly that Jack Childs has an obligation to communicate them to Kosmo under Model Rule 1.4(a)(3) and to seek his input. Model Rules 1.2 and 1.4 require a lawyer to communicate offers of settlement and to defer to clients' judgments about them. Even if Jack Childs thought the offer was worth far more than $75,000 (which would net Kosmo $50,000 after deducting Jack Childs's fee), he should have communicated it to Kosmo.

Release the Hounds, but Not the Information

9. **Monty's Initial Plan.** Klutz cannot, under Model Rule 1.2(d), assist a client in committing a fraud. In this case, Barns has not yet made any representation, so no fraud yet exists. But it is easy to imagine the conversation Barns is planning, and it is clear that Barns intends to commit fraud. Ultimately, Klutz would be unable to represent Barns in the action if Barns goes forward with his initial plan. But withdrawal is a measure of last — not first — resort here.

Klutz's first effort should almost certainly be to try to talk Barns out of his plan. For example, Klutz could explain that he would be unable to continue to represent Barns for the reasons stated above. Klutz could explain the legal consequences of Barns's planned fraud. Klutz could also explain that, as a practical matter, it is quite unlikely that the lie would even be successful, given the ease with which discovery is conducted. Klutz could discuss the "moral, economic, social, and political factors" that counsel against lying in this context. In short, before contemplating withdrawal, Klutz should counsel Barns against his proposed course of action.

10. **Monty Barns, Man of His Word.** Klutz cannot assist Barns in committing fraud. And the problem is that Barns has made a statement that is clearly a knowing misrepresentation of material facts, intended to cause detrimental reliance. The comment to Model Rule 1.2(d) described this sort of situation as "especially delicate." And yet, the bottom line is clear: Klutz cannot assist Barns to commit fraud.

Before considering the possibility of withdrawing from the representation, Klutz should probably take steps to see whether Barns will correct his misstatement, and therefore, not commit fraud. Klutz could easily ask to take a break in the mediation, so that he could consult with Barns. In a private meeting, Klutz could explain the situation to Barns and encourage him to recant the story he just made up. If Barns agrees and recants, no fraud has occurred because fraud requires detrimental reliance (which has not occurred yet because Leeza has taken no steps based on the account Barns just provided), so Klutz could continue to represent Barns.

If Barns refuses, however, Klutz will be required to withdraw from representing him. Before the recent amendments to Model Rule 1.6, there may have been a difficult question about whether Klutz could withdraw "quietly," providing no indication of the cause of his withdrawal to Leeza and her lawyer, or "noisily." The combination of the revised Rule 1.6(b)(2) and Comment [3] to Model Rule 4.1(b) — both of which appear earlier in this chapter — make it clear that an attorney may be required to disclose information in order to prevent a client's crime or fraud. Therefore, if Klutz is unable to convince Barns to correct his own fraudulent statements, Klutz must withdraw, and must do so in a way that corrects Leeza's misunderstanding.

11. **Not a Penny More!** Barns's statement to the mediator may or may not be strategically wise (and you as his lawyer may want to take a break to talk to him about this), but it certainly does not constitute fraud. Indeed, it is possible that something has caused Barns to change his mind about the most he is willing to offer, and there's nothing wrong with that from an ethical perspective. As we discussed in Chapter 2, statements about reservation values almost never constitute fraud, because they are deemed "mere puffery," rather than statements about material facts. Further, Barns owes no duty of candor (a heightened standard above merely avoiding fraud) to the mediator. Klutz, therefore, is not constrained by the Model Rules here. Klutz may counsel Barns to adopt a different tactic, but nothing in the ethical rules requires Klutz to do so.

Analyzing Settlement Decisions

§11.1 INTRODUCTION

Some aspects of negotiation are undeniably psychological, emotional, and deeply interpersonal. No understanding of negotiation is complete if it ignores the human experience of the disputants. Further, real-world negotiators' interests often extend far beyond the simple maximization of dollars.

At the same time, negotiations often involve decisions with important financial implications. As a negotiation's stakes increase, the complexity of those implications also often increase. A tourist haggling over the correct price for a trinket in a market understandably uses a less sophisticated decision-making process than a litigant assessing the implications of settling a multimillion dollar lawsuit.

In this chapter, we examine two concepts commonly associated with analyzing relatively complex financial decisions in dispute resolution processes. First, we outline the basic mechanisms involved in decision analysis. Second, we provide an outline of some of the ways in which time factors into disputants' financial analyses. Each of these topics could occupy an entire book, if examined in depth. We aim here to provide enough of a foundation so that you can perform the kinds of basic analyses you might be expected to perform in a Dispute Resolution course.

§11.2 DECISION ANALYSIS

The process by which some disputants attach a particular value to a course of action (for example, taking a case to trial) involves mathematical calculations. In making these calculations, some negotiators employ a graphically based process of laying out current and future decisions, along with their probable outcomes. This method of calculation has the generic label *decision analysis*.

Decision analysis helps compare decisions over time, in circumstances in which the future may hold a variety of possible outcomes, each of which has a different likelihood of occurring. For example, you might want to place a bet on your favorite team to win the Super Bowl at the end of the NFL season. Your choice right before the Super Bowl — your team will win or your team will lose — is a much simpler choice than at the beginning of the season. Right before the Super Bowl, you need only to have an assessment of the likelihood of this single victory. At the beginning of the season, you need to calculate the likelihood that your team will win enough games to make the playoffs, *and* the likelihood of them making it through the playoffs, *before* you can make the final assessment about how likely they are to win the Super Bowl.

Calculating how you will do at trial is similarly complex. Although one might view a prediction to win or lose at trial as a simple either/or choice, in fact there are multiple steps along the way to trial victory. Decision analysis helps to put those choices into perspective so that you can make wise decisions about whether to accept a settlement offer (or put one forward). Consider the following example of a simple lawsuit:

> You sustained certain injuries in an accident at a retail store. You believe you were entirely without fault, and you brought suit against the store, claiming $50,000 in damages. The store's insurer has offered you $10,000 to settle the case. Should you accept it?

The answer, of course, depends on many variables. Perhaps your decision will hinge entirely on nonfinancial considerations. Perhaps you want to "teach the store a lesson." Perhaps you want an opportunity to air your frustrations in a public forum. Alternatively, perhaps you have such a pressing and immediate need for cash that you feel you cannot afford to do anything but accept the offer. Or perhaps you have reason to want to stay out of the public spotlight. In any of these events, you might not have any need to engage in any calculations. For many litigants, however, the settlement decision might hinge on their expectations about the risks and opportunities presented by litigation. Decision trees aid in making that kind of assessment.

§11.2.1 Building a Decision Tree

"Decision trees" are graphic constructs that can facilitate the math involved when there are multiple variables or future events with various payouts and probabilities. You certainly do not need to construct decision trees in order to arrive at mathematical assessments of these decisions. But the step-by-step nature of decision trees helps many people to visualize the implications of and connections between what might otherwise appear to be an impossibly complex set of factors.

Certain standard conventions apply in constructing decision trees. For example, time moves from left to right as you follow the various paths the future might take. At every branch in the tree, something happens. If you face a decision (for example, "shall I accept this settlement offer or not?"), you place a square (called a "decision node"). If you face an uncertain outcome that is beyond your control (for example, "will the jury find in my favor or not?") you place a circle (called a "chance node"). At the point where each branch of the tree has reached its logical end (the end for purposes of your analysis), you place a triangle (called a "terminal node"). And where, along the way, you incur costs, you place a funny looking little gate (appropriately called a "cost gate"). Once the tree is constructed, you can then insert the payouts each of the eventualities would provide and the probabilities associated with each of the chance nodes. The last step is using the decision tree to aid you in doing the math that produces an expected value for the litigation.

Decision Tree Graphics	
Decision node	□
Chance node	○
Terminal node	◁
Cost gate	⊟

Returning to the accident case, then, the question you are being asked is "shall I accept this settlement offer or not?" In constructing the decision tree, the first thing to do is lay out the choice graphically.

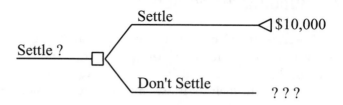

It is clear what happens if you accept the settlement. But we need more information about what happens if you go to trial. For our purposes of illustration, we will assume that the litigation would be highly simplistic. Assume the defendant has filed a summary judgment motion against you. If you lose on that motion, you are done. If you win, you proceed to trial, and you believe you have an 80 percent chance of defeating the defendant's summary judgment motion. In either event, assume that it will cost you $5,000 in unrecoverable attorneys' fees to defend against the summary judgment motion. At trial, you believe you have a 50-50 chance of winning. If you win, you'll recover $50,000, and if you lose, you recover nothing. And assume as well that going to trial will cost you another $5,000 in unrecoverable attorneys' fees. The completed decision tree would then look like this:

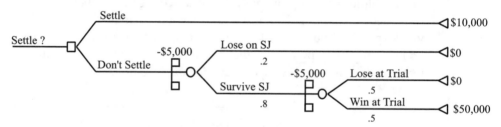

Once the tree is constructed, you have the opportunity to do some basic math to help you to understand the expected value of taking this case to trial. Called "rolling the tree back," it involves taking the expected payout (at the far right side of the tree) and multiplying it by the probability of that branch occurring. Below you'll see how the math at each stage works out.

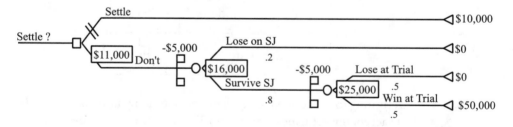

To understand how the tree arrives at the figures in the boxes, begin reading from the right-hand side of the tree. The payout of a branch is multiplied by the probability of that branch occurring. For example,

"Win at Trial" has a payout of $50,000, which is then multiplied by .5. That produces $25,000. "Lose at Trial" has a payout of $0, which is then multiplied by .5, which produces $0. The $25,000 and the $0 are added together to produce the $25,000 that appears in the box just to the right of the chance node related to trial.

The same logic applies then to the rest of the process of rolling the tree back. The $25,000 has to rollback through the cost gate, and after subtracting $5,000 becomes $20,000. That figure is then multiplied by the probability for "Survive SJ." Because $20,000 × .8 = $16,000, and because $0 × .2 = $0, the value $16,000 ($16,000 + $0) appears in the box related to surviving summary judgment. We then roll that back through one more cost gate ($16,000 − $5,000) and arrive at the expected value of not settling: $11,000.

The last step in using a decision tree, of course, is to figure out what meaning to make of the number(s) your analysis produces. In our case, we are particularly interested in the final values the tree assigns to the two branches stemming off of the decision node. The tree suggests that the expected value of settling is $10,000, while the expected value of not settling is $11,000. Graphically, therefore, the path leading to the less favorable outcome is marked with little bars, indicating that the decision tree does not recommend making that choice.

Few clients would base their decisions entirely on such numbers, of course, particularly when the two choices produce very similar figures. The expected value is only that — an expectation. It is no certainty. Perhaps if you have reliable information, and perhaps if you had a thousand of these cases to litigate, you would notice that on *average* each case returns about $11,000. But that doesn't necessarily tell you whether to roll the dice on litigating this case.

§11.2.2 The Limits of Decision Analysis

Decision analysis is used every day by sophisticated businesses to make important decisions. As a tool, it has gained extraordinary acceptance as a component in business practices. But there are limits on the contributions mathematical decision analysis (even when it is conducted properly) can provide to decision makers. Below, we outline four of the most significant of these limitations. Again, none of these is a reason not to conduct an analysis of a deal's implications. But each provides reason to put a decision tree's conclusions in perspective.

Garbage In, Garbage Out Even if you do all of the modeling and the arithmetic correctly, if you have unreliable estimates about the likelihood of various outcomes, you have good reason to be cautious about a decision tree's conclusions. Insurance companies and other repeat players have enough experiences with different scenarios that they often have relatively high confidence in the quality of their predictions. Similarly, although often less formally, experienced attorneys develop a "sense" of cases, based on their years of practice. This is not to suggest that decision trees have no value without perfect information. We *never* have perfect information, yet we have to make decisions all the time, and we should try to make them the best way we can. Still, the more unreliable the data you are putting into the equations, the more cautiously you should consider the equations' conclusions.

Anchoring Risks   As a basic psychological phenomenon, our brains often cling to the first numbers to which they are exposed. (The psychology literature calls this the "anchoring effect.") Because decision trees reduce complex decisions to a single number (and often even, a single choice), there is some risk that decision makers will lock onto that final number unhelpfully. In the case of something like a piece of complex litigation, the landscape shifts frequently. Ideally, decision makers would update their assessments along the way, but the anchoring effect makes doing so difficult.

Ignoring Value Creation Opportunities and Nonmonetary Interests Decision trees ask, rather narrowly, about dollars and probabilities. As you know from Chapter 1, negotiations almost always involve more complex interests than just money. And even in cases in which both sides care principally about money, there are many different ways to structure agreements beyond a simple, one-time lump-sum payment. Those who use decision trees must take care not to forget the availability of these efficient, value-maximizing strategies.

Ignoring the Impact of Time   These simple versions of decision trees (yes, there are more complex versions for those of you who adore math) do not take into account things like the question "when would I get this money?" In a more complex model, you would also include the time value of money — figuring out how much that $10,000 offer today would earn you in interest during the time you would otherwise be waiting for a final outcome in the courts.

Despite these various caveats, a decision tree can help to provide decision makers with some insight into the magnitude of the tradeoffs they are considering. A key lesson for you or your client in the scenario we described above, for example, is that, despite the ability to win $50,000 at trial, the expected value of all of that time and effort is merely $1,000 more than you could receive tomorrow. For most people, who can get focused on what they *might* win at trial, discovering the calculated expected value is an eye-opening experience.

§11.3 TIME AND THE VALUE OF MONEY

As a basic proposition, in almost all circumstances, everyone would prefer to receive a dollar today instead of receiving a dollar a year from now. Maybe we want the dollar now because we are afraid the other side will not pay up a year from now. Or maybe we want the dollar today because we have an immediate need for cash. Or maybe we just want the dollar today because we could invest it and expect to have more than a dollar by the time next year rolls around.

Consider a basic scenario in which you are a plaintiff in a lawsuit, and the defendant has offered you $100,000 to settle the case. You have done your research and you have concluded that you have a 50-50 chance of winning the case at trial. Assume also, for simplicity's sake, that you know you will recover $200,000 if you win and nothing if you lose. Finally, assume away (for simplicity's sake) the impact of any attorneys' fees. You probably do not even need a decision tree to tell you that your expected return on going to court equals $100,000.

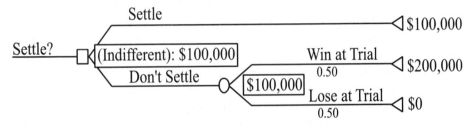

From the perspective of a decision tree, therefore, you might appear to be indifferent between settling for $100,000 or litigating (with its expected return of $100,000). But what if the court's docket is such that you should not expect to complete the trial and receive any award until two years from today? In theory, you should be able to earn some sort of return on any money you invest. Assume for purposes of this section (though not necessarily for purposes of your own financial planning) that you could make a 5 percent annual return on any money you invest. Comparing the two choices then looks more like this:

	Expected Value of Settling	Expected Value of Litigating
Today	$100,000	
One Year from Today	$105,000	
Two Years from Today	$110,250	$100,000

This is not a book on finance, of course. But even the most basic concepts of interest make clear that when you receive or pay a particular sum of money can have a large impact on how valuable or costly that money is.[1]

And in the real world, of course, the circumstances are even more complex. If we add back in attorneys' fees, for example, it would not only make the math more complicated, it would also invite us to examine the effects of time on those expenditures as well. (You could have done something else with those attorneys' fee dollars during the two years this will take to litigate, for example.)

We might also look at the **cash-flow** implications of the decision to press forward with litigation. Even though you expect to win $100,000 with this litigation, what if the attorneys' fees will cost you $20,000 and you do not have that kind of money available? Unless the attorneys agree to take your case on a contingent fee basis, your decision will probably not only be driven by the eventual expected payout. Instead, it will be based on what you can afford to pursue right now.

Each side in a dispute would prefer money today rather than money next year. The plaintiff would rather have its money today so that it can invest the money and enjoy the benefits of the interest on that money. The defendant would rather keep its money today, so that it can continue to earn interest on the money. (Or in some cases, the defendant would rather pay later because, in order to pay the plaintiff, it is going to have to borrow money, and pay a bank some interest rate on that money.) Sometimes, the two sides will have utterly equal opportunities for investing and borrowing money, in which case, the time factor is less significant. In most circumstances, however, one side or the other places more value on having the money immediately and so is willing to pay a premium (in effect) to have the money now.

This basic principle underlies the increasingly common use of **structured settlements** to resolve claims. Structured settlements typically involve one or more financial instruments (such as annuities) to provide payment over time. Depending on the parties' financial circumstances, such arrangements may create more total benefit for each party than a simple one-time lump-sum payment, because their structure and terms include calculations

---

1. The mathematical formula for calculating the effects of compound interest is:

$$A = P\left(1 + \frac{r}{n}\right)^{nt}$$

where P is the initial principal amount
       r is the interest rate
       n is the number of times per year the interest is compounded
       t is the number of years
       A is the amount the principle will be worth t years from now, given that interest rate.
So in our example:

$$110,250 = 100,000\left(1 + \frac{.05}{1}\right)^{(1 \times 2)}$$

based on what each party would have done with the money in the interim periods. For example, if the defendant (the party making the payments) expects greater returns on the money than the plaintiff (the party receiving the payments), it may be more efficient to have the defendant hold onto more of the money, for longer, in exchange for paying out a greater total to the plaintiff over time.

Examples

The Apartment of Ralph's Nightmares

Ralph entered into a one-year rental agreement with Laura. During his first week in the new apartment, Ralph became violently ill. Based on some initial tests performed by his physician, Ralph became convinced that his poor health was being caused by exposure to a toxin of some sort. Ralph called Laura and accused her of exposing him to "deadly chemicals and other toxins" in the apartment, and Ralph told Laura that he considered the rental agreement to be void. The next day, Ralph moved out of the apartment.

Two days after moving out, Ralph filed a lawsuit against Laura, alleging that she knowingly exposed him to unsafe living conditions. In his complaint, Ralph demanded $10,000 for medical and moving expenses, plus pain and suffering compensation of $50,000. Laura denied that the apartment contains any toxins, denied all liability, and filed a counterclaim for the approximately $18,000 Ralph still owed her in rent for the coming year. Neither side has yet engaged in any discovery in the case.

Ralph's Choices

Ralph and his attorney (a good friend of Ralph, who gave him a discounted fee for her services) made the following estimates about their prospects in litigation: Ralph's case will hinge exclusively on the question of whether the apartment contains toxins capable of causing an illness like Ralph's. To determine this, Ralph will need to hire an expert to conduct tests on the apartment. Ralph's attorney gave him the following summary of the likelihood of various outcomes at trial: "If your expert finds toxins, we're a lock to win our claim for $60,000, and there's no way Laura's counterclaim will succeed. If, on the other hand, the expert finds no toxins, you're out of luck—Laura's claim will succeed and yours will fail." In either event, Ralph would owe the expert $10,000 and he would owe $5,000 to his attorney. Ralph has admitted to his attorney that he might have been exposed to toxins elsewhere, and they therefore estimate that there is only a 50 percent chance that the expert's report will show the presence of toxins in the apartment.

1. **Ralph's Reservation Value.** Based on the information above, what do you think Ralph's reservation value would be in a negotiation with Laura over settling these claims?

Ralph's attorney returns to him the next day and says, "I've done some more research, and I have some good news and some bad news. The bad news is that there's a chance you won't be able to receive the pain and suffering award, even if you win your claim. I'd say there's about a 60 percent chance you'd get the full award amount if you win. Otherwise, you would just receive the $10,000 of actual damages. The good news is this: Even if you lose your claim and Laura wins hers, there is a 90 percent chance that she would only be able to recover about $3,000 from you, because she almost certainly has a duty to mitigate her losses by renting to someone else. That leaves only a 10 percent chance she can recover the full amount she's demanding in her counterclaim."

2. **Ralph's Revised Reservation Value.** How does this new information affect your estimate of Ralph's reservation value in his negotiations with Laura?

Laura's Choices

Laura has hired an attorney who has agreed to handle the preliminary aspects of this case for no charge, but if the case proceeds to trial, it will cost Laura $10,000 in legal expenses. Laura and her attorney have privately assessed the risks and opportunities present in the litigation with Ralph. Laura believes that there is only a 25 percent chance that Ralph's expert will find toxins in the apartment. She would be even more confident than that, but she recently heard about another local landlord — one whom Laura considers very trustworthy — finding toxins present in a unit similar to the one Laura rented to Ralph. If Ralph's expert finds toxins, Ralph will surely win his claim and Laura will lose her counterclaim. In the event he wins, Ralph has a 50 percent chance of recovering the full amount he has claimed, and a 50 percent chance he will receive only the actual damages of $10,000. If Ralph's expert finds no toxins, Laura and her attorney are absolutely confident that they will recover the full amount of the counterclaim, $18,000.

3. **Laura's Reservation Value.** Based on this information, what do you estimate Laura's reservation value to be in her negotiations with Ralph over these claims?

After reviewing her attorney's analysis of the risks and opportunities present in litigation, Laura says to her attorney, "Things look really bad for me if Ralph's expert finds toxins. If that happens, don't you think I should hire my own expert to check the results of that analysis?" Laura's attorney tells her that an expert would cost $10,000, and that the results of the tests for toxins are 90 percent likely to come back the same. If Laura's expert confirms the presence of toxins, the same set of probabilities as described above would apply: a 50 percent chance of full recovery for Ralph, and a 50 percent chance of only actual damages for Ralph. If, however, Laura's expert found no toxins, the fact finder would have to choose to believe one expert or the other — and Laura's attorney sees no reason why one would be more credible than the other, making it a 50-50 chance that the fact finder would side with Laura. If the fact finder believes Laura's expert, she would expect to recover the full $18,000 she claimed. If the fact finder sided with Ralph's expert, Ralph would again have a 50 percent chance of receiving full damages and a 50 percent chance of receiving only actual damages.

4. **Laura's Own Expert.** Based on this information, how would you respond to Laura's question about whether she should plan to hire a competing expert, in the event Ralph's expert finds toxins in the apartment?

Pay Me Now, Pay Me Later

Assume that Ralph and Laura have each learned some new information, leading them each to revise their expectations about the likely outcome of litigating their dispute. Assume that both of them have decided to proceed without attorneys, eliminating those possible expenses.

After rerunning his numbers, Ralph has concluded that his expected benefit from litigating is $14,000. Unfortunately, Ralph has not managed his finances well up until this point, and he is carrying tens of thousands of dollars of credit card debt right now, on which he is paying an annual interest rate of 19 percent.

After rerunning her numbers, Laura has concluded that the expected result of litigating would be that she would owe Ralph $12,000. Laura's real estate business has more than enough funds to cover any judgment against her. At the moment, she has her company's reserves invested in an account that yields 6 percent interest per year.

5. **ZOPA?** Based on each party's expected trial outcome, if the trial were to take place immediately, does it appear that Laura and Ralph have a zone of possible agreement?
6. **Time Cures All?** Assume that the current backlog of cases in the local courts means that any judgment in this case would not occur until two years from today. What effect, if any, might this two-year court delay have on the parties' ability to find a mutually agreeable lump-sum settlement today?

Explanations

Ralph's Choices

1. **Ralph's Reservation Value.** One way to analyze Ralph's reservation value would be to construct a decision tree to reflect the various costs, opportunities, and risks involved in the litigation Ralph faces. The facts tell us that going to litigation will cost Ralph $15,000, regardless of the outcome. According to the facts, the entire litigation hinges on whether the expert finds toxins, so the decision tree should include a chance node — one branch showing a victory for Ralph, and the other showing a loss for Ralph. If Ralph wins, he stands to gain $60,000. If he loses, he would wind up owing Laura $18,000.

   The facts tell us that Ralph estimates the odds at 50-50. Of course, Ralph might have reason to doubt the precision of such an estimate. To say that something is 50 percent likely to happen (as opposed to 45 percent or 60 percent likely) has questionable reliability. Still, because these are the figures we are given, we should use them at least for a basis of getting a sense of the magnitude of Ralph's decision. The tree below shows how one might lay out the probabilities and set up the basic arithmetic involved in estimating Ralph's expected payout if he pursues the litigation.

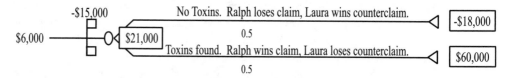

   According to this decision tree, Ralph's expected benefit from pursuing litigation is $6,000. (That is (−$18,000)*.5 + ($60,000*.5) − $15,000.) One might imagine, therefore, that Ralph's reservation value in a negotiation with Laura would be $6,000. If we knew more about Ralph, we might be able to judge the accuracy of this estimate. How risk averse is Ralph? How important is it to him to see Laura "punished" by the justice system? How badly does Ralph need the money *now* (recalling that he would not see any dollars from litigation for some time)? How confident is Ralph in his estimates of the probabilities and the payoffs involved? Based on the information we have been given, though, we might reasonably assume that Ralph would be willing to settle for anything above $6,000, but might prefer to litigate if Laura's offer is below that figure.

   Note that we are assuming that Ralph's reservation value is a function of his BATNA, translated into dollars. Ralph's actual medical and moving expenses in this case may already be greater than this amount. By stating that this is Ralph's reservation value, we are not saying that this is an amount that Ralph would feel happy about, an amount that would make Ralph "whole," or an amount that is based on some vision of fairness. A reservation value estimates the point at which a party would be

indifferent between two courses of action — in this case settling or litigating. If we assume that Ralph is economically rational (an assumption
that is surely worthy of testing), and that his primary motivator is net
expected dollars (again, an assumption worth testing), his reservation
value should not be far from $6,000.

2. **Ralph's Revised Reservation Value.** Ralph's revised reservation value
   should take into account these two new variables — the probability that
   recovery would be less than complete for either Ralph or Laura, in the
   event of a victory at trial. Modifying the decision tree described above
   yields the following:

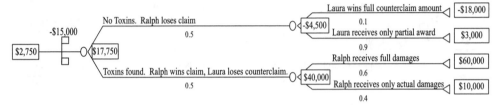

So, according to this analysis, Ralph's reservation value would drop
to under $3,000.

To make the math explicit:

$$.10* (-\$18,000) = -\$1,800$$
$$.90* (-\$3,000) = -\$2,700$$
$$(-\$1,800) + (-\$2,700) = -\$4,500$$

$$.5* (-\$4,500) = -\$2,750$$

$$\$17,750 - \qquad .5* \$40,000 = \$20,000$$
$$\$15,000 = \$2,750 \qquad \$20,000 + (-\$2,750)$$
$$= \$17,750$$

$$.6 * \$60,000 = \$36,000$$
$$.4* \$10,000 = \$4,000$$
$$\$36,000 + \$4,000 = \$40,000$$

As with the analysis above, if we were counseling Ralph, we would
caution him not to attach too strong a meaning to the particular figure
this analysis yields. It is difficult to estimate probabilities with great
reliability. To say that something is unlikely to happen may be correct.
To distinguish something that is 10 percent likely to happen from
something that is 15 percent likely to happen is questionable, at best.
Further, this analysis does not take into account Ralph's personal preference for or tolerance of risk. And it does not take into account any value
Ralph places on his own time. (How many hours will Ralph spend in
litigation that he might have spent doing something else?) In sum, what
this analysis can tell us is that Ralph's expected net benefit from going to
trial is only modestly above zero.

259

Laura's Choices

3. **Laura's Reservation Value.** The point at which she would be indifferent to continuing with litigation and settling would be in the neighborhood of $5,250. That is, if she were basing her decision purely on expected economic opportunities and costs, she would be willing to pay slightly over $5,000 to settle this case. To arrive at this figure, the decision tree below sets out the attorneys' fees, the probability that Ralph's expert will find toxins, and the various expected payouts and probabilities at trial.

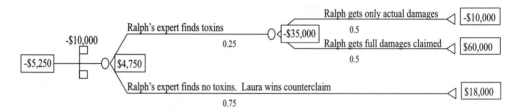

Note that the value of this calculation depends on the quality of the estimates Laura and her attorney generated. However, based on the facts provided, this is the best estimate we can produce. (Of interest here also is the fact that Laura's expected net benefit/liability from litigation is positive before we factor in the attorneys' fees. That is, if she could get the same odds at trial without hiring a lawyer, she might prefer to go to trial.)

4. **Laura's Own Expert.** Laura's instinct to want to get her own expert to verify the findings of toxicity is understandable, since everything essentially rides on this one finding. The transaction costs of hiring an expert, however, make it financially unwise for Laura to invest the extra money—at least from the perspective of its effects on the expected outcome of this litigation. According to the decision tree below, hiring her own expert only improves her expected outcome in litigation by a few thousand dollars, while the expert costs ten thousand dollars.

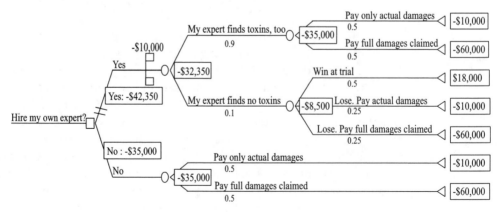

Laura's choice boils down to this: Hiring her own expert brings down her expected loss at trial from $35,000 to $32,350. But the expert would cost $10,000, far outweighing the expected benefits the expert would bring.

As always with decision trees, this analysis is sensitive to the probability estimates created by Laura and her attorney. The tree also does not take into account any interests Laura may have beyond the net expected payouts in this piece of litigation. Perhaps Laura is willing to incur the additional expenses of having an expert because she has several other units that would be susceptible to the same kind of claim. Perhaps she places a premium on her reputation — and would therefore either pay for a confidentiality agreement (see Chapter 4 for a discussion of the legality and enforceability of such provisions in settlements) or would be willing to take on greater risk at trial, rather than admit liability. And so on. Based on the information provided, however, if Ralph's expert finds toxins in the apartment, Laura should not bother to hire a competing expert.

Pay Me Now, Pay Me Later

5. **ZOPA?** No. If we look only at what each expects to happen at trial, and if the trial and judgment occur immediately, there appears to be no zone of possible agreement. Ralph would want more than he expects to receive by going to trial ($14,000), and Laura would want to pay less than she expects to pay by going to trial ($12,000).

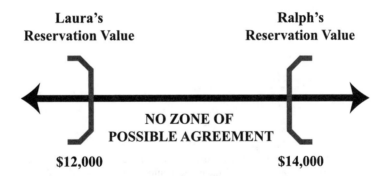

6. **Time Cures All?** This is a classic situation in which the parties both prefer money today, but differ in the rates at which they prefer money sooner rather than later. Because Ralph is paying such a high interest rate on his debt right now — far higher than the interest rate Laura is receiving — the most efficient agreement between the two would be one in which Laura pays Ralph quickly. Ralph will, in effect, be willing to take a discount from Laura (or depending on your perspective, pay a premium to Laura) in exchange for getting the money now.

To illustrate this proposition mathematically, consider how each party would assess a lump-sum settlement today of $10,000. Ralph would, theoretically at least, be able to use that money to pay off some of his credit card debt. Since he is paying 19 percent interest on his debt, if he were to pay $10,000 of his debt today, it would save him from having to pay $11,900 a year from today. So, today, the $10,000 would be worth $10,000 to Ralph. But to Ralph, receiving that $10,000 today would be the equivalent of receiving $11,900 a year from today. ($10,000 × 1.19 = $11,900.) And that, in turn, is the equivalent of Ralph receiving $14,161 two years from today. ($11,900 × 1.19 = $14,161.) The miracles of compound interest! Laura would, of course, prefer to keep her money, so that she can continue to earn the 6 percent interest on it. If she were to keep her $10,000 and invest it this year, it would be worth $10,600 to her a year from today. ($10,000 × 1.06 = $10,600.) And a year later, it would be worth, $11,236 to her. ($10,600 × 1.06 = $11,236.)

Now compare each party's expectation of what trial would yield two years from now with how each party values $10,000 today.

What does all of this mean for a ZOPA analysis for Laura and Ralph, if we are looking two years down the road? Absent the time consideration, these two parties had no apparent ZOPA. But by factoring in the effects of interest over time, these two parties could arrive at a settlement (for example, a flat $10,000 payment today) each would find more financially attractive than going to court and getting an outcome two years from now.[2]

---

2. To calculate how each party's reservation value shifts under the effects of time and interest (and therefore, to calculate the contour of any possible ZOPA), the relevant formula would be:

$$PV = \frac{FV}{(1 + r)^n}$$

PV = present value
FV = future value
r = interest rate
n = number of periods

Applying this formula to the figures in this case suggests that a trial one year away still produces no ZOPA. (Laura's maximum would be $11,321 and Ralph's minimum would be $11,765.) If trial is two years away, however, a ZOPA emerges. Laura's maximum is $10,680 and Ralph's minimum is $9,886. Any number between $9,886 and $10,680 should, at least theoretically, be more attractive to each party than continued litigation.

Ralph's Choice		Laura's Choice	
Amount of expected award two years from now	$14,000	Amount of expected liability two years from now	$12,000
Value two years from now of an immediate $10,000 lump-sum payment	$14,161	Cost two years from now of an immediate $10,000 lump-sum payment	$11,236

The dollar figures in this case are not terribly large, of course. It is not clear that either party would necessarily make a decision about settlement based on just a few hundred dollars difference in expected cost of benefit. But the principle is there. And if you consider the potential implications of these analyses in cases that involve millions (rather than thousands) of dollars, you can imagine why this becomes important.

Uniform Mediation Act

Drafted by the National Conference of Commissioners on Uniform State Laws

SECTION 1. TITLE.

This [Act] may be cited as the Uniform Mediation Act.

SECTION 2. DEFINITIONS.

In this [Act]:

(1) "Mediation" means a process in which a mediator facilitates communication and negotiation between parties to assist them in reaching a voluntary agreement regarding their dispute.

(2) "Mediation communication" means a statement, whether oral or in a record or verbal or nonverbal, that occurs during a mediation or is made for purposes of considering, conducting, participating in, initiating, continuing, or reconvening a mediation or retaining a mediator.

(3) "Mediator" means an individual who conducts a mediation.

(4) "Nonparty participant" means a person, other than a party or mediator, that participates in a mediation.

(5) "Mediation party" means a person that participates in a mediation and whose agreement is necessary to resolve the dispute.

(6) "Person" means an individual, corporation, business trust, estate, trust, partnership, limited liability company, association, joint venture, government; governmental subdivision, agency, or instrumentality; public corporation, or any other legal or commercial entity.

(7) "Proceeding" means:

(A) a judicial, administrative, arbitral, or other adjudicative process, including related pre-hearing and post-hearing motions, conferences, and discovery; or

(B) a legislative hearing or similar process.

(8) "Record" means information that is inscribed on a tangible medium or that is stored in an electronic or other medium and is retrievable in perceivable form.

(9) "Sign" means:

(A) to execute or adopt a tangible symbol with the present intent to authenticate a record; or

(B) to attach or logically associate an electronic symbol, sound, or process to or with a record with the present intent to authenticate a record.

SECTION 3. SCOPE.

(a) Except as otherwise provided in subsection (b) or (c), this [Act] applies to a mediation in which:

(1) the mediation parties are required to mediate by statute or court or administrative agency rule or referred to mediation by a court, administrative agency, or arbitrator;

(2) the mediation parties and the mediator agree to mediate in a record that demonstrates an expectation that mediation communications will be privileged against disclosure; or

(3) the mediation parties use as a mediator an individual who holds himself or herself out as a mediator, or the mediation is provided by a person that holds itself out as providing mediation.

(b) The [Act] does not apply to a mediation:

(1) relating to the establishment, negotiation, administration, or termination of a collective bargaining relationship;

(2) relating to a dispute that is pending under or is part of the processes established by a collective bargaining agreement, except that the [Act] applies to a mediation arising out of a dispute that has been filed with an administrative agency or court;

(3) conducted by a judge who might make a ruling on the case; or

(4) conducted under the auspices of:

A) a primary or secondary school if all the parties are students or

B) a correctional institution for youths if all the parties are residents of that institution.

(c) If the parties agree in advance in a signed record, or a record of proceeding reflects agreement by the parties, that all or part of a mediation is not privileged, the privileges under Sections 4 through 6 do not apply to the mediation or part agreed upon. However, Sections 4 through 6 apply to a mediation communication made by a person that has not received actual notice of the agreement before the communication is made.

SECTION 4. PRIVILEGE AGAINST DISCLOSURE; ADMISSIBILITY; DISCOVERY.

(a) Except as otherwise provided in Section 6, a mediation communication is privileged as provided in subsection (b) and is not subject to discovery or admissible in evidence in a proceeding unless waived or precluded as provided by Section 5.

(b) In a proceeding, the following privileges apply:

(1) A mediation party may refuse to disclose, and may prevent any other person from disclosing, a mediation communication.

(2) A mediator may refuse to disclose a mediation communication, and may prevent any other person from disclosing a mediation communication of the mediator.

(3) A nonparty participant may refuse to disclose, and may prevent any other person from disclosing, a mediation communication of the nonparty participant.

(c) Evidence or information that is otherwise admissible or subject to discovery does not become inadmissible or protected from discovery solely by reason of its disclosure or use in a mediation.

SECTION 5. WAIVER AND PRECLUSION OF PRIVILEGE.

(a) A privilege under Section 4 may be waived in a record or orally during a proceeding if it is expressly waived by all parties to the mediation and:

(1) in the case of the privilege of a mediator, it is expressly waived by the mediator; and

(2) in the case of the privilege of a nonparty participant, it is expressly waived by the nonparty participant.

(b) A person that discloses or makes a representation about a mediation communication which prejudices another person in a proceeding is precluded from asserting a privilege under Section 4, but only to the extent necessary for the person prejudiced to respond to the representation or disclosure.

(c) A person that intentionally uses a mediation to plan, attempt to commit or commit a crime, or to conceal an ongoing crime or ongoing criminal activity is precluded from asserting a privilege under Section 4.

SECTION 6. EXCEPTIONS TO PRIVILEGE.

(a) There is no privilege under Section 4 for a mediation communication that is:

(1) in an agreement evidenced by a record signed by all parties to the agreement;

(2) available to the public under [insert statutory reference to open records act] or made during a session of a mediation which is open, or is required by law to be open, to the public;

(3) a threat or statement of a plan to inflict bodily injury or commit a crime of violence;

(4) intentionally used to plan a crime, attempt to commit or commit a crime, or to conceal an ongoing crime or ongoing criminal activity;

(5) sought or offered to prove or disprove a claim or complaint of professional misconduct or malpractice filed against a mediator;

(6) except as otherwise provided in subsection (c), sought or offered to prove or disprove a claim or complaint of professional misconduct or malpractice filed against a mediation party, nonparty participant, or representative of a party based on conduct occurring during a mediation; or

(7) sought or offered to prove or disprove abuse, neglect, abandonment, or exploitation in a proceeding in which a child or adult protective services agency is a party, unless the

[Alternative A: [State to insert, for example, child or adult protection] case is referred by a court to mediation and a public agency participates.]

[Alternative B: Public agency participates in the [State to insert, for example, child or adult protection] mediation.].

(b) There is no privilege under Section 4 if a court, administrative agency, or arbitrator finds, after a hearing in camera, that the party seeking discovery or the proponent of the evidence has shown that the evidence is not otherwise available, that there is a need for the evidence that substantially outweighs the interest in protecting confidentiality, and that the mediation communication is sought or offered in:

(1) a court proceeding involving a felony [or misdemeanor]; or

(2) except as otherwise provided in subsection (c), a proceeding to prove a claim to rescind or reform or a defense to avoid liability on a contract arising out of the mediation.

(c) A mediator may not be compelled to provide evidence of a mediation communication referred to in subsection (a)(6) or (b)(2).

(d) If a mediation communication is not privileged under subsection (a) or (b), only the portion of the communication necessary for the application of the exception from nondisclosure may be admitted. Admission of evidence under subsection (a) or (b) does not render the evidence, or any other mediation communication, discoverable or admissible for any other purpose.

SECTION 7. PROHIBITED MEDIATOR REPORTS.

(a) Except as required in subsection (b), a mediator may not make a report, assessment, evaluation, recommendation, finding, or other communication regarding a mediation to a court, administrative agency, or other authority that may make a ruling on the dispute that is the subject of the mediation.

(b) A mediator may disclose:

(1) whether the mediation occurred or has terminated, whether a settlement was reached, and attendance;

(2) a mediation communication as permitted under Section 6; or

(3) a mediation communication evidencing abuse, neglect, abandonment, or exploitation of an individual to a public agency responsible for protecting individuals against such mistreatment.

(c) A communication made in violation of subsection (a) may not be considered by a court, administrative agency, or arbitrator.

SECTION 8. CONFIDENTIALITY.

Unless subject to the [insert statutory references to open meetings act and open records act], mediation communications are confidential to the extent agreed by the parties or provided by other law or rule of this State.

SECTION 9. MEDIATOR'S DISCLOSURE OF CONFLICTS OF INTEREST; BACKGROUND.

(a) Before accepting a mediation, an individual who is requested to serve as a mediator shall:

(1) make an inquiry that is reasonable under the circumstances to determine whether there are any known facts that a reasonable individual would consider likely to affect the impartiality of the mediator, including a financial or personal interest in the outcome of the mediation and an existing or past relationship with a mediation party or foreseeable participant in the mediation; and

(2) disclose any such known fact to the mediation parties as soon as is practical before accepting a mediation.

(b) If a mediator learns any fact described in subsection (a)(1) after accepting a mediation, the mediator shall disclose it as soon as is practicable.

(c) At the request of a mediation party, an individual who is requested to serve as a mediator shall disclose the mediator's qualifications to mediate a dispute.

(d) A person that violates subsection [(a) or (b)] [(a), (b), or (g)] is precluded by the violation from asserting a privilege under Section 4.

(e) Subsections (a), (b), [and] (c), [and] [(g)] do not apply to an individual acting as a judge.

(f) This [Act] does not require that a mediator have a special qualification by background or profession.

[(g) A mediator must be impartial, unless after disclosure of the facts required in subsections (a) and (b) to be disclosed, the parties agree otherwise.]

SECTION 10. PARTICIPATION IN MEDIATION.

An attorney or other individual designated by a party may accompany the party to and participate in a mediation. A waiver of participation given before the mediation may be rescinded.

SECTION 11. INTERNATIONAL COMMERCIAL MEDIATION.

(a) In this section, "Model Law" means the Model Law on International Commercial Conciliation adopted by the United Nations Commission on International Trade Law on 28 June 2002 and recommended by the United Nations General Assembly in a resolution (A/RES/57/18) dated 19 November 2002, and "international commercial mediation" means an international commercial conciliation as defined in Article 1 of the Model Law.

(b) Except as otherwise provided in subsections (c) and (d), if a mediation is an international commercial mediation, the mediation is governed by the Model Law.

(c) Unless the parties agree in accordance with Section 3(c) of this [Act] that all or part of an international commercial mediation is not privileged, Sections 4, 5, and 6 and any applicable definitions in Section 2 of this [Act] also apply to the mediation and nothing in Article 10 of the Model Law derogates from Sections 4, 5, and 6.

(d) If the parties to an international commercial mediation agree under Article 1, subsection (7), of the Model Law that the Model Law does not apply, this [Act] applies.

SECTION 12. RELATION TO ELECRONIC SIGNATURES IN GLOBAL AND NATIONAL COMMERCE ACT.

This [Act] modifies, limits, or supersedes the federal Electronic Signatures in Global and National Commerce Act, 15 U.S.C. Section 7001 et seq., but this [Act] does not modify, limit, or supersede Section 101(c) of that Act or authorize electronic delivery of any of the notices described in Section 103(b) of that Act.

SECTION 13. UNIFORMITY OF APPLICATION AND CONSTRUCTION.

In applying and construing this [Act], consideration should be given to the need to promote uniformity of the law with respect to its subject matter among States that enact it.

SECTION 14. SEVERABILITY CLAUSE.

If any provision of this [Act] or its application to any person or circumstance is held invalid, the invalidity does not affect other provisions or applications of this [Act] which can be given effect without the invalid provision or application, and to this end the provisions of this [Act] are severable.

SECTION 15. EFFECTIVE DATE.

This [Act] takes effect _____.

SECTION 16. REPEALS.

The following acts and parts of acts are hereby repealed:

(1)

(2)

(3)

SECTION 17. APPLICATION TO EXISTING AGREEMENTS OR REFERRALS.

(a) This [Act] governs a mediation pursuant to a referral or an agreement to mediate made on or after [the effective date of this [Act]].

(b) On or after [a delayed date], this [Act] governs an agreement to mediate whenever made.

The Model Standards of Conduct for Mediators

The *Model Standards of Conduct for Mediators* was prepared in 1994 by the American Arbitration Association, the American Bar Association's Section of Dispute Resolution, and the Association for Conflict Resolution. A joint committee consisting of representatives from the same successor organizations revised the Model Standards in 2005. Both the original 1994 version and the 2005 revision have been approved by each participating organization.

PREAMBLE

Mediation is used to resolve a broad range of conflicts within a variety of settings. These Standards are designed to serve as fundamental ethical guidelines for persons mediating in all practice contexts. They serve three primary goals: to guide the conduct of mediators; to inform the mediating parties; and to promote public confidence in mediation as a process for resolving disputes.

Mediation is a process in which an impartial third party facilitates communication and negotiation and promotes voluntary decision making by the parties to the dispute.

Mediation serves various purposes, including providing the opportunity for parties to define and clarify issues, understand different perspectives, identify interests, explore and assess possible solutions, and reach mutually satisfactory agreements, when desired.

NOTE ON CONSTRUCTION

These Standards are to be read and construed in their entirety. There is no priority significance attached to the sequence in which the Standards appear.

The use of the term "shall" in a Standard indicates that the mediator must follow the practice described. The use of the term "should" indicates that the practice described in the standard is highly desirable, but not required, and is to be departed from only for very strong reasons and requires careful use of judgment and discretion.

The use of the term "mediator" is understood to be inclusive so that it applies to co-mediator models.

These Standards do not include specific temporal parameters when referencing a mediation, and therefore, do not define the exact beginning or ending of a mediation.

Various aspects of a mediation, including some matters covered by these Standards, may also be affected by applicable law, court rules, regulations, other applicable professional rules, mediation rules to which the parties have agreed and other agreements of the parties. These sources may create conflicts with, and may take precedence over, these Standards. However, a mediator should make every effort to comply with the spirit and intent of these Standards in resolving such conflicts. This effort should include honoring all remaining Standards not in conflict with these other sources.

These Standards, unless and until adopted by a court or other regulatory authority do not have the force of law. Nonetheless, the fact that these Standards have been adopted by the respective sponsoring entities should alert mediators to the fact that the Standards might be viewed as establishing a standard of care for mediators.

STANDARD I.   SELF-DETERMINATION

A. A mediator shall conduct a mediation based on the principle of party self-determination. Self-determination is the act of coming to a voluntary, uncoerced decision in which each party makes free and informed choices as to process and outcome. Parties may exercise self-determination at any stage of a mediation, including mediator selection, process design, participation in or withdrawal from the process, and outcomes.

1. Although party self-determination for process design is a fundamental principle of mediation practice, a mediator may need to balance such party self-determination with a mediator's duty to conduct a quality process in accordance with these Standards.

2. A mediator cannot personally ensure that each party has made free and informed choices to reach particular decisions, but, where appropriate, a mediator should make the parties aware of the importance of consulting other professionals to help them make informed choices.

B. A mediator shall not undermine party self-determination by any party for reasons such as higher settlement rates, egos, increased fees, or outside pressures from court personnel, program administrators, provider organizations, the media or others.

STANDARD II.   IMPARTIALITY

A. A mediator shall decline a mediation if the mediator cannot conduct it in an impartial manner. Impartiality means freedom from favoritism, bias or prejudice.

B. A mediator shall conduct a mediation in an impartial manner and avoid conduct that gives the appearance of partiality.

1. A mediator should not act with partiality or prejudice based on any participant's personal characteristics, background, values and beliefs, or performance at a mediation, or any other reason.

2. A mediator should neither give nor accept a gift, favor, loan or other item of value that raises a question as to the mediator's actual or perceived impartiality.

3. A mediator may accept or give de minimis gifts or incidental items or services that are provided to facilitate a mediation or respect cultural norms so long as such practices do not raise questions as to a mediator's actual or perceived impartiality.

C. If at any time a mediator is unable to conduct a mediation in an impartial manner, the mediator shall withdraw.

STANDARD III.   CONFLICTS OF INTEREST

A. A mediator shall avoid a conflict of interest or the appearance of a conflict of interest during and after a mediation. A conflict of interest can arise from involvement by a mediator with the subject matter of the dispute or from any relationship between a mediator and any mediation participant, whether past or present, personal or professional, that reasonably raises a question of a mediator's impartiality.

B. A mediator shall make a reasonable inquiry to determine whether there are any facts that a reasonable individual would consider likely to create a potential or actual conflict of interest for a mediator. A mediator's actions necessary to accomplish a reasonable inquiry into potential conflicts of interest may vary based on practice context.

C. A mediator shall disclose, as soon as practicable, all actual and potential conflicts of interest that are reasonably known to the mediator and could reasonably be seen as raising a question about the mediator's impartiality. After disclosure, if all parties agree, the mediator may proceed with the mediation.

D. If a mediator learns any fact after accepting a mediation that raises a question with respect to that mediator's service creating a potential or actual conflict of interest, the mediator shall disclose it as quickly as practicable. After disclosure, if all parties agree, the mediator may proceed with the mediation.

E. If a mediator's conflict of interest might reasonably be viewed as undermining the integrity of the mediation, a mediator shall withdraw from or decline to proceed with the mediation regardless of the expressed desire or agreement of the parties to the contrary.

F. Subsequent to a mediation, a mediator shall not establish another relationship with any of the participants in any matter that would raise questions about the integrity of the mediation. When a mediator develops personal or professional relationships with parties, other individuals or organizations following a mediation in which they were involved, the mediator should consider factors such as time elapsed following the mediation, the nature of the relationships established, and services offered when determining whether the relationships might create a perceived or actual conflict of interest.

STANDARD IV.   COMPETENCE

A. A mediator shall mediate only when the mediator has the necessary competence to satisfy the reasonable expectations of the parties.

1. Any person may be selected as a mediator, provided that the parties are satisfied with the mediator's competence and qualifications. Training, experience in mediation, skills, cultural understandings and other qualities are often necessary for mediator competence. A person who offers to serve as a mediator creates the expectation that the person is competent to mediate effectively.

2. A mediator should attend educational programs and related activities to maintain and enhance the mediator's knowledge and skills related to mediation.

3. A mediator should have available for the parties information relevant to the mediator's training, education, experience and approach to conducting a mediation.

B. If a mediator, during the course of a mediation determines that the mediator cannot conduct the mediation competently, the mediator shall discuss that determination with the parties as soon as is practicable and take appropriate steps to address the situation, including, but not limited to, withdrawing or requesting appropriate assistance.

C. If a mediator's ability to conduct a mediation is impaired by drugs, alcohol, medication or otherwise, the mediator shall not conduct the mediation.

STANDARD V.   CONFIDENTIALITY

A. A mediator shall maintain the confidentiality of all information obtained by the mediator in mediation, unless otherwise agreed to by the parties or required by applicable law.

1. If the parties to a mediation agree that the mediator may disclose information obtained during the mediation, the mediator may do so.

2. A mediator should not communicate to any non-participant information about how the parties acted in the mediation. A mediator may report, if required, whether parties appeared at a scheduled mediation and whether or not the parties reached a resolution.

3. If a mediator participates in teaching, research or evaluation of mediation, the mediator should protect the anonymity of the parties and abide by their reasonable expectations regarding confidentiality.

B. A mediator who meets with any persons in private session during a mediation shall not convey directly or indirectly to any other person, any information that was obtained during that private session without the consent of the disclosing person.

C. A mediator shall promote understanding among the parties of the extent to which the parties will maintain confidentiality of information they obtain in a mediation.

D. Depending on the circumstance of a mediation the parties may have varying expectations regarding confidentiality that a mediator should address. The parties may make their own rules with respect to confidentiality, or the accepted practice of an individual mediator or institution may dictate a particular set of expectations.

STANDARD VI.   QUALITY OF THE PROCESS

A. A mediator shall conduct a mediation in accordance with these Standards and in a manner that promotes diligence, timeliness, safety, presence of the appropriate participants, party participation, procedural fairness, party competency and mutual respect among all participants.

1. A mediator should agree to mediate only when the mediator is prepared to commit the attention essential to an effective mediation.

2. A mediator should only accept cases when the mediator can satisfy the reasonable expectation of the parties concerning the timing of a mediation.

3. The presence or absence of persons at a mediation depends on the agreement of the parties and the mediator. The parties and mediator may agree that others may be excluded from particular sessions or from all sessions.

4. A mediator should promote honesty and candor between and among all participants, and a mediator shall not knowingly misrepresent any material fact or circumstance in the course of a mediation.

5. The role of a mediator differs substantially from other professional roles. Mixing the role of a mediator and the role of another profession is problematic and thus, a mediator should distinguish between the roles. A mediator may provide information that the mediator is qualified by training or experience to provide, only if the mediator can do so consistent with these Standards.

6. A mediator shall not conduct a dispute resolution procedure other than mediation but label it mediation in an effort to gain the protection of rules, statutes, or other governing authorities pertaining to mediation.

7. A mediator may recommend, when appropriate, that parties consider resolving their dispute through arbitration, counseling, neutral evaluation or other processes.

8. A mediator shall not undertake an additional dispute resolution role in the same matter without the consent of the parties. Before providing such service, a mediator shall inform the parties of the implications of the change in process and obtain their consent to the change. A mediator who undertakes such a role assumes different duties and responsibilities that may be governed by other standards.

9. If a mediation is being used to further criminal conduct, a mediator should take appropriate steps including, if necessary, postponing, withdrawing from or terminating the mediation.

10. If a party appears to have difficulty comprehending the process, issues, or settlement options, or difficulty participating in a mediation, the mediator should explore the circumstances and

potential accommodations, modifications or adjustments that would make possible the party's capacity to comprehend, participate and exercise self-determination.

B. If a mediator is made aware of domestic abuse or violence among the parties, the mediator shall take appropriate steps including, if necessary, postponing, withdrawing from or terminating the mediation.

C. If a mediator believes that participant conduct, including that of the mediator, jeopardizes conducting a mediation consistent with these Standards, a mediator shall take appropriate steps including, if necessary, postponing, withdrawing from or terminating the mediation.

STANDARD VII.   ADVERTISING AND SOLICITATION

A. A mediator shall be truthful and not misleading when advertising, soliciting or otherwise communicating the mediator's qualifications, experience, services and fees.

1. A mediator should not include any promises as to outcome in communications, including business cards, stationery, or computer-based communications.

2. A mediator should only claim to meet the mediator qualifications of a governmental entity or private organization if that entity or organization has a recognized procedure for qualifying mediators and it grants such status to the mediator.

B. A mediator shall not solicit in a manner that gives an appearance of partiality for or against a party or otherwise undermines the integrity of the process.

C. A mediator shall not communicate to others, in promotional materials or through other forms of communication, the names of persons served without their permission.

STANDARD VIII.   FEES AND OTHER CHARGES

A. A mediator shall provide each party or each party's representative true and complete information about mediation fees, expenses and any other actual or potential charges that may be incurred in connection with a mediation.

1. If a mediator charges fees, the mediator should develop them in light of all relevant factors, including the type and complexity of the matter, the qualifications of the mediator, the time required and the rates customary for such mediation services.

2. A mediator's fee arrangement should be in writing unless the parties request otherwise.

B. A mediator shall not charge fees in a manner that impairs a mediator's impartiality.

1. A mediator should not enter into a fee agreement which is contingent upon the result of the mediation or amount of the settlement.

2. While a mediator may accept unequal fee payments from the parties, a mediator should not use fee arrangements that adversely impact the mediator's ability to conduct a mediation in an impartial manner.

STANDARD IX.   ADVANCEMENT OF MEDIATION PRACTICE

A. A mediator should act in a manner that advances the practice of mediation. A mediator promotes this Standard by engaging in some or all of the following:

1. Fostering diversity within the field of mediation.

2. Striving to make mediation accessible to those who elect to use it, including providing services at a reduced rate or on a pro bono basis as appropriate.

3. Participating in research when given the opportunity, including obtaining participant feedback when appropriate.

4. Participating in outreach and education efforts to assist the public in developing an improved understanding of, and appreciation for, mediation.

5. Assisting newer mediators through training, mentoring and networking.

B. A mediator should demonstrate respect for differing points of view within the field, seek to learn from other mediators and work together with other mediators to improve the profession and better serve people in conflict.

The Federal Arbitration Act

9 U.S.C. 1 ET SEQ.

SECTION 1. "MARITIME TRANSACTIONS" AND "COMMERCE" DEFINED; EXCEPTIONS TO OPERATION OF TITLE

"Maritime transaction," as herein defined, means charter parties, bills of lading of water carriers, agreements relating to wharfage, supplies furnished vessels or repairs to vessels, collisions, or any other matters in foreign commerce which, if the subject of controversy, would be embraced within admiralty jurisdiction; "commerce," as herein defined, means commerce among the several States or with foreign nations, or in any Territory of the United States or in the District of Columbia, or between any such Territory and another, or between any such Territory and any State or foreign nation, or between the District of Columbia and any State or Territory or foreign nation, but nothing herein contained shall apply to contracts of employment of seamen, railroad employees, or any other class of workers engaged in foreign or interstate commerce.

SECTION 2. VALIDITY, IRREVOCABILITY, AND ENFORCEMENT OF AGREEMENTS TO ARBITRATE

A written provision in any maritime transaction or a contract evidencing a transaction involving commerce to settle by arbitration a controversy thereafter arising out of such contract or transaction, or the refusal to perform the whole or any part thereof, or an agreement in writing to submit to arbitration an existing controversy arising out of such a contract, transaction, or refusal, shall be valid, irrevocable, and enforceable, save upon such grounds as exist at law or in equity for the revocation of any contract.

SECTION 3. STAY OF PROCEEDINGS WHERE ISSUE THEREIN REFERABLE TO ARBITRATION

If any suit or proceeding be brought in any of the courts of the United States upon any issue referable to arbitration under an agreement in writing for such arbitration, the court in which such suit is pending, upon being satisfied that the issue involved in such suit or proceeding is referable to arbitration under such an agreement, shall on application of one of the parties stay the trial of the action until such arbitration has been had in accordance with the terms of the agreement, providing the applicant for the stay is not in default in proceeding with such arbitration.

SECTION 4. FAILURE TO ARBITRATE UNDER AGREEMENT; PETITION TO UNITED STATES COURT HAVING JURISDICTION FOR ORDER TO COMPEL ARBITRATION; NOTICE AND SERVICE THEREOF; HEARING AND DETERMINATION

A party aggrieved by the alleged failure, neglect, or refusal of another to arbitrate under a written agreement for arbitration may petition any United States district court which, save for such agreement, would have jurisdiction under Title 28, in a civil action or in admiralty of the subject matter of a suit arising out of the controversy between the parties, for an order directing that such arbitration proceed in the manner provided for in such agreement. Five days' notice in writing of such application shall be served upon the party in default. Service thereof shall be made in the manner provided by the Federal Rules of Civil Procedure. The court shall hear the parties, and upon being satisfied that the making of the agreement for arbitration or the failure to comply therewith is not in issue, the court shall make an order directing the parties to proceed to arbitration in accordance with the terms of the agreement. The hearing and proceedings, under such agreement, shall be within the district in which the petition for an order directing such arbitration is filed. If the making of the arbitration agreement or the failure, neglect, or refusal to perform the same be in issue, the court shall proceed summarily to the trial thereof. If no jury trial be demanded by the party alleged to be in default, or if the matter in dispute is within admiralty jurisdiction, the court shall hear and determine such issue. Where such an issue is raised, the party alleged to be in default may, except in cases of admiralty, on or before the return day of the notice of application, demand a jury trial of such issue, and upon such demand the court shall make an order referring the issue or issues to a jury in the manner provided by the Federal Rules of Civil Procedure, or may specially call a jury for that purpose. If the jury find that no agreement in writing for arbitration was made or that there is no default in proceeding thereunder, the proceeding shall be dismissed. If the jury find that an agreement for arbitration was made in writing and that there is a default in proceeding thereunder, the court shall make an order summarily directing the parties to proceed with the arbitration in accordance with the terms thereof.

SECTION 5. APPOINTMENT OF ARBITRATORS OR UMPIRE

If in the agreement provision be made for a method of naming or appointing an arbitrator or arbitrators or an umpire, such method shall be followed; but if no method be provided therein, or if a method be provided and any party thereto shall fail to avail himself of such method, or if for any other reason there shall be a lapse in the naming of an arbitrator or arbitrators or umpire, or in filling a vacancy, then upon the application of either party to the controversy the court shall designate and appoint an arbitrator or arbitrators or umpire, as the case may require, who shall act under the said agreement with the same force and effect as if he or they had been specifically named therein; and unless otherwise provided in the agreement the arbitration shall be by a single arbitrator.

SECTION 6. APPLICATION HEARD AS MOTION

Any application to the court hereunder shall be made and heard in the manner provided by law for the making and hearing of motions, except as otherwise herein expressly provided.

SECTION 7. WITNESSES BEFORE ARBITRATORS; FEES; COMPELLING ATTENDANCE

The arbitrators selected either as prescribed in this title or otherwise, or a majority of them, may summon in writing any person to attend before them or any of them as a witness and in a proper case to bring with him or them any book, record, document, or paper which may be deemed material as evidence in the case. The fees for such attendance shall be the same as the fees of witnesses before masters of the United States courts. Said summons shall issue in the name of the arbitrator or arbitrators, or a majority of them, and shall be signed by the arbitrators, or a majority of them, and shall be directed to the said person and shall be served in the same manner as subpoenas to appear and testify before the court; if any person or persons so summoned to testify shall refuse or neglect to obey said summons, upon petition the United States district court for the district in which such arbitrators, or a majority of them, are sitting may compel the attendance of such person or persons before said arbitrator or arbitrators, or punish said person or persons for contempt in the same manner provided by law for securing the attendance of witnesses or their punishment for neglect or refusal to attend in the courts of the United States.

SECTION 8. PROCEEDINGS BEGUN BY LIBEL IN ADMIRALTY AND SEIZURE OF VESSEL OR PROPERTY

If the basis of jurisdiction be a cause of action otherwise justiciable in admiralty, then, notwithstanding anything herein to the contrary, the party claiming to be aggrieved may begin his proceeding hereunder by libel and seizure of the vessel or other property of the other party according to the usual course of admiralty proceedings, and the court shall then have jurisdiction to direct the parties to proceed with the arbitration and shall retain jurisdiction to enter its decree upon the award.

SECTION 9. AWARD OF ARBITRATORS; CONFIRMATION; JURISDICTION; PROCEDURE

If the parties in their agreement have agreed that a judgment of the court shall be entered upon the award made pursuant to the arbitration, and shall specify the court, then at any time within one year after the award is made any party to the arbitration may apply to the court so specified for an order confirming the award, and thereupon the court must grant such an order unless the award is vacated, modified, or corrected as prescribed in sections 10 and 11 of this title. If no court is specified in the agreement of the parties, then such application may be made to the United States court in and for the district within which such award was made. Notice of the application shall be served upon the adverse party, and thereupon the court shall have jurisdiction of such party as though he had appeared generally in the proceeding. If the adverse party is a resident of the district within which the award was made, such service shall be made upon the adverse party or his attorney as prescribed by law for service of notice of motion in an action in the same court. If the adverse party shall be a nonresident, then the notice of the application shall be served by the marshal of any district within which the adverse party may be found in like manner as other process of the court.

SECTION 10. SAME; VACATION; GROUNDS; REHEARING

(a) In any of the following cases the United States court in and for the district wherein the award was made may make an order vacating the award upon the application of any party to the arbitration

(1) where the award was procured by corruption, fraud, or undue means;

(2) where there was evident partiality or corruption in the arbitrators, or either of them;

(3) where the arbitrators were guilty of misconduct in refusing to postpone the hearing, upon sufficient cause shown, or in refusing to hear evidence pertinent and material to the controversy; or of any other misbehavior by which the rights of any party have been prejudiced;

(4) where the arbitrators exceeded their powers, or so imperfectly executed them that a mutual, final, and definite award upon the subject matter submitted was not made.

(b) If an award is vacated and the time within which the agreement required the award to be made has not expired, the court may, in its discretion, direct a rehearing by the arbitrators.

(c) The United States district court for the district wherein an award was made that was issued pursuant to section 580 of title 5 may make an order vacating the award upon the application of a person, other than a party to the arbitration, who is adversely affected or aggrieved by the award, if the use of arbitration or the award is clearly inconsistent with the factors set forth in section 572 of Title 5.

SECTION 11. SAME; MODIFICATION OR CORRECTION; GROUNDS; ORDER

In either of the following cases the United States court in and for the district wherein the award was made may make an order modifying or correcting the award upon the application of any party to the arbitration:

(a) Where there was an evident material miscalculation of figures or an evident material mistake in the description of any person, thing, or property referred to in the award.

(b) Where the arbitrators have awarded upon a matter not submitted to them, unless it is a matter not affecting the merits of the decision upon the matter submitted.

(c) Where the award is imperfect in matter of form not affecting the merits of the controversy.

The order may modify and correct the award, so as to effect the intent thereof and promote justice between the parties.

SECTION 12. NOTICE OF MOTIONS TO VACATE OR MODIFY; SERVICE; STAY OF PROCEEDINGS

Notice of a motion to vacate, modify, or correct an award must be served upon the adverse party or his attorney within three months after the award is filed or delivered. If the adverse party is a resident of the district within which the award was made, such service shall be made upon the adverse party or his attorney as prescribed by law for service of notice of motion in an action in the same court. If the adverse party shall be a nonresident then the notice of the application shall be served by the marshal of any district within which the adverse party may be found in like manner as other process of the court. For the purposes of the motion any judge who might make an order to stay the proceedings in an action brought in the same court may make an order, to be served with the notice of motion, staying the proceedings of the adverse party to enforce the award.

SECTION 13. PAPERS FILED WITH ORDER ON MOTIONS; JUDGMENT; DOCKETING; FORCE AND EFFECT; ENFORCEMENT

The party moving for an order confirming, modifying, or correcting an award shall, at the time such order is filed with the clerk for the entry of judgment thereon, also file the following papers with the clerk:

(a) The agreement; the selection or appointment, if any, of an additional arbitrator or umpire; and each written extension of the time, if any, within which to make the award.

(b) The award.

(c) Each notice, affidavit, or other paper used upon an application to confirm, modify, or correct the award, and a copy of each order of the court upon such an application.

The judgment shall be docketed as if it was rendered in an action.

The judgment so entered shall have the same force and effect, in all respects, as, and be subject to all the provisions of law relating to, a judgment in an action; and it may be enforced as if it had been rendered in an action in the court in which it is entered.

SECTION 14. CONTRACTS NOT AFFECTED

This title shall not apply to contracts made prior to January 1, 1926.

SECTION 15. INAPPLICABILITY OF THE ACT OF STATE DOCTRINE

Enforcement of arbitral agreements, confirmation of arbitral awards, and execution upon judgments based on orders confirming such awards shall not be refused on the basis of the Act of State doctrine.

SECTION 16. APPEALS

(a) An appeal may be taken from

(1) an order

(A) refusing a stay of any action under section 3 of this title,

(B) denying a petition under section 4 of this title to order arbitration to proceed,

(C) denying an application under section 206 of this title to compel arbitration,

(D) confirming or denying confirmation of an award or partial award, or

(E) modifying, correcting, or vacating an award;

(2) an interlocutory order granting, continuing, or modifying an injunction against an arbitration that is subject to this title; or

(3) a final decision with respect to an arbitration that is subject to this title.

(b) Except as otherwise provided in section 1292 (b) of title 28, an appeal may not be taken from an interlocutory order

(1) granting a stay of any action under section 3 of this title;

(2) directing arbitration to proceed under section 4 of this title;

(3) compelling arbitration under section 206 of this title; or

(4) refusing to enjoin an arbitration that is subject to this title.

Table of Authorities

Table of Authorities

Table of Authorities

Index